# GROUNDBREAKERS

# GROUNDBREAKERS

## HOW OBAMA'S 2.2 MILLION VOLUNTEERS TRANSFORMED CAMPAIGNING IN AMERICA

**ELIZABETH McKENNA**

**HAHRIE HAN**

FOREWORD BY JEREMY BIRD

OXFORD
UNIVERSITY PRESS

# OXFORD

## UNIVERSITY PRESS

Oxford University Press is a department of the
University of Oxford. It furthers the University's objective
of excellence in research, scholarship, and education
by publishing worldwide.

Oxford   New York

Auckland   Cape Town   Dar es Salaam   Hong Kong   Karachi
Kuala Lumpur   Madrid   Melbourne   Mexico City   Nairobi
New Delhi   Shanghai   Taipei   Toronto

With offices in

Argentina   Austria   Brazil   Chile   Czech Republic   France   Greece
Guatemala   Hungary   Italy   Japan   Poland   Portugal   Singapore
South Korea   Switzerland   Thailand   Turkey   Ukraine   Vietnam

Oxford is a registered trade mark of Oxford University Press
in the UK and certain other countries.

Published in the United States of America by
Oxford University Press
198 Madison Avenue, New York, NY 10016

© Elizabeth McKenna and Hahrie Han 2014

Library of Congress Cataloging-in-Publication Data
McKenna, Elizabeth.
Groundbreakers : how Obama's 2.2 million volunteers transformed campaigning in
America / Elizabeth McKenna, Hahrie Han ; foreword by Jeremy Bird.
pages   cm
ISBN 978-0-19-939459-3 (hardback)—ISBN 978-0-19-939460-9 (paperback)
1. Presidents—United States—Election—2008.   2. Presidents—United States—
Election—2012.   3. Political campaigns—United States.   4. Obama, Barack.
5. Political participation—United States.   6. United States—Politics and government.
I. Han, Hahrie.   II. Title.
JK5262008 .M35   2015
324.973'0931—dc23          2014013637

1  3  5  7  9  8  6  4  2

Printed in the United States of America
on acid-free paper

# CONTENTS

**PART THREE**
**OBAMA FOR AMERICA'S LEGACY**

# FOREWORD
## *An Organizer's Perspective on This Book*

### JEREMY BIRD

In the early morning hours of November 6, 2012, thousands of neighborhood team leaders arrived at their local staging locations hours before the polls opened to begin running their Election Day operations. Based in makeshift get-out-the-vote centers ranging from houses to garages to community rooms, these volunteer leaders—5,171 in all—ran President Barack Obama's reelection campaign.

The neighborhood team leaders welcomed the phone bank captains who ran their call centers, canvass captains who managed the door-to-door canvasses, and polling location captains who ran the monitoring of the polling sites throughout the day. They reported their progress to their Obama campaign field organizer.

For these volunteer team leaders and their captains—who had spent years building their local organization and honing their ground game—it was Game Day. They had registered the new voters, persuaded the undecided voters, and talked to the "sporadic" voters on their lists. They knew the volunteers who flooded into their staging locations personally. And on that one important day, they were executing their program for their president, one last time.

Much has been written about Barack Obama's reelection campaign from the perspective of the 50,000-square-foot headquarters overlooking Millennium Park in Chicago. But, the untold story of that campaign—

and of the historic 2008 election before it—was how those grassroots get-out-the-vote staging locations came to be.

This book tells that story.

When Liz McKenna and Hahrie Han first approached me about this book in late 2012, I was humbled by and excited about their project. In the wake of our groundbreaking campaign to reelect President Barack Obama, my colleagues and I were already deep into the process of culling best practices and analyzing the lessons learned from our work.

As we took stock of the grassroots organization we built together—not just in 2012 but over the preceding six years—one absolute truth we all agreed on was that none of the successes we shared would have been possible without the boundless passion and tireless efforts of the millions of volunteers who sacrificed their time to support the president. In telling their stories—and making clear the critical role grassroots volunteers played in making and remaking history in this country—Liz and Hahrie offer a glimpse at the complicated dynamics behind our volunteer-led grassroots campaign.

This book is an important contribution to the continued dialogue around politics in America. In their postmortem analyses of recent elections from the national to the local level, news reporters and political scientists have often focused disproportionately on the inner circle of campaign senior advisers or the big data and game-changing technology that paved the way to victory. These things are critically important, but so are the contributions of volunteers and the often misunderstood and underappreciated field program that enabled the Obama campaigns to use that big data and technology and to spread the message block by block, neighborhood by neighborhood.

The campaigns of the future should be modern and cutting-edge and continue to be impacted by the latest innovations—but they should also be about people. There are incredibly important lessons to be gleaned from telling the story of the 2.2 million grassroots volunteers who brought the plans on paper to life—at the doors, on the phones, in barbershops and community centers—in communities around the country this past presidential election.

In evaluating the outcomes of the Obama reelection campaign, many observers have looked at things from a quantitative perspective and centered their work on the technological or data-analytics advances achieved by our team. Where these analysts failed to explore the fundamentals of creating a bottom-up campaign, Liz and Hahrie instead dive wholeheartedly into the advantages and challenges of relying on grassroots volunteers to engage their neighbors in the democratic process. Their assessment of our operation is insightful, honest, and, at times, necessarily critical. One thing the authors make clear that others have omitted: It's hard, grueling, and often messy work to build a truly grassroots national organization—and that is why so few campaigns choose to do it.

Since 2012, some campaigns, consultants, and reporters have driven a false narrative about the off-the-shelf products and technology tools campaigns can purchase for immediate, Obama-like success. The truth is that there is no shortcut, no silver bullet, and no special sauce to building a winning campaign in the 21st century.

The real lesson from both of the Obama campaigns is that winning elections requires an integrated campaign that raises the money necessary to win from multiple revenue streams; develops a winning message true to the candidate's personal narrative; invests in a robust digital program to raise money, get out the message, and mobilize voters; uses cutting-edge technology across departments; fully embraces data and analytics to make metrics-based decisions across the campaign; and focuses on building a field campaign driven by volunteers who are trained and developed as leaders and empowered to represent the campaign in their own communities.

It's this last piece that Liz and Hahrie carefully study and write about in this book. It's this last piece that is so often dismissed as only important at the margins and as inferior to paid television ads and direct mail. It's this last piece that President Obama and his top advisers believed in and invested in like no other presidential campaign in history.

It was a big gamble to put field organizers on the ground in February of 2007 and April of 2011 when the national media and other insiders were advising the campaign to save its resources for the final paid media blitzes. But this commitment—this philosophical belief in the power of organizing at the local level—is exactly what brought me to the Obama campaign in early spring of 2007 and what kept me with the Obama organization for the next six years.

Many of the volunteers who showed up to run those staging locations on Election Day 2012 had been trained and tested for years, and they ran a more professional ground game than any of us could have imagined. But it didn't happen overnight. It took years of refining our organizing approach, learning from our many failures, and continually building a culture of learning and testing. It took a belief that volunteer leaders—when trained and empowered to own their piece of the campaign—were more effective in the short term and that running the campaign this way was, unequivocally, more effective in the long term.

By telling the story through the eyes of these volunteers and recognizing their impact on the two campaigns, this book offers would-be grassroots campaigners a real picture of the Obama organizing model—and a roadmap for building even better, people-focused, metrics-driven, and digitally sophisticated campaigns in the years to come.

# ACKNOWLEDGMENTS

We owe thanks to many people who helped make this book possible. First and foremost, we want to thank all the volunteers, leaders, and staff from OFA who participated in interviews with us. This list includes Nina Anziska, Rick Baer, Hayden Barnes, Sara Bean Duncan, Jeremy Bird, Dorien Blythers, Jenni Boyle-Smith, Andrew Brau, Shirley Bright, Austin Brookley, Pat Bruner, Matt Caffrey, Ann Cherry, Anna Cooper, Patrick Cronin, Kate Cummings, Colleen Cunningham, Joy Cushman, Zack Davis, Lan Diep, Laura Diviney, Howard Dolginoff, Cheryl Ellis, Shenelle Fabio, Patrick Frank, Kara Freeman, Sarah Frost, Ellen Gangnon, Sally Gasior, Lulu Gould, Dan Grandone, Bobbie Gustine, Garry Hayworth, Jennifer Herrington, Greg Jackson, Jyoti Jasrasaria, Daniel Johnson, Katie Keating, Michelle Kleppe, Harlan Kutscher, Nicholas LaCava, Judi Lanza, Eric Leufroy, Gabe Lifton-Zoline, Samantha Link, Kate Malloy, Marlon Marshall, Felesia Martin, Terrell Martin, Stephanie Monahon, Jorge Neri, Staci O'Brien, Blanca O'Leary, Alex Peña, Mary Pizzariello, Deidre Reynolds, Lodro Rinzler, Dylan Roberts, Alyssa Roberts, Erin Roediger, Tony Speare, Alex Steele, Mitch Stewart, Maria-Teresa Liebermann, Clinton Thomas, Suzanne Trask, Alex Watters, Sarah Weinstein, Buffy Wicks, Allison Zelman, and others who wished to remain anonymous. Not only did we learn a tremendous amount from talking with each of you, we were inspired by the commitment, creativity, and courage you showed. We have tried throughout the book to let your voices come through to remain true to what you told us. This book is your story.

Many colleagues gave us support, encouragement, and feedback on the project. We benefited tremendously from the insightful feedback people gave us on our ideas at all stages of the project, as well as comments on earlier drafts of the manuscript. We appreciated the kindness with which this feedback was delivered, and hope that we were able to address those comments with equal grace. All errors that remain are, of course, our own. This group includes Joy Cushman, Ryan Enos, Dan Grandone, Peter Han, Sunshine Hillygus, Michael Jeffries, Matt Levendusky, Rasmus Kleis Nielsen, Kristee Paschall, John Sides, Jessica Stiles, Jake Waxman, the Leading Change Network leadership team and three anonymous reviewers. Peter Han deserves special thanks for coming up with the title of this book while riding around in a taxi cab in Korea. The inimitable Hines family of Port Clinton and Marlene Beierle of Columbus were warm and generous hosts throughout the 2008 and 2012 election cycles, respectively.

We owe particular thanks to Jeremy Bird and Marshall Ganz, without whom this book (and perhaps the story within it) would not have happened. Having spoken separately with each of us, Marshall introduced us to each other in November 2012, suggesting that perhaps we could work together. He then provided important feedback throughout the project, from giving us rich historical information about how the campaign unfolded to incisive comments on the manuscript itself. For many years, Marshall has taught us both a tremendous amount through his mentorship and unwillingness to accept anything less than the very best from us and the world we are trying to create. Jeremy believed in the project from the start and helped it get off the ground by introducing us to many of the people we interviewed. He also sat through several long interviews with us, speaking with candor and insight about his experiences on the campaign. In addition, Jeremy provided important feedback on early drafts, correcting factual errors and identifying places where we needed to think more deeply about our findings. And, despite his busy schedule, he did it all with good cheer. The book also tells the story of Jeremy's leadership on the campaign; we are grateful for the ways his leadership helped this project come to fruition.

Writing this book was a true (and joyous) partnership, in which we both contributed fully to its intellectual development and writing, learning from and pushing each other to sharpen the ideas in the book. As a field organizer and regional field director for the Obama campaigns in 2008 and 2012, Liz alone led data collection as a participant-observer.

As with most big projects, there is also an important team of research assistants, editors, and other supporters to thank. An able team of students from Wellesley College helped us conduct the interviews, including Ava Bramson, Jessica Camacho, Candice Evers, Callie Furmaniuk, Esther Gonzalez, Justyna Jakubaszek, Sapna Jain, Cristina Lucas, Veronica Martinez, Katie McCann, Ace Wang, Alexa Williams, Jiezhen Wu, and Kirstin Yanisch. Michaela Ross also conducted several interviews. Barbara Alihosseini from New England Transcript transcribed the interviews with speed and accuracy. Kathryn Sargent Ciffolillo edited the manuscript with care. Angela Chnapko at Oxford University Press was a supporter of the project from its very early incarnations and helped lead it from conception to publication. We are grateful for the support for this project we received from the Barnette Miller Fund at Wellesley College.

Finally, we thank our friends and families who supported us in many intangible ways throughout the project. Liz is indebted to her parents, Michael and Susan McKenna, her siblings, and Alexandre. Hahrie owes special thanks to Hunter, Kaya, and Jaemin. None of this work would be meaningful without your presence in our lives. We hope it goes without saying how much we value your support.

By telling the story of how the Obama campaign invested in developing the capacity of volunteers and leaders, we hope this book will support the millions of people and organizations continuing to make our democracy work in communities around the globe. It is to those people—those who worked on, volunteered for, and were inspired by the Obama campaign—that we dedicate this book.

# TABLES AND FIGURES

# GLOSSARY

| | |
|---|---|
| **527** | A tax-exempt entity organized under section 527 of the U.S. Internal Revenue Code. 527s fundraise and execute political activities, including voter mobilization and issue advocacy. Political action committees (PACs) fall under this broad definition of a 527. |
| **50-State Strategy** | In 2005, under Howard Dean's leadership, the Democratic Party launched an effort to invest in winning elections outside of the traditional roster of swing states, including deploying organizers to states like Idaho, Texas, and Mississippi. |
| **72-Hour Program** | (Also sometimes referred to as the "72-Hour Task Force.") After the disputed 2000 election, Karl Rove designed this voter mobilization program to marshal grassroots forces for the GOP in the final three days of the 2004 campaign. |
| **ACT** | Americans Coming Together; a political action 527 that worked on behalf of Democratic candidates in the 2004 elections. It had a staff of 4,000 and upward of 45,000 paid canvassers. It was dismantled following John Kerry's loss. |
| **AFL-CIO** | The American Federation of Labor and Congress of Industrial Organizations, the largest federation of unions in the United States. |
| **Camp Obama** | Two- to three-day-long intensive training sessions for OFA volunteers. First held in California in the summer of 2007, participants learned the history of grassroots organizing, public narrative, and leadership skills necessary for building their own local teams of volunteers. *continued* |

| | |
|---|---|
| **CTM** | Core team member, one of the four volunteer leadership roles in an OFA neighborhood team snowflake. Most commonly, those who were responsible for running phone banks or recruiting and confirming shifts, canvass captains, and data-entry volunteers were considered CTMs. |
| **DFD** | Deputy field directors—anywhere between two and seven—were deployed to battleground states to support field directors. Regional field directors (RFDs) reported to them. |
| **Early Vote** | In an effort to increase enfranchisement and decrease crowding on Election Day, eligible voters in many states have the opportunity to cast their ballot prior to the scheduled election. Early Vote became a key part of the Obama field strategy, which aimed to turn out supporters either in person at designated polling sites in October, or by mail via absentee ballot. The details and duration of Early Voting periods vary by state and jurisdiction. |
| **FD** | Field director; the highest-ranking field staffer in each state with an OFA presence. |
| **FO** | Field organizer; responsible for implementing the OFA field program by building an average of four neighborhood teams in an assigned geographic area, called turf. |
| **Focus on the Family** | A conservative nonprofit organization based in Colorado Springs, Colorado. |
| **GOTV** | Get-out-the-vote; the widely used acronym that refers to a campaign's efforts to mobilize its supporters to the polls on or just before Election Day. |
| **Meetup** | Founded in 2001, the website Meetup.com aims to connect like-minded strangers in social settings. Meetups became one of the key organizing tools the 2004 Dean campaign used to galvanize its "netroots," or online supporters. |
| **NationalField** | A software platform developed by OFA staffers in Georgia in 2008. It was designed to streamline, simplify, and consolidate information for both in-the-field organizers and campaign management. In 2013, NGP VAN acquired NationalField. |

| | |
|---|---|
| Neighborhood team | Referred to interchangeably as a "snowflake," OFA neighborhood teams were composed of local volunteers in interdependent roles. Neighborhood teams took responsibility for running the Obama campaign locally. |
| NTL | Neighborhood team leader; the volunteer who took responsibility for overseeing all of the activities of the neighborhood team. |
| OFA, Obama for America | The original Obama campaign organization, founded in 2007. |
| OFA, Organizing for America | Following Obama's first inauguration in 2009, Organizing for America (also called "OFA 2.0") incorporated as the grassroots organizing arm of the Democratic National Committee. The group sought to mobilize volunteers, supporters, and voters on behalf of Obama's legislative priorities, most notably, health care reform. It then became the legal name for the field arm of the 2012 campaign ("OFA 3.0"). |
| OFA, Organizing for Action | Established after Obama's second inauguration, "OFA 4.0" is a registered as a 501(c)(4) and may advocate for legislation but cannot support political candidates. Its organizational infrastructure consists of local chapters that help define issue priorities. |
| PAC | Political action committee; a type of organization that pools financial contributions and donates the funds for or against candidates, ballot initiatives, and/or legislation. Different classifications of PACs exist. Following the 2010 Supreme Court decision *Citizens United*, for example, the colloquially named Super PACs were granted the right to engage in unlimited political fundraising and spending. |
| Public narrative | Developed by Marshall Ganz, public narrative is a leadership practice that uses stories of "self, us, and now" to inspire collective action. |
| RFD | Regional field director, reported to deputy field directors and coached and managed between 5 and 15 field organizers. |
| Rockwood Leadership Institute | A nonprofit organization that trains social change leaders. One of its consultants coached Jeremy Bird for the duration of the 2012 election cycle. |

*continued*

| | |
|---|---|
| **Sierra Club** | One of the largest grassroots environmental organizations in the United States. |
| **Staging location** | Often a volunteer's garage, a church basement, or a field office, staging locations were the temporary local hubs from which OFA's GOTV operations were launched. |
| **STOMP** | Strategic Task Force to Organize and Mobilize People, the GOP's 2001–2004 effort to build a grassroots field program in a large swath of states to counteract the Democrats' ground game. |
| **Super Tuesday** | The Tuesday in February or March of a presidential election year when the largest number of states hold primary elections or caucuses to select delegates who, in turn, nominate candidates at party conventions. |
| **Texas two-step** | Texas voters select their party's nominee in a primary and caucus sequence; to be eligible to participate in the latter, he or she must cast a vote in the former. The process differs for Republicans and Democrats. |
| **Turf** | The geographic area for which an OFA field organizer was responsible. Its size varied dramatically depending on the phase of the campaign (and therefore, the number of field staff in a given state). |
| **VAN** | Voter Activation Network, also referred to as VoteBuilder by OFA field staff and volunteers. Owned by the private company NGP VAN, it was the Obama campaign's primary database in both 2008 and 2012 and remains the biggest political technology provider for Democratic and progressive campaigns and organizations. |

# GROUNDBREAKERS

# 1.

# OBAMA FOR AMERICA
## *Stronger People and*
## *Stronger Communities*

Our campaign was not hatched in the halls of Washington; it began in the backyards of Des Moines and the living rooms of Concord and the front porches of Charleston.... It drew strength from the young people who rejected the myth of their generation's apathy, who left their homes and their families for jobs that offered little pay and less sleep. It drew strength from the not-so-young people who braved the bitter cold and scorching heat to knock on the doors of perfect strangers, and from the millions of Americans who volunteered and organized, and proved that more than two centuries later, a government of the people, by the people, and for the people has not perished from the earth. This is your victory.

—*Barack Obama, November 4, 2008, Grant Park, Chicago*

Something [we] always talked about was: We're organizing to win an election, but at the end of the day, you're going to want to leave behind stronger people and stronger communities than when you got there.

—*Alex Steele, Deputy Field Director, Colorado for Obama 2012*

According to its own numbers, the campaign to reelect Barack Obama engaged 2.2 million volunteers in 2012. More than 30,000 of those volunteers accepted responsibility for leading 10,000 neighborhood teams that organized their communities in swing states across America. In a post-election survey that garnered more than 1 million responses, 60 percent of these volunteer leaders and 20 percent of team members reported investing more than 10 hours per week in the campaign.[1] Together, these volunteers, teams, and leaders held 24 million conversations with prospective voters and registered 1.8 million new voters.

For many of the people who were part of the campaign, however, the experience was about much more than just the numbers. As Ellen Gangnon, 64, a neighborhood team leader from Wisconsin, said, "I had never been involved before, and so by participating in that election process—it impacted me so many different ways because, for the first time in my life, I felt I had a voice and I could make a positive change in our local community, in the state, and in the nation." Gangnon was not alone. Thousands of people like Gangnon working on the front lines, including the paid field staff supporting the volunteer neighborhood teams and leaders, reported that their participation in the campaign was a transformative experience. Approximately 95 percent of neighborhood team leaders and 75 percent of volunteers in Obama for America (OFA)[2] said that they will continue to volunteer in their communities as a result of their involvement in the campaign.[3] One in 10 survey respondents—approximately 100,000 people—indicated interest in using the organizing skills they acquired through their work with OFA to run for public office. Campaign leaders note that these are the statistics that make them proudest: For them, these numbers signal that the Obama campaign not only helped elect a president, it also reinvigorated the art and the practice of democratic politics in communities across America.

How did they do it? How did Obama's ground game engage so many people in the campaign in such leadership-intensive ways? In a time of rising citizen disaffection with politics, when organizations and campaigns increasingly turn to paid staff to do the grassroots work that people used to do voluntarily, the 2008 and 2012 Obama campaigns did something different.[4] They harnessed the energy of regular people to produce concrete outcomes for an electoral campaign. Mainstream outlets like the *Wall Street Journal* called Obama's field operation "his campaign's trademark...of a size unprecedented in presidential politics, stunning even seasoned veterans."[5] Howard Dean declared OFA "the best campaign I've seen in all my life in politics."[6] Even conservative commentators hailed "the brilliant way in which [the Obama campaign] mobilized volunteers to personally contact like-minded supporters."[7] Many scholars agree that the Obama campaign achieved an unparalleled breadth and depth of volunteer commitment.[8] But how?

This book helps answer that question by analyzing how the 2008 and 2012 campaigns to elect Barack Obama president created, tested, and scaled innovations in field campaigning that enabled millions of ordinary citizens to engage meaningfully in the democratic process. Many have described the inner workings of the OFA electoral machine, but few have told the story of how the campaign developed its groundbreakers: the volunteers who were at the core of the Obama field operation. As president-elect Obama noted in his acceptance speech in 2008, the "millions of Americans who volunteered and organized" formed the backbone of his campaign. This book explains how the campaign recruited, motivated, trained, managed, and deployed citizens as the campaign's ambassadors in every county of every battleground state.

In describing the mechanics of the Obama ground game, this book also shows how modern campaigns—sometimes regarded as nothing more than high-tech marketing operations—have the potential to repair rather than undermine democracy. By investing in its volunteers, developing them as leaders, and teaching them to organize their communities, the Obama campaign aimed to do more than earn 50 percent plus 1 of the vote share. They sought, as deputy field director Alex Steele noted, to "win an election...but [also to] leave behind stronger people and stronger communities."

## GROUNDBREAKERS

On January 20, 2013, the day before Obama's second inauguration, his campaign staff and volunteers filled the ballroom in the Washington, D.C., Hilton. They had traveled from all over the country to gather with each other and celebrate their work. A neighborhood team leader from

Toledo, Ohio, Cathy Johns, stood before the crowd to reflect on her experience:

> The friendships that we all forged were the secret ingredient in how we were able to pull off the most formidable ground game that this country has ever witnessed. We are family...
>
> I wish you could see our headquarters now. It was a storefront in a strip mall, not even on a main street. The paint is gone. The office is vacant. My heart skips a beat every time I drive by. Each of you has that same experience. The heart of where your campaign experience took place. It could have been a storefront or a church or a home. It is so important for us to remember that it wasn't the place. It was all of us that brought the campaign alive. We were transformed by our common belief, common passion, common goals. We didn't just show up, we interrupted our lives....
>
> It was late October in northwest Ohio. Our opponent began to flood our region with ads, warning that Jeep [the main employer in our community] was going to close down. Jobs would be moved to China. They were going to win Ohio through deception and fear.
>
> Something they had not calculated or anticipated was that lurking in strip centers and offices and churches and homes was a force. An army of experienced, well-trained, confident, fired-up-and-ready-to-go volunteers and staff who would respond without blinking an eye and squash those lies with conversations—one at a time. Our "snowflakes" [meaning, our neighborhood teams] were in place. We knew our turf. We knew who our undecideds were and we knew where they lived.
>
> We in Ohio delivered Ohio. Along the way we realized we could do anything. So, with deepest respect, Mr. President, "Bring it on."[9]

As with thousands of other volunteers around the country, Johns "interrupted" her life to become a neighborhood team leader on the Obama campaign. With other supporters from her community, she toiled to organize her "turf," the specified geographic area she was responsible for turning out, for no monetary return. Johns and her team trained other volunteers to register voters, recruit supporters, and speak face-to-face with the voters whom the analytics team in Chicago had deemed "persuadable." They built relationships with voters and with each other to sustain themselves through the long days. When it came time to deliver, they were ready. "[W]ithout blinking an eye," Johns and Obama's "army of experienced, well-trained, confident, fired-up-and-ready-to-go volunteers and staff" beat back challenges from Mitt Romney's campaign "one [conversation] at a time." In the process, Johns describes how the volunteers in her community discovered their own power. "We in Ohio delivered Ohio." Johns notes they did not depend on paid staff or outsiders to mobilize their community—they did it themselves. Johns realized that she was not only helping win a national election, but she was also being "transformed." After the campaign ended, she was ready to use her newfound organizing skills to fight for her beliefs—even standing up to the president she helped elect. As she put it, "[W]ith deepest respect, Mr. President, 'Bring it on.'"

Johns's experience was not unique. Unlike many previous campaigns, OFA made a long-term, organizational investment in developing the leadership potential of volunteers like Johns. Working with volunteers, however, is not easy. For decades, most campaigns relied more heavily on staff because, they thought, only paid staff could be pushed to put in the long tedious hours needed to make voter contact.[10] Volunteers were considered too risky because they could not be depended on to show up consistently or to produce the phone calls and door knocks the candidate needed. As one campaign manager for a 2010 congressional race said, "It is more important that we do field [voter contact] than that we have volunteers do it."[11] In short, many political campaigns did not entrust their volunteers with meaningful responsibilities.

The OFA leaders we interviewed described the gamble they had taken. They bet that if they developed the motivations, skills, and capacities of ordinary Americans to organize their communities, they could win. They bet that with volunteers, they could enfranchise, persuade, and turn out more voters than the opposition. They bet, in other words, that they could do with local volunteers what most previous campaigns had done with staff. One Ohio training document from 2008 read, "Volunteer recruitment and retention is the most important aspect of our field program. We cannot achieve the sheer volume of what we need in order to win without their help." Ohio field organizer Tony Speare explained,

> Rather than trying to do all the work ourselves, the idea was to spend the majority of our time building up volunteer teams and then making them self-sufficient so that by the end of the campaign, volunteers were calling other volunteers to recruit them. They were running all the trainings. They were entering all the data. They were making all the phone calls, knocking on all the doors. And by the end, the last four days we were able to remove ourselves and just coordinate with all of the teams but let them run their own operation.

The Obama volunteers thus became the groundbreakers who demonstrated the power of an alternative way of running field campaigns in America.

Once they committed to a volunteer-driven program, the field campaign's central challenge became figuring out how to motivate, train, support, and manage them. To meet this challenge, OFA applied principles of community organizing. Community organizing is an approach to social change that works by developing power within individuals, organizations, and communities to enable them to enact the change they want. Organizers build power not by raising more money, creating a better product, or crafting a more compelling message. Instead, they build power by developing the leadership capacities of individuals, and bringing those individuals together to engage strategically in collective action.[12] By integrating principles of community organizing in an electoral setting, OFA practiced a distinct model of grassroots politics.

So how did OFA do it? When we listen to the words and stories of those on the ground, we learn how OFA built a field operation that gave volunteers the responsibility, training, and interpersonal support needed to take charge of their own communities. They created a structure of neighborhood teams—also called "snowflakes"—composed of volunteers who worked with each other in interdependent roles to organize their communities. These teams became the fabric of the Obama field campaign.

Instead of asking volunteers to make rote phone calls, stuff envelopes, or distribute yard signs, OFA asked them to become leaders and to take responsibility for measureable electoral outcomes. Rather than spend their time attempting to persuade voters, staff like field organizer Speare invested in growing volunteer capacity, so that local supporters—not out-of-state staffers—could speak with voters in their neighborhoods. Steele, deputy field director for Colorado, drew the contrast between OFA-trained field organizers and a staffer from another campaign. "[The other campaign staffer] made 700 dials in a day and that was celebrated. They were like, 'Holy smokes! This guy is amazing!' and I thought to myself, 'That's not amazing at all. What is this guy doing?... Instead of building the organization, he's on the phone all day.'" In contrast to previous campaigns, OFA called staffers "organizers," a title they wore with pride. Volunteers who proved their leadership capabilities became "neighborhood team leaders," a role many took so seriously that they included it in their email signatures and on business cards.

The difference between the way traditional campaigns and OFA treated staff becomes evident through the story of Alex Watters, a field organizer for OFA in Iowa in 2012. When asked why he got involved in OFA, he told a story. "In 2004," Watters said, "I was two weeks into my freshman year of college. I was actually on a golf scholarship to Morningside College. I wanted to be a golf pro. And I met these girls—they were going up to my hometown, and I live in a resort community in Iowa, Okoboji, and they're known for their lakes and stuff like that—and they were going up for a family reunion and they asked if I'd join." His story continued,

It was about midnight and we were hanging out, playing catch with a football, singing campfire songs, and we decided we wanted to go swimming. And I was with one of their little brothers on the dock and my hat blew off into the water and I was about 150 feet out on the dock, a long ways out. And I knew I was next to a boat so I figured I knew the depth and I dove in after it. And it was only 18 inches deep and so it snapped my neck instantly. I was just paralyzed. My body went into shock, I couldn't swim, I couldn't turn over, and I remembered hearing a break and not really knowing what happened, but knowing that I wasn't swimming. And so the little boy, the brother, he knew something was wrong, went and got the girls.

To make a long story short, I ended up having surgery, being life-flighted down to Sioux City to have surgery to stabilize my neck. That was followed by six months of rehabilitation at Craig Hospital in Englewood, Colorado, to learn what my body was going to be like, what I could do, what I would be able to do, everything like that. I use a power wheelchair to get around because I have no movement from about my chest down and have very limited use of my arms and hands.

Zack Davis, a regional field director in Iowa, interviewed Watters for an open field organizer position in the summer of 2012. Davis was impressed and recalls, "When I went to hire him [my superiors] were like, 'Oh, he can't knock doors and this, that and the other.' I said, 'Are you asking me to hire a doorknocker or a phone-caller or are you asking me to hire an organizer? Because I believe this kid can organize and I believe with the right coaching we can organize him.'"

Watters had the same concerns about taking the job as a field organizer for the president's reelection campaign. "It was very scary for me going into this job knowing how much emphasis is put on going door-to-door, how you want to go above and beyond," Watters said. "Even down to the little things, you know, kept me up at night initially...how am I going to get the paper out of the printer, and how am I going to plug in the phones, you know? I can't even turn on the lights from where they were. Things like that were really nerve-wracking."

Watters voiced some of these concerns to Davis. "I'll never forget, my boss, Zack, talking to me," Watters recalled. "[Davis said], 'I don't need a person to do door-to-door, I don't need a person that can make endless phone calls. I need an organizer, and I need a person that can organize these individuals, these volunteers, to know what's at stake so that *they're* knocking your doors and *they're* making your phone calls, because I never expect you to do all of this. You'll never meet all of your goals if you rely on yourself.'" Watters interpreted Davis's words as an affirmation of his own leadership potential, as well as a nod to the underlying values of OFA's field program. "It was that moment," Watters remembered, when he learned that Davis "didn't need someone to do all that, he needed someone to inspire the individuals and the volunteers to be able to go out and reach those [voter contact] numbers" that he accepted the responsibility of organizing his turf. According to Davis, he far exceeded expectations: despite his mobility restrictions, Watters was "one of my best organizers with one of the largest volunteer capacities…he built one of the biggest [neighborhood] teams in the state."

## WHY DO WE CARE?

So what? So what if Obama invested more in volunteers than previous campaigns? So what if staff infused principles of community organizing into electoral campaigns? Why do we care about unpacking the mechanics of the Obama ground game? There are a number of reasons. First, from a practical standpoint, OFA introduced a model for grassroots campaigning that other campaigns have already begun to emulate in local, domestic, and international settings. Second, it informs popular discussions about the Obama campaign that have thus far overlooked *how* OFA was able to generate so much high-quality volunteer involvement. Third, unpacking the Obama ground game has implications for scholarship in a wide range of fields seeking to understand how organizations of any kind recruit, motivate, and develop volunteers, leaders, and staff. Finally, from a normative standpoint, it provides a model for revitalizing people's capacity to engage actively with our democracy. This case therefore carries important lessons for civic engagement and participation in American politics.

Starting first with a practical perspective, understanding the Obama ground game helps elucidate what many other campaigns and grassroots organizations around the world are starting to do. The Obama field model has been adopted wholesale by multiple local, state, national, and international organizing efforts. Often, down-ballot electoral races or issue-based advocacy campaigns work with smaller budgets and thus depend more heavily on volunteer activity. When these campaigners saw the Obama campaign's ability to generate an unprecedented breadth and depth of volunteer commitment, they paid attention. Kristee Paschall, national political director of PICO (People Improving Communities through Organizing), observed in 2013 that "from [voter contact] scripts to program design there has been a lot of adoption by the [501] c3 and [501]c4 community of the Obama model."[13] This book will provide a detailed primer on how the Obama ground game achieved both quality and scale, employing strategies that can be adapted to grassroots campaigns, electoral and otherwise.

Second, in both popular and scholarly literatures, the dominant discourse about the Obama campaign has paid little attention the importance of its human resources—the staff and volunteers in the trenches. Nearly all accounts of OFA acknowledge its sophisticated use of technology, analytics, social media, and beta testing to refine its fundraising and voter contact programs.[14] Many top-level staffers made data and analytics one of OFA's defining narratives in 2012. "Big data is here," campaign manager Jim Messina said. "I could tell exactly who was undecided. I could tell you exactly who of your friends on Facebook was undecided," Messina said to an auditorium full of college students at George Washington University.[15] Analytics gave the campaign more confidence in its decision-making and allowed OFA to allocate its resources more efficiently to targeted television, direct mail, Internet ads, and finely honed walk and call lists.

But how did the campaign put all of that information to use on the ground? We will argue that the legacy of the 2008 and 2012 Obama campaigns is far more than just its data infrastructure and digital presence. Future campaigns that hope to model themselves on OFA by becoming a "high-tech political start-up"[16] at the expense of their people operation will find themselves with accurate lists of voters and nobody to do the work of speaking with them. Unlike previous work, we highlight the symbiotic relationship between the ground game and targeting and analytics. The number-crunchers in Chicago used a persuadability index to categorize voters and identified the best ways to target messages to particular constituencies. But the volunteers printed the lists generated by these data, brought democracy to voters' doorsteps, and gathered information that helped refine the lists to create the valuable targeting resource that Messina describes. These same volunteers used the information from Obama's database to talk to voters, build relationships with them, and, as Cathy Johns said, "squash those lies with conversations—one [voter] at a time." One undervalued aspect of big data, therefore, is that campaigns cannot put analytics as powerful as the Obama campaign's to use without having first invested in an army of people on the ground to help clean the lists and contact voters in person once the lists are culled. Focusing only on OFA's technology and analytics provides an incomplete picture of the campaign's innovations.

Third, by providing an analysis of how the campaign learned, developed, and scaled a different model of field campaigning, this book also has lessons for scholars interested in a wide range of issues, including political campaigns, participation and civic engagement, movement building, organizational learning, volunteerism, and leadership. Campaigns, movements, and organizations of all kinds face the challenge of recruiting, motivating, and developing high-quality human capital, whether it be volunteers, leaders, or staff. The case of Obama for America is relevant to a number of these literatures. Researchers working across multiple fields examine the sources of civic and political action. Scholars studying volunteerism, community organizing, social movements, participation, and civic associations examine the strategies democratic organizations can use to generate involvement.[17] A growing body of experimental literature has examined the value of interpersonal contact and social networks in generating involvement, focusing particularly on get-out-the-vote (GOTV) efforts in electoral campaigns.[18] Scholars of organizational behavior examine how organizational leaders manage staff and volunteers in ways that foster commitment and create the conditions for more effective and distributed leadership.[19] Understanding how OFA was able to generate a high degree of volunteer commitment has implications for all of these literatures and, more broadly, for our understanding of organizational change, leadership, and the sources of political action.

Finally, for those who care about reinvigorating the power of people in our democracy, the Obama ground game shows one way to do so. Prior to OFA, electoral campaigns often parachuted legions of paid canvassers into communities to create a temporary voter turnout machine for the election. When the election was over—win or lose—the campaign apparatus would disappear, leaving nothing behind. The Obama campaign, in contrast, sought to build a campaign that drew its power from volunteer teams that took responsibility for organizing their own neighborhoods. By integrating the principles and practices of community organizing with electoral politics, OFA tried to build a campaign that also enhanced the long-term democratic capacities of local communities.

Jeremy Bird, national field director of OFA 2012, said, "The real story of the campaign is not in the numbers," but in the "millions of volunteers who saw their power and became real leaders." The Obama ground game gave citizens the opportunity to be effective participants in their democracy, to create community, and to exercise their collective power. By showing how the Obama campaign built power through voluntary commitment, this book provides insight into one pathway for creating more citizen voice in American politics.

The book is not, then, an analysis of the effect of the Obama ground game on electoral outcomes, nor is it an effort to determine how many votes Obama earned through fieldwork. A large literature in political science argues that campaigns overall, and field operations in particular, may matter only at the margins, if at all.[20] Volunteers working inside the campaign disagree: several interviewees noted that in the United States, campaigns are regularly won and lost on the margins, recalling that George W. Bush was named the winner in 2000 by a margin of just 537 votes out of nearly 6 million cast in the state of Florida.[21] Looking out from inside the campaign, Blanca O'Leary, a volunteer leader in Colorado, was unequivocal. "The unsung part of [the campaign] was the field work, because that's what makes a bigger difference than everything else. That's why we win and that's why we're going to continue to win."

We do not attempt to adjudicate between scholarly analyses of campaign effects and the felt experience of volunteers. We put aside the question of the net effect of field activity on campaign outcomes. Instead, our book takes as its starting point the degree of commitment that OFA generated from ordinary citizens and, according to our data, the transformative effect it had on both those who got involved and the way in which people-powered campaigns can be executed. The felt experience of power among millions of volunteers is, we argue, an important outcome worth understanding. By describing the substance of the field operation, our book thus tries to unpack *how* the campaign developed and scaled an approach to field campaigning that engaged so many people with such depth.

Understanding how OFA achieved that outcome has numerous implications for grassroots activism, organizational learning, political participation, and our grasp of democracy. To make this case, we begin in part I by highlighting the need for innovation that early Obama campaign staff confronted in early 2007. We found that a handful of campaign staffers introduced solutions—such as distributing real responsibility to volunteers—that contained a core paradox: On one hand, they sought to build a movement based on the power of millions of local volunteers exercising their own agency in their local communities. On the other hand, they were introducing these ground-level innovations within the strictures of a top-down campaign. We describe how the campaign struggled with this tension—of empowering local people but doing it at scale—and the ways in which the campaign's approach to volunteer empowerment and methodical systems of accountability worked in concert and in contradiction with one another at different times. This book thus describes how OFA experimented with and codified its distinctive electoral organizing model, but also identifies what the innovations themselves were and how they worked on the ground.

## OBAMA FOR AMERICA: A CASE STUDY

Our book is an in-depth exploration of the Obama ground game: how the organization was built and how it worked. We chose to take a case study approach because we wanted to provide a thick, textured description of not just *what* the campaign did, but also *how*. How did staffers recruit so many volunteers? How did they motivate and transform volunteers into leaders, and organize them into collective teams? How did they train them? How did they hold them accountable to campaign goals, to produce meaningful work for the campaign? How did they learn to do all of this?

The Obama campaign is a useful case to study because it blended new and old organizing tactics to generate deep and widespread volunteer enthusiasm in the modern era. As such, we argue that the Obama campaign is what some scholars call an "extreme case" or a "crucial case," important to study because of its unique results on an outcome of interest (in this analysis, the quantity and quality of citizen action).[22] Our study relies on within-case variation to spell out the mechanisms that enabled OFA to achieve these results. Naturally, relying on one case raises the possibility that our findings are dependent on features exceptional to that case, such as the unique background and reputation of Barack Obama and the coalition he was seeking to build. We discuss these limitations and implications for other citizen-based organizations in our conclusion.

Our data consist of in-depth interviews with staff and volunteers, historical research, 10 months of participant-observation during both the 2008 and 2012 campaigns, and analysis of nearly 100 internal campaign documents. At the core of our data are more than 4,500 minutes of in-depth interviews with 46 OFA field staff and 25 volunteers. We conducted most of these interviews between January and April of 2013, with one interview conducted in November 2013. We used a third-party service to professionally transcribe the interviews and conducted a close read and coding of the transcripts for our analysis. To identify interviewees, we used purposive and chain-referral sampling such that we had representation across campaign roles and geography. Our goal in sampling was not distribution, but instead saturation: The last individuals interviewed provided very little new or surprising information.[23]

Popular accounts of campaigns often center on the drama of the candidates themselves or, in some cases, take the point of view of top campaign operatives who are many steps removed from the field.[24] Scholarly accounts often take broad sweeps of data, missing some of the granularity of particular campaigns. We suggest that understanding the Obama ground game depends on capturing the experiences of the people on the front lines. To understand how the campaign transformed people and campaigns' capacities for democratic action, we have to look, as Obama said in his victory speech, "in the backyards of Des Moines and the living rooms of Concord and the front porches of Charleston."

As with any small-n qualitative study, our sample of interviews has (at least) two important biases. First, our interviewee pool likely over-samples those who had the most positive experiences with the campaign. We began our study by interviewing high-level staff from all 10 battleground states. We asked these field leaders to identify regional field directors or field organizers from a range of turf-types within their state for us to interview. From there, we continued to ask each interviewee for the names of other OFA staff and volunteers in their area. We should note that we still found that people were open about their critiques of the campaign, which we chronicle throughout the book. Yet, the possibility of bias remains. Second, our interviews were all done retrospectively, risking the possibility that victory colored their recollections.

Given these limitations, we sought to triangulate findings from the interviews with other data sources, specifically historical research, participant observation, and analysis of campaign materials. We drew on a range of scholarship and written accounts to inform the description of the historical evolution of field campaigns in part I of our book. In addition, one of us—Elizabeth McKenna—served as a field organizer with the 2008 Obama campaign and a regional field director with the 2012 campaign in Ohio. Finally, we carefully read and analyzed as many internal campaign documents and email threads as we could access to provide a fuller picture of the way the Obama field operation worked.

## MAPPING THE BOOK

Unlike campaigns that came before it, Obama for America invited millions of volunteers to, as one of our interviewees, Felesia Martin, put it, "be a part of the campaign—and not just to cast the vote—but actually get in on the ground and become a part of something bigger than yourself." Volunteers like Martin were the groundbreakers because, together, they found sources of power they did not know they had, and in so doing, developed a new model for ground campaigns. One field organizer in Ohio, Patrick Cronin, recalled a volunteer who canvassed for six hours at a time in the sweltering August heat while fasting for Ramadan—not because he had asked her to, but because she had promised her team that she would. Ellen Gangnon, the neighborhood team leader from Wisconsin, vowed to "never ask people to do more than what I would do myself," and so would trudge door-to-door in the snow during the brutal Wisconsin winters in solidarity with the volunteers on her team. In Nevada, Mary Pizzariello said that she found inspiration—and continues to organize her community—because of the commitment she saw in her fellow volunteers. She remembers working with an 88-year-old woman who, nearly blind, would take the bus to and from team meetings and phone banks.

Withstanding the oppressive summer heat, the blizzards of the Midwest, and navigating public transit as an octogenarian required volunteers to tap previously undiscovered sources of commitment. Volunteers report that being part of the campaign transformed them because they were entrusted with local responsibility for a national project. Field organizer Erin Roediger said, "We are beginning to see in the last four years, six years, just how powerful our voice can be and how much it can make a difference in our politics." The Obama campaign not only carried an improbable candidate to office, but it also demonstrated that electoral campaigns can be run differently: They can be run in ways that include citizens in the work of democracy.

We start our story by providing a historical overview of field campaigns in America. Part I provides historical context for the role of field operations in the broader campaign structure, and shows how different strategies have ebbed and flowed over time. Chapter 2 shows how some of the roots of the Obama field campaign can be found in previous campaigns, but also how it is distinct from them. Chapter 3 chronicles the evolution of the OFA field program. Focusing particularly on the 2008 presidential primaries, this chapter shows how OFA's commitment to working with volunteers grew out of necessity: Short on staff, resources, and momentum in the hard-fought primary against Hillary Clinton, OFA had no choice but to rely on volunteers. The process by which the leaders of Obama's ground game figured out how to make it work was messy, frenetic, and full of setbacks. Staff in an array of primary states were learning sometimes overlapping and sometimes divergent lessons. Buffy Wicks, one of Obama's earliest field staffers and 2012 national Operation Vote director, said that OFA's electoral-organizing structure was launched "on a wing and a prayer" in 2008. In some ways, we discover, being the underdog allowed OFA to take risks in its field program design, engendering a spirit of creativity necessary for innovation.

Part II examines the features of the OFA field program that made it work, all of which are interrelated. We study how OFA built and sustained relationships to organize communities (chapter 4), how it structured its work and distributed leadership through neighborhood teams (chapter 5), and how it used metrics to distribute meaningful responsibility to volunteers, while maintaining accountability loops (chapter 6). Although we unpack each of the practices in separate chapters, they were all inextricably intertwined in making the field program successful. Each element we describe is effective only in harmony with the others; that is, success is possible only when relational organizing, public narrative, leadership teams, strategic goals, and measured action are combined. Thus, we urge readers—and especially practitioners who hope to adopt and adapt this model—to consider these chapters not a stepwise manual, but rather an account of strategies and tactics to be understood and practiced in an integrated fashion. Taken together, these practices formed a new kind of field campaign. Throughout these chapters, our task is to describe, operationalize, exemplify, and critically analyze these organizing practices in ways that the prevailing literature has not. In so doing, we show how the Obama volunteers were groundbreaking.

**PART ONE**

# THE HISTORICAL ROOTS OF THE OBAMA FIELD OPERATION

# 2.

# THE WAY THINGS WERE

Before the 2008 Obama campaign, many political operatives treated community organizing and electioneering as mutually exclusive endeavors. While iconic social movements in America from the Temperance movement to the Civil Rights movement have long used practices of community organizing to achieve their purpose, electoral campaigns have not. Instead, most political campaigns functioned like "medieval war machine[s]," mobilizing the votes they need to win only to be "[dismantled] after battle."[1]

Neglecting the long-term base building that characterizes community organizing, most contemporary electoral campaigns focus on creating a temporary voter turnout machine that disappears when the election is over. These campaigns win without investing in citizens' capacity to make change, or to be leaders in their communities. Staff drive mobilization efforts with titles like "field activist," "field coordinator," or "volunteer supervisor." In such campaigns, volunteers, when available, do not have responsibility for any real outcomes and are sometimes viewed as a drain on resources rather than an asset.

In 2008, the conditions were ripe for OFA to break from the norm and blend practices of grassroots organizing with electoral campaigning. The late 1990s had seen a revived interest in the power of the ground game. With each federal election cycle, campaigns on both sides of the political spectrum tried new field strategies, learned from their mistakes, and refined their work for the next election. In most of these campaigns, however,

23

the focus of the field operation was on the period between Labor Day and Election Day, when staff deployed to competitive states and cities, spent little more than a month trying to persuade voters, and then focused exclusively on get-out-the-vote (GOTV) mobilization. OFA built on this tradition, but started organizing much earlier—in some places, more than a year before the election. Instead of using field efforts only to orchestrate a short-term turnout operation, OFA sought to develop a ground strategy that built capacity within local communities. It did so by registering new voters, building leadership among volunteers, and, finally, deploying those leaders' teams to turn out their own communities. In this way, OFA did not run a traditional ground operation. It ran what the New Organizing Institute would later term an "engagement campaign."[2]

## PUTTING THE GROUND GAME IN CONTEXT

The word "campaign" derives from Campania, a region in Southern Italy, one of the "greatest breadbasket[s] in antiquity," and the site of the Roman Empire's annual wartime operations.[3] In their terminology, electoral campaigns retain vestiges of this militaristic origin: strategy, tactics, mobilization, chain-of-command, war rooms, and zero-sum winners and losers. Academics define campaigns as communication and mobilization events with a finite beginning and end.[4] They combine strategy, organization, and message to accomplish their singular goal, which, in the case of presidential elections, is winning 270 electoral votes.

Electoral campaigns are heterogeneous. One may be unrecognizable from the next, contingent on where decision-makers invest a campaign's limited resources. Some rely on highly specialized professionals. Others, often local and less well-resourced candidates, rely more on organic sources of labor and small numbers of grassroots volunteers. Presidential campaigns, which tend to have access to vast financial resources, have relied on both professionals and volunteers to varying degrees and in qualitatively different ways.

However professionalized or well-resourced a campaign might be, the top strategist's main job is to win an election. Embedded in this goal are three intermediate objectives: to inform, to persuade, and to turn out voters. The fundraising, media, and outreach "assemblages" they construct are dedicated to achieving those three objectives.[5] To that end, candidates and their staff construct impermanent operations that are organized around four interrelated categories: management, money, message, and mobilization. Table 2.1 elaborates these four categories.

The "field" campaign, which focuses on in-person voter contact, is only one part of a much larger campaign apparatus. Campaign managers have to analyze the circumstances of the particular race to develop a winning strategy and create a team to implement it. They also need funding, and extensive fundraising operations are dedicated to raising resources. They must develop a winning message and get that message out to voters, working with a team of media and public relations experts

TABLE 2.1: **Campaign Schema**

| Category | Management | Money | Message | Mobilization |
|---|---|---|---|---|
| Goal | Implementation | Resources | Persuasion | Voter contact |
| Means | • Operations<br>• Human resources<br>• Advance and scheduling | • Bundling<br>• Online fundraising<br>• PACs<br>• Public financing<br>• Events<br>• Budgeting | • Traditional media (print, TV, radio)<br>• New media, social media, and digital outreach<br>• Candidate and surrogate events<br>• Issue and opposition research<br>• Data targeting and analytics | • Field operation (door-to-door, calling, registration, literature drops, community meetings, candidate events)<br>• GOTV drives<br>• Data targeting and analytics |
| Actors | • Campaign managers<br>• Consultants | • Wealthy individuals<br>• Online donors<br>• Fundraising professionals | • Paid staff<br>• Mainstream media<br>• Consultants<br>• "Blogosphere" | • Paid field staff<br>• Out-of-state volunteers<br>• Local volunteers |

*A schematized campaign organization chart. Table based on information in Thurber and Nelson 2010 and Cushman et al. 2010.*

to do so. Alongside money, management, and messaging, campaigns seek to make contact with voters, relying on their on-the-ground presence—their field operation—to accomplish this objective.

The importance of field campaigns has waxed and waned in recent history. For instance, after the 1994 midterm elections, political scientist Paul Herrnson's survey of hundreds of congressional campaigns found that staffers rated in-person canvassing well below paid and earned media in terms of impact and importance. Field operations remained "in the shadows in conversations about electioneering and campaign communications."[6] When Herrnson repeated the study in 2002, he found that operatives saw field practices as "among the most effective means of communication, more so than television advertisements, email, or the Internet."[7]

The fluctuating importance of field campaigning can be understood in light of three interrelated trends in the 20th and 21st centuries: the decline of local party organizations, the rise of mass marketing and new forms of media, and, finally, the resurgence of interest in ground campaigns in the early 21st century. These historical forces are among the factors that shaped the development of the Obama ground game.

### The Decline of Local Party Organizations

Until the 1970s, the bedrock of most presidential field operations was a network of precinct captains. The precinct captain model originated with strong local party bosses who used to rule the electoral process. Drawing on her study of 600 precinct captains in the greater Chicago area, Sonya Forthal wrote in her 1946 book *Cogwheels of Democracy,*

> Each captain corresponded to the constituency he served, was to an extent conditioned by it. The more successful possessed a bluff personality, a flair for politics, and above all, the professional capacity to seem to be everybody's friend, especially before a primary or election, and to seem to serve the voter while serving himself.[8]

The title of Forthal's book and her analysis convey the essence of the precinct captain model: a party functionary "served" the party constituents in his community and traded favors for votes, grinding the "cogwheels of democracy." Political scientist V. O. Key further describes the manner in which precinct captains ruled their precincts:

> Especially in the poorer neighborhoods, [the precinct executive] is likely to become a sort of social agency, distributing food to the needy and from time to time paying their rent and furnishing them with coal.... Beyond services of this kind the precinct executive serves as a buffer between governmental agencies and the voters of his precinct. He steers the alien through the naturalization procedure. He aids in obtaining governmental employment for the people of his precinct and private employment as well. He may see the judge and attempt to mix mercy with justice. In all these relationships the precinct captain may from time to time obtain treatment for his friends that amounts to favoritism, but in a substantial portion of these services he is primarily a guide.... Yet when he can have the traffic ticket "fixed" he can create a great obligation to himself. By these various means, the working precinct executive can build up a substantial bloc of votes in his precinct, a bloc that can be swung to the support of the organization slate.[9]

Through the services they provided for their constituents, precinct captains built a strong base of voters to support their party. Candidates seeking votes in a particular neighborhood would rely on their party's precinct captains to turn the voters out.

The local party organization was thus responsible for implementing a campaign's ground game through its network of precinct captains and county chairs.[10] In many communities across America, citizens' primary contact with politics occurred by way of the local incarnation of the Democratic or Republican Party. Affinity associations like labor unions, churches, and issue-based organizations also played an important role in negotiating the relationship between politicians and voters. Along with the local parties, these intermediate organizations—often referred to on the Left as "organized liberalism"—became crucial allies in electoral campaigns after the Second World War and central to the blueprint for Democratic field operations for decades to come.[11]

The precinct model of electioneering worked because of the strength of the local party organizations. In his canonical *Making of the Presidency 1960*, Theodore White argues that John F. Kennedy won the 1960 Democratic nomination because he leveraged his connections to the local party bosses who ruled the Northern political machine. Indeed, it was these party insiders who dictated the outcomes of presidential campaigns, by "[selecting the] delegates to the party conventions—and hence the [choosing] party nominees."[12] National parties nominated their presidential candidates with "slavish obedience to state bosses."[13] Party conventions twice turned down "ambitious mavericks"—Estes Kefauver in 1952 and Eugene McCarthy in 1968—who "campaigned vigorously for the nomination and won significant popular support" but lacked support of local party bosses.[14]

The 1968 Democratic Convention was a paradigmatic case of an invisible primary, so named because voting was a mere consummation of boss decree. Delegates chose Hubert Humphrey as their nominee, despite the fact that he had not even launched a public campaign and had only entered one primary race. While McCarthy and Bobby Kennedy were competing for delegates in primary elections across the country, Humphrey was "making big gains in back rooms and secret caucuses where delegates were chosen in ways that were closed to the public and not ideally democratic."[15] None of the nominees of this era—Dewey, Kennedy, Nixon, Humphrey—"forced the hand of the party; rather, party insiders were choosing them over rivals who also wanted to be nominated."[16]

Humphrey's humiliating loss to Richard Nixon in the 1968 general election, however, prompted reform-minded Democrats to release the grip of party insiders by adopting binding primary elections. George McGovern, who would go on to become the Democratic nominee in 1972, spearheaded a commission that defined the new rules for delegate selection, giving the electorate greater influence. "Practicality and patronage" began to mix with "idealism and issue orientation."[17] This transition, scholars contend, spurred significant changes in American political processes and consciousness. It was McGovern's eponymously named Senate Commission that devised the new system, designed to "open party participation, especially in nominating candidates, to women, minorities, and young people."[18]

These reforms weakened local party organizations and opened presidential primaries to greater popular pressure. In 1952, there were presidential primaries in only 16 states; in 1976, there were primaries in over two dozen. In 2008, all 50 states had primaries or caucuses. Obama and Clinton carried 29 and 21 primary or caucus states, respectively, nearly all of which were consequential in the final tally of delegates. The need to build public support also became evident in the increasing length of campaigns. John F. Kennedy's campaign lasted 310 days; Obama's 2008 campaign was twice that.[19] The pressures of mass democracy supplanted, at least in part, the proverbial smoke-filled back room and meant that campaigns had to adopt new strategies for voter enfranchisement and engagement.

Obama's nomination in 2008 would have been almost inconceivable had the invisible primary system—or the system of control by local party leaders—persisted. In 2007, the Democratic machine backed Clinton, the ultimate party insider. The Obama campaign knew that it could not rely on an existing precinct captain infrastructure, thus forcing it to innovate.

The declining influence of the party machine and electoral reforms fundamentally changed the ways in which campaigns conducted their field operations. Nowadays, many precinct captain seats are vacant, or filled by volunteers who no longer hold the same sway over their constituents. Today, precinct captains (also sometimes called precinct judges, executives, committee officers, or clerks depending on the local county party infrastructure) are still elected by ballot, establishing a formal link between their political party and the voters in a given electoral district. They subdivide the residential areas in their purview and appoint what are sometimes called section captains to canvass voters and initiate turnout drives on Election Day. The Obama campaign did not call on them to oversee its field operation. Rasmus Kleis Nielsen reports that in 2000, the Democratic ground infrastructure in Mahoning County, Ohio, like many other precincts nationwide, was considered "'in disarray,' 'weak,' [and] 'poor.' "[20] Many county parties, especially suburban and rural ones, were "in shambles" by 2000. This "disarray" contrasted with elections as recent as the 1992 campaign to elect Bill Clinton, whose campaign "could count on the remnants of a traditional political machine."[21]

Because precinct captains do not have the patronage power or organizational infrastructure they once had, many modern campaigns have essentially replaced the precinct captain with hired staff. Precinct captains used to base their power in deep local relationships and kickbacks. With these relationships in place, much of what the captains had to do to turn out voters was call their contacts to remind them to vote. In modern campaigns, what paid staff lacked in local knowledge, they made up for with more aggressive voter contact. Out-of-state staff do not have the deep local relationships needed to make the precinct captain model work, nor the ability to "fix" traffic tickets or serve as "a buffer between governmental agencies and the voters." By coordinating with the local party, however, campaign staff gain access to lists of partisan voters, and spend much of their time calling and knocking through those lists to turn out votes.

## The Rise of Mass Marketing

As party organizations declined and campaigns increased their reliance on paid staff, political operatives began to rely more heavily on paid media. In 1950, only 11 percent of American homes had a television; by 1960, that number had increased to 88 percent. In the late 1980s, 15 percent of American homes had a computer. In 2004, more than 65 percent did—almost all of which had access to the Internet—and in 2011 three quarters of American households were connected to the World Wide Web. Because television and social media have the capacity to reach millions of voters at once, campaigns spend enormous resources managing a candidate's media appearances.[22]

Mass communications thus eclipsed the importance of direct communication on political campaigns. From the 1970s to the 1990s, shoe-leather politics gradually faded away.[23] Local ward heelers were replaced with phone banks and direct mail firms, whose standardized messages meant that "operations could be started with very short lead-time and deployed virtually anywhere on an enormous scale."[24] Research by Donald Green and Alan Gerber explains why: "Television reaches vast audiences, and even a small effect goes a long way."[25] Canvassing can increase turnout by anywhere from 7 to 18 percent but is far more costly. "Perhaps the biggest challenge," Green and Gerber argue, "is bringing a door-to-door campaign 'to scale.'" They continue: "It is one thing to canvass 3,600 voters, and quite another to canvass 36,000 or 360,000." The "more personal the interaction," they conclude, "the harder it is to reproduce on a large scale" because of the extensive human resources— paid or volunteer—that it would require.[26]

The "new media" and data revolutions of the 2000s changed the information landscape around campaigns again. With more sophisticated technology to identify voters' concerns, some campaigns invested more resources in sending voters targeted mail or leaving robocall messages prior to the election, using field efforts primarily to mobilize voters on Election Day itself. This process, called "microtargeting," is hardly new. Doris Kearns Goodwin's biography of Lincoln provides what could be mistaken for a modern field strategy: "Our intention is to organize the whole State, so that every Whig can be brought to the polls." Lincoln's campaign manual "outlined a plan whereby each county would be divided into small districts, each responsible for making 'a perfect list' of all their voters, designating which names were likely from past behavior."[27] Campaigns still engineer "the perfect lists" of voters, but they use algorithms to model how past behavior might predict electoral preferences and the type of information that voters may find persuasive. Microtargeting is a more sophisticated way of leveraging a fraction of what is now fashionably called "big data" or the more than 2.5 quintillion bytes of data humans produce each day.[28] The goal of modern campaigning, writes political scientist Daniel Shea, is to "tailor the appropriate message to each voter, to find the right button to push."[29] Technology facilitates mass mailing, robo-dials, and targeted ads via television and social media even as it attempts to optimize the canvassing routes of campaign staff and volunteers.

Accompanying the rise of mass media in electoral politics is the inexorable rise of money. The cost of the 2012 election exceeded the cost of all presidential elections from 1960 to 1984—seven campaign cycles—combined. The Obama campaign, the Democratic Party, and their major super PAC, Priorities USA Action, spent over a billion dollars in 2012. Romney's campaign, the Republican Party, and the Restore our Future Super PAC spent $992 million. For the GOP, this was $870 million more than what McCain had spent in 2008. The vast majority of this money went to paid media. Each campaign spent nearly 60 percent of its budget on advertising.[30] Campaign consultants represent a second significant category of campaign expenditures: "Each technological innovation produced a new expert—or 'consultant'—who provided access to the new tool for a fee."[31] As mass communications expanded, so did campaign budgets.

The constantly escalating battle for dollars often meant that campaigns invested resources in fundraising and media instead of their field program. Jeremy Bird said that he and other top staff in Chicago knew "*Citizens United* was going to change the game." *Citizens United v. Federal Election Commission* (130 S. Ct. 876, 2010) was a January 2010 Supreme Court case that permitted corporations, interest groups, unions, and wealthy individuals to pour unregulated sums of money into campaigns.[32] Bird was aware that, with the promise of large sums of money after *Citizens*, the Romney campaign was "spending a lot of money early," which meant that it was "always a fight over how much money [OFA] got to put into the field program."

## A Resurgence of Interest in the Ground Game

While television delivers scripted messages and still consumes the majority of campaign budgets, the Internet, some argue, is credited with reviving the "older forms of political communication."[33] Paradoxically, observes Ari Berman, "it took the emergence of the Internet—a medium everyone thought would turn its users into antisocial automatons—to make old-school organizing relevant again and reestablish the sense of community that TV destroyed."[34]

Although congressional candidates still lean on the party establishment to reach voters,[35] by 2002, the shifting role of money, mass media, geopolitics, and "cybernetic technology" had further weakened the relationship between the party and local citizens.[36] Lacking support from the precinct captains, most voter contact operations were contingent on the amount of paid staff a campaign could hire or the capacity of outside 527 political organizations like the one John Kerry's campaign enlisted to provide much of his ground game's manpower.[37] Face-to-face contact with voters was ancillary to paid media, and voter contact fell under the purview of paid staff and, when available, traditional civic organizations such as churches, unions, gun clubs, and the local party infrastructure. Some scholars argue that because the technology- and consultant-driven campaign apparatus that emerged out of the 1990s "devalue[d] all forms of political activism except for giving money, the role of the political volunteer [was] all but eliminated."[38] Others note that non-donation-based activism still occurred even with the rise of this "consultocracy," but that the volunteers were drawn from pools of party loyalists who were asked to do little more than provide "GOTV/field services"—that is, calling and canvassing voters in the final days before the election.[39]

Near the turn of the 21st century, campaign field strategies began to shift. During the 1998 congressional elections, the AFL-CIO ran a series of experiments that showed the power of in-person voter contact, reviving interest in field campaigns.[40] A body of experimental research began to emerge showing that personal conversations can be remarkably effective in turning out voters.[41] The topline finding again comes from Green and Gerber's book, *Get Out the Vote: How to Increase Voter Turnout*.[42] According to their synthesis of more than 100 controlled experiments, their conservative estimate is that face-to-face canvassing can yield "one additional vote for every 14 people," or a 7.1-percent increase in turnout.[43] They argue that this figure likely understates the effectiveness of door-to-door canvassing because "about 60 percent of the direct impact of canvassing appears to be transmitted to voters' housemates."[44] For these reasons, they argue that door knocks are the "gold-standard mobilization tactic," despite the high cost-per-voter-reached, as compared to paid media.[45] Most of the field experiments Green and Gerber analyzed, however, reflect the work of paid canvassers, which is different from OFA's local volunteer-driven model.[46] Nevertheless, these experimental studies reinforced previous research demonstrating that personal recruitment has a powerful effect on turning out voters.[47]

All of these factors—the erosion of the party establishment, the attendant unraveling of the precinct captain infrastructure, the rise of mass media, and increased attention to the power of direct voter contact—presented a ripe opportunity for a new kind of field campaigning. We turn next to the salient elements of the ground campaigns that immediately preceded OFA 2008: Howard Dean's mobilization of progressive online communities, called his "netroots," his campaign's New Hampshire house meetings, John Kerry's outsourced canvassing efforts, and George W. Bush's much-acclaimed 72-hour voter mobilization blitz. According to most observers, the 2004 election marked a fundamental shift in how campaigns organized their in-person contact operations.[48]

## A NEW ERA OF FIELD CAMPAIGNING:
## THE 2004 GROUND GAME

In 2004, Howard Dean, then a little-known governor from Vermont, made an unlikely run for the presidency. Although he lost, the unexpected enthusiasm he generated made campaign strategists pay attention. In multiple ways, Dean's team laid the foundation for Obama's success. Berman writes,

> Dean's run for the presidency embraced and amplified a few unique notions that profoundly altered modern American politics, namely, that committed volunteers are cheaper and more effective than the same old crew of professional campaign consultants; that small donations in large numbers can do more than large donations in small numbers; that the Internet and new social-networking tools could level the playing field for seemingly quixotic candidacies and attract hordes of new people into politics for the first time; and that Democrats needed to compete everywhere, including in the hinterlands of long-forgotten red America, stand up for some core principles, and stick with them.[49]

Despite its loss, the 2004 Dean campaign built a host of new digital tools, found clever ways to use social networking sites like Meetup.com, and, perhaps most important, revamped the Democrats' voter database, which is still in use today. It also served as the electoral baptism for many of the organizers who would later develop the 2008 OFA field organizing model, which we describe in chapter 3.

In discussing Dean's innovations, many have focused on the Dean campaign's pioneering use of the Internet. Joe Trippi, Dean's campaign manager, famously declared, "There is only one tool, one platform, one medium that allows the American people to take their government back, and that's the Internet."[50] The Dean campaign's obsession with the Internet was summed up in this anecdote from the campaign's headquarters in Vermont: "Trippi scribbled four things on a giant whiteboard: Iowa, New Hampshire, Internet, and $. If you came in to talk to him about anything else, he said, 'Get the fuck out of my office.' "[51]

Many of Dean's key digital staff joined the Obama campaign in 2008, carrying the netroots legacy with them. "We pioneered it," Trippi later said, "and Obama perfected it."[52] Dean's director of Internet organizing, Zephyr Teachout, contends that in the four, feverish months preceding the 2004 Democratic primary, "all of the seeds of what then became the Obama campaign were created."[53] In 2005, when Dean became chair of the Democratic National Committee, he brought with him his team of "young Deaniacs" to develop VoteBuilder, which became the Democratic National Committee's—and then OFA's—database in both 2008 and 2012.[54]

As Berman recounts, however, it was not just Dean's Meetups and his use of the Internet to fundraise that signaled a sea change in American presidential campaigns. As effective as his online efforts were, campaigns had been using online technologies as a tool for nearly a decade before Dean.[55] Nielsen agrees: Most organizations (not just political ones), he argues, already leveraged information technology to "supplement, extend, and augment existing practices, not to transform them."[56]

A lesser-known innovation of the Dean campaign can be traced back to its New Hampshire field operation. According to Marshall Ganz, the organizer-turned-Harvard-professor who some consider the silent giant behind the Obama team model, Dean's New Hampshire effort was "the real 'starting point' for the [Obama] organizing approach."[57]

Bird, who would later be one of the main conduits through which the neighborhood team model was introduced to the Obama campaign, worked under Dean's New Hampshire director Karen Hicks in 2004. Hicks had been "running a pretty traditional campaign, relying on under-paid college students to knock on doors in support of Dean."[58] It was not working. After "knocking on seventeen-thousand doors during the spring and summer, the campaign netted only three-hundred new supporters, a disappointing return rate."[59] Hicks paid a visit to Ganz at Harvard.

As legend has it, Hicks told Ganz: "We're not getting the numbers we need. What if we tried community organizing?" "Oh, that would be interesting," Ganz responded. "We haven't done that for a while in elec-toral politics."[60] Ganz recounted the meeting:

> [Hicks] came down to see me [in July 2003] with a tale of woe about the canvassing operation that they were doing with their enthusiastic young organizers but that was going nowhere and asked if I could help her bring an organizing approach into it. This led to a one-day workshop that I did with her crew of 35 or so in an almost intolerably hot yurt on the [University of New Hampshire] campus.

Under Ganz's guidance, Hicks's New Hampshire team launched a house meeting program, an approach built on legendary community organizer Fred Ross's strategy to engage directly with voters in their homes. The house meeting philosophy called for generating local capacity by turning young canvassers into organizers, sharing personal stories, and building a structure for collective action out of relational networks. Ross pioneered the house meeting in the Mexican community of East Los Angeles as a tactic for building capacity where none existed and first recruited Cesar Chavez at a house meeting in San Jose.[61]

The house meeting approach worked remarkably well in New Hampshire. One poll found that "a third of New Hampshire voters reported being invited to a Dean meeting" and "for the first time in many years, the organizers and the supporters, rather than just the candidate, became the stars of the campaign."[62] In another key moment that summer, Ganz "recommended Jeremy [Bird] to Karen [Hicks] and Karen to Jeremy." Bird had been one of Ganz's teaching assistants at Harvard the year before. The house-meeting model that Dean's New Hampshire team began to use with great success—and which would become very familiar to Obama organizers in 2008 and 2012—included "telling your story, one-on-ones leading to house meetings, and very intensive data collection and analysis on the actual organizing," said Ganz.

Dean's field campaign in New Hampshire was markedly different from his Iowa operation, where a young organizer named Buffy Wicks was stationed. "Buffy called me to try to figure out how to do what we were doing in New Hampshire in Iowa," Bird said. In Iowa, the campaign sent out-of-state staffers and volunteers in droves to attempt to persuade and turn out voters. One *New York Times* reporter observed,

> Dr. Dean has run as the quintessential political outsider, and his campaign has by far the most workers from outside Iowa. Every weekend since Christmas, fresh batches of volunteers have arrived from as far away as Texas, Virginia, and Mississippi. They get fluorescent orange knit hats, cellphones, purple identification wristbands and 45 minutes of training in the nuts and bolts of caucus procedure, then are sent out to stump as part of what they call the Iowa Perfect Storm.[63]

A Pew Research Center survey that randomly sampled a list of nearly 12,000 Dean supporters found that, "as befits a population heavily involved in politics," they were, "more interested and engaged in politics, more ideological, and better educated than the average citizen or their fellow partisans."[64]

Instead of expanding his support in Iowa, however, some argue that Dean's out-of-state volunteers "repelled caucus voters who resented being told how to vote by a bunch of kids from out-of-state wearing bright orange hats."[65] For many reasons—including, as many postmortem analyses said, Dean's fumbling field operation—John Kerry and John Edwards defeated Dean resoundingly in Iowa. Cohen and colleagues write,

"Despite their disadvantage, Kerry and Edwards finished well ahead of the two candidates [Dean and Dick Gephardt] with the commanding organizations."[66]

Dean's loss in Iowa and the subsequent demise of his campaign meant that the campaign "didn't get a chance to test [the New Hampshire electoral-organizing model] in the general election," OFA's 2012 deputy national field director Marlon Marshall said. As a result, it was not until Obama was elected in 2008 that "people really woke up," Marshall noted, to the potential electoral gains to be won from building local capacity in the way Ganz and Hicks had introduced to the Dean campaign in 2003 and 2004. Even Obama's 2004 Senate campaign—which was predicated on his roots as a community organizer—resembled a traditional political operation. Ganz remembered that Bird "had gone out to check out [Obama's Senate campaign], expecting to see an organizing operation, but found nothing close to it." It took until 2008 for people to realize that volunteer- and team-based organizing could "work in terms of a large-scale presidential election," Marshall argues.

When Bird and Wicks assumed leadership roles in key states in Obama's primary election in 2007 and 2008, they designed their field programs with their divergent experiences on the Dean campaign in mind. While Bird had his first encounter with the precursor to what would later become the OFA way in New Hampshire, Wicks had worked for Dean in Iowa, where she protested the campaign's reliance on out-of-state volunteers to no avail. While Hicks and her team in New Hampshire held more than 1,000 house meetings and recruited hundreds of Granite State natives to do outreach for them, Dean's Iowa effort had imported thousands of out-of-state supporters to rally voters—ultimately unsuccessfully—to the caucuses.

## John Kerry's Outsourced Operation

In contrast to the Dean campaign's experimentalism, Kerry's 2004 operation embraced a textbook model of field campaigning. Staff built an in-state volunteer operation in Iowa but relied primarily on precinct captains, the labor movement, and party faithful to help make phone calls, deliver yard signs, and give rides to the polls. During the general election, Kerry's operation outsourced much of its voter contact to the newly established 527 group America Coming Together (ACT), funded by billionaire George Soros. ACT spent about $80 million hiring roughly 4,000 full-time staffers, 45,000 paid part-time canvassers, and enlisting approximately 70,000 volunteers in 17 battleground states.[67]

At the same time, MoveOn, the largest of the online progressive groups at the time, hired 500 organizers to run a $5 million "neighbor-to-neighbor" program. Pro-Kerry (or anti-Bush) partisans thus channeled their energy into these progressive interest groups. The Democrats attempted to reach beyond the party establishment to engage a larger cross-section of liberal activists. The strategy, however, had drawbacks. First, because of campaign finance laws, ACT, MoveOn, and other allied groups were not considered part of Kerry's federally financed expenditures. They were therefore forbidden to explicitly state the candidate's name when making phone calls and canvassing voters. Instead, they "armed themselves with Palm Pilots that play[ed] 'issue' videos."[68] Perhaps unsurprisingly, ACT disbanded after the election. As Nielsen writes, "less than a year after the election, the largest 527 group of the 2004 cycle was effectively no more."[69]

All told, the *Almanac of American Politics* reports that the Democratic National Committee enlisted 233,000 volunteers in 2004 in addition to the 115,000 activists from ACT and MoveOn. With just shy of 350,000 ground campaigners on behalf of Kerry in a roster of swing states, this was, according to many political observers, "traditional, industrial-era politics, well executed."[70]

### George W. Bush's 72-Hour Program

On the Republican side, by contrast, the *Almanac* observes that more than 1.4 million people volunteered for GOP candidates on Election Day in 2004. Unlike Kerry's outsourced and staff-driven voter turnout drive, the Bush campaign "depended on volunteers persuading people with whom they had something in common to get out and vote." Barone and Cohen provide one illustration: "If a Bush volunteer was a Hispanic accountant active in the Boy Scouts, the campaign would reach out through him to other Hispanics, accountants and their clients, and Boy Scout volunteers."[71]

After the 2000 election, George W. Bush's campaign strategists identified the ground war as one of its top priorities for the reelection. They admitted that they had been out-muscled on the ground by the unions' heavy mobilization efforts on behalf of Gore. At the 2002 election postmortem conference at Harvard, Bush's chief campaign strategist Karl Rove observed that "one of the Gore campaign's greatest unsung successes [was] Election Day."[72] He went on to praise Donna Brazile, Gore's campaign manager, in this statement:

> Early on, literally in 1999 when we knew that she was going to be associated with the campaign, we started studying what Donna would do about getting out the vote. So we began early, building a huge get-out-the-vote apparatus. And we did. We built the largest, biggest, baddest, best-funded get-out-the-vote operation on the Republican side.... Our mistake was that we assumed that this would be big enough to overcome [the Democratic] efforts. It wasn't.[73]

With this in mind, during Bush's first term, Rove masterminded two different ground strategies for 2004: the 72-Hour Program to boost voter turnout and STOMP—the Strategic Taskforce to Organize and Mobilize People. RNC insider Blaise Hazelwood was chosen to spearhead both efforts in an attempt to reintroduce grassroots campaigning to the GOP. In 2003, Hazelwood described her commitment to face-to-face campaigning: "I always heard stories about my grandmother. It was all personal contact, and it obviously worked."[74] In advance of Bush's reelection campaign, the Republicans invested more than $1 million in 50 field experiments to test how best to contact voters and refine turnout lists.[75]

The 72-Hour Program drew inspiration from the American Way (Amway)'s famous direct sales model, a marketing scheme used to sell commercial products to consumers via face-to-face contact.[76] Campaign volunteers were charged with canvassing voters who shared some affiliation, such as a neighborhood, church, or NRA (National Rifle Association) chapter. In this way, Republican activists recruited local volunteers to personally contact targeted voters. The project, which was pioneering in its use of a local, self-replicating model on an electoral campaign, sought to flood Republican swing voters with turnout messages in the three days leading up to the election.[77]

STOMP was a GOP-wide organizational vehicle that diverted money, staff, and volunteers from safe districts into competitive races and precincts across the country. Through a combination of the 72-Hour Program and STOMP, by February 2004, "the RNC knew precisely how many volunteers it needed on the ground in Ohio, where they would be, and what they'd be doing" on Election Day.[78] "In 2004," Nielsen writes, Rove "had few reasons to envy the Democrats and their allies anything."[79]

Indeed, as Dean observed in the wake of the 2004 election on *Meet the Press*, "We [the Democrats and Kerry campaign] sent 14,000 people into Ohio from elsewhere. [Bush] had 14,000 from Ohio talking to their neighbors, and that's how you win rural states and rural America."[80] In fact, as Berman points out, using local volunteers can be a winning field strategy everywhere. Subsequent experimental research validated what Dean's trouncing in Iowa and Bush's victory in Ohio suggest, that is, "Voters are less likely to be influenced by campaigners from other communities."[81]

Rove and Hazelwood were praised for these ground game innovations. Whereas the Bush-Cheney campaign had mobilized 450,000 volunteers in 2000, STOMP and the 72-Hour Program increased that number more than threefold in 2004. "By assembling a core of 1.4 million volunteers," write Barone and Cohen, the Bush campaign "created a quantum of social connectedness that the Republican nominee can build on; a long-lasting asset for the Republican Party."[82] After this feat, the GOP spoke of a lasting Red America, "built on razor-thin electoral majorities, donor largesse, and effectively institutionalized and highly disciplined political organizing."[83]

OFA's ground game built on important lessons from the 2004 Bush-Cheney field campaign. First and foremost, the 2004 Republican 72-Hour Program demonstrated the ability of national campaigns to run locally led volunteer programs. Second, just as Rove's operation sought to target each voter with a custom-made message—"Coors beer and bourbon drinkers, college football television viewers, Fox News viewers, people with caller ID"[84]—so too the Obama campaign sought out the farmers market, Volvo-driving, and MSNBC faithful. Third, "just as Sam Walton figured he could make huge profits selling things to people in low-income rural areas," the Bush campaign calculated that it could "wring votes out of areas that most political strategists and political reporters ignored."[85] The Kerry campaign relied on labor unions, paid staff, and 527s to turn out votes in urban strongholds, while the Bush and Obama campaigns built sprawling operations with a heavy volunteer presence in cities as well as in the heartlands and hinterlands of America.

## LAYING THE FOUNDATION FOR 2008

According to its internal count, the Obama campaign dwarfed all of these numbers, engaging 2.2 million volunteers in 2012. Unlike previous campaigns, the Obama field model did not rely on the party infrastructure, the labor movement, out-of-state volunteers, 527s, or a last-minute GOTV blitz. Instead, in 2008, OFA cobbled together an electoral-organizing strategy, one that embraced the gritty but necessary work of recruiting local volunteers and testing their voter contact capacity well in advance of the election. In so doing, OFA revived elements of the shoe-leather politics that had characterized older campaigns, even as it built on the cutting-edge mobilization research and technology that had emerged from the 2004 election.

The context within which the field innovations of the Obama campaign emerged reflected three important shifts, which we have outlined in this chapter: the dissolution of the traditional party system in the twentieth century; the rise of new, paid, and mass media; and the resurgent interest in the efficacy of face-to-face, targeted communication in the early 2000s. These forces converged in the 2004 election, albeit in different ways in the Democratic and Republican camps. In 2008, key players on the Obama team studied lessons from both sides, tested different approaches, and then sought to sharpen them.

As we detail in the next chapters, OFA learned as an organization to invest in and develop its *human* resources (not just its financial or technological resources) and, in doing so, transformed the people who were a part of it. Rick Baer of Colorado, for example, described himself as a "lifelong Democrat" but drew stark contrasts between his campaign volunteering experiences before and after OFA:

> I've supported other candidates and worked for Democrats when I had time, but it usually ended up being just like a Saturday afternoon walk in the precinct, or something like that, a few days during the campaign. I knocked on doors and canvassed. I worked on the Kerry campaign, but I really didn't have the passion, I guess you would say, that I did with the Obama campaign. I just really submerged myself into it.

In the next chapters, we explore why volunteers like Cathy Johns, introduced in chapter 1, "interrupted [their] lives" for OFA, and why otherwise minimally engaged Democrats like Baer "submerged" themselves in the Obama campaign. By taking a gamble on volunteers and by eschewing campaign models that outsourced voter contact to the party, to unions, and to impermanent 527s, OFA developed a new kind of American field campaign. In part II of this book, we will see how the Obama campaign adopted and adapted the principles of community organizing to scrupulously build a field program that engaged an estimated 200 volunteers per paid organizer. The result was both an electoral victory for Obama and, for many first-time volunteers, a resurgence of the kind of deep political engagement Alexis de Tocqueville admired centuries ago when he first observed American democracy.

# 3.

# DISCOVERY AND DIFFUSION

All these staff recognized that the volunteers were important and needed to be heard and their opinions valued. [OFA's motto was] respect, empower, include...and they did. And I think that that made a difference because a lot of people would talk about volunteering on other campaigns and saying they never felt like they were part of anything; that they were just called up at the last minute and say go here or go do that and weren't valued.

*—Deidre Reynolds, Nashua, NH, Neighborhood*
*Team Leader, OFA 2012*

One of the most distinctive features of the OFA ground game was its sustained reliance on volunteers. The campaign's motto, "respect, empower, include," gave OFA an aura—especially in 2008—of being more like a social movement than an electoral campaign. Incorporating volunteers in substantial ways, however, was not a foregone conclusion at the outset of the campaign. In 2007 and 2008, OFA leaders had to learn to trust, motivate, and manage volunteers. This chapter describes that journey.

When Obama announced his candidacy on a frigid February morning in 2007, he reminded the teeming crowd in Springfield of how he had arrived in Illinois. Just out of college, he came to Chicago "without money or family connections." At the time, he said, "a group of churches had offered me a job as a community organizer for the grand sum of $13,000 a year." Obama continued, "I accepted the job, sight unseen, motivated then by a single, simple, powerful idea: that I might play a small part in building a better America." This was the same kind of step that thousands of others would take when they decided to work for the Obama campaign in 2008.

At the time, Obama was a long shot candidate running against the formidable resources, experience, and star power of the Clinton machine. Hillary Clinton's chief strategist Mark Penn said, "For starters, her husband was not only a popular former president but also widely considered among the savviest strategists in all of politics.... Veterans of past Clinton campaigns owned Washington's Democratic turf. Rank-and-file Democrats adored the Clinton brand.... We have the highest levels of early enthusiasm for any Democratic candidate in modern history—people don't just like Hillary Clinton, they love her."[1] Obama, by contrast, was polling as the top choice for just 14 percent of Iowa Democrats in January of 2007. *Real Clear Politics*' nationwide average of polls showed that Clinton had twice the support Obama did.

Being the underdog forced OFA leaders to innovate. Whether by design or benign neglect, the Obama's 2008 primary campaign became a laboratory of ground game strategies, what Buffy Wicks called a "petri dish" of different possibilities. Throughout the bitterly fought primary campaign between Obama and Clinton, OFA organizers were identifying, testing, and modifying different approaches to running a field operation.

The 2008 national field director, Jon Carson, created what Bird called "a culture of learning and experimenting. He was patient, and if you proved it worked, he would go with it." Bird argues that this was central to the campaign's ability to innovate: "[I'm] not sure how to give this guy more credit—but the fact that he was giving his staff the opportunity to succeed is actually huge, and a big departure from the old-school model." "On a different campaign," said Joy Cushman, one of the early Obama field staffers and another protégé of Ganz, "[the field staff] would have just been told what to do." The tumultuous 16-month stretch from Obama's announcement to his acceptance of the nomination was thus an unintentional testing ground for what would become OFA's electoral-organizing field program.

This chapter describes the discovery process that occurred through-out the 2008 primary season, charting the journey toward the field model that OFA implemented nationwide in 2012. How did OFA decide to start relying on volunteers? How did campaign staff figure out ways to identify, recruit, and support those volunteers? We show how the field model emerged not through premeditated planning, but instead by an iterative process of trying new things, learning from mistakes, and trying again. In showing how the field program developed, we also uncover some of the core elements of OFA's unique electoral-organizing model: neighborhood team structures that make collective action possible, relationships that motivate and inspire commitment, and a focus on enabling volunteers to take responsibility for outcomes. We elaborate all of these elements further in part II of the book.

We describe this journey through the eyes of OFA's earliest field staff—including Jeremy Bird, Buffy Wicks, and 2008 Iowa caucus director Mitch Stewart—who joined hundreds of others who left school and steady jobs to work for a long-shot candidate. Many of these people came to the campaign with a passion for organizing. Wicks told us, "We all recognize *now* the value of organizing, but I think prior to the Obama world it wasn't taken as seriously. Pre-Obama," she continued, "[volunteers] on political campaigns were often treated like, 'Oh we have to kind of deal with them.'" In the "Obama world," Wicks said, "we were like, 'Oh this is our strength, this is part of our strategy, this is how we are going to win.'" This chapter shows how these early field staff applied organizing lessons they had learned elsewhere to the campaign in order to take advantage of the flood of Obama supporters, and in the process, hone an alternative model for field campaigning in America.

## LEARNING THROUGH THE 2008 PRIMARIES

As Wicks observed, the innovations that emerged from the 2008 prima-ries were rooted in the Obama campaign's basic need to rely on volun-teers. Whether the campaign depended on them because non-Iowans were not allowed in the caucus counting areas, or because they had only six paid organizers in the entire state of California, OFA had to figure out how to turn Obama's base of supporters into an electoral ground game. Entrusting volunteers with great responsibility is risky, however, because unpaid recruits are notorious for being unreliable. Even those who consistently show up may not have or be willing to learn the skills the campaign needs, or they may have narrow personal agendas that differ from the overarching electoral goal. How could the campaign build and maintain motivation among volunteers? What kind of support did volunteers need to do their work? How could campaign staff hold volunteers accountable?

Community organizers and social movements have grappled with these challenges for years. Community organizing facilitates social change by building power within an aggrieved constituency. It is an approach to social change that develops the capacity of people in a given constituency to act as leaders and to enable others to achieve their shared purpose.[2] As Ganz teaches, community organizing works by investing in the motivations, skills, and capacities of volunteers; transforming volunteers into leaders; building community around those leaders; and harnessing power from within that community.

Community organizing practices have been largely absent from modern field programs because, as described in the previous chapter, campaigns were often viewed as temporary machines created to get voters to the polls—not to build their capacity for leadership and collective action. OFA, by contrast, *did* want to build the capacity of volunteers, originally out of necessity. In many cases, the organization needed volunteers to do the work of staff. Thus, several rogue OFA field staff in a handful of primary states began to integrate practices of community organizing into their work.

The story that unfolds shows how the campaign learned to transform volunteers into an asset, and in so doing, transform the volunteers themselves. Although we describe the lessons sequentially to better illuminate the core points, the actual process of learning within the campaign was often messy and circuitous. OFA leaders were trying out new approaches on the ground, failing often, and starting over to attempt entirely new approaches. Over time, through this frenzy of activity, several key practices began to emerge.

First, OFA staff had to learn to trust volunteers. In Iowa in particular, they learned that well-trained supporters would show up and could produce real results if they were taken seriously. Second, they had to figure out how to identify, recruit, and motivate more supporters to take on leadership roles. In South Carolina and California, early OFA staff found that if they invested time in building relationships with volunteers, and organizing those relationships into neighborhood teams, they created a motivational and self-replicating basis for growing their capacity. Volunteers may have come to the campaign because they cared about Obama, but they stayed because they were committed to the people with whom they worked, as 28 of our interviewees articulated. Third, OFA had to figure out how to equip and support volunteers. They developed a training model in California that would eventually spread to the entire country. Fourth, they had to figure out how to hold volunteers accountable for real outputs—measured in calls, knocks, and voter registration forms—and to give them access to the data they needed to get that work done. Finally, early Obama campaign staff had to figure out how to take their electoral-organizing model to scale. Although the program emerged because of scarcity—some primary states had only a handful of staff—the challenge eventually became one of abundance. Without a clear reporting structure and accountability loops, OFA would not have been able to manage all of the people who were eager to get involved. Could OFA take the principles of community organizing, which often operates at a hyper-local level, and create a national program?

The 2008 primary season was one of the most complicated nomination processes in American electoral history. Table 3.1 provides a roadmap to serve as a reference tool for this chapter. We include only those states for which we have data on the ground campaign as it related to the discovery and diffusion of the OFA electoral-organizing model. The narrative of this chapter tracks loosely with the chronology of the primaries and seeks to highlight the key lessons that OFA's leaders extracted in each state.

## TABLE 3.1: Nomination Contest, 2008 (Obama vs. Clinton)

| Date, 2008 | State | Pledged delegates *from election* (cumulative)* | | Key lessons for OFA field |
|---|---|---|---|---|
| | | *Obama* | *Clinton* | |
| January 3 | Iowa | 16 | 15 | • Respect, empower, include volunteers<br>• Nontraditional, local volunteers will deliver<br>• Field organizers' long-term immersion is critical |
| January 8 | New Hampshire | 25 | 24 | • Command-and-control model of field failed to deliver and demotivated staff |
| January 19 | Nevada | 38 | 36 | |
| January 26 | South Carolina | 63 | 48 | • First pilot of the relationship-based, neighborhood team model<br>• Learn to develop metrics that measure capacity and hold volunteer teams accountable |
| February 5 | Super Tuesday (23 primaries/caucuses) | 910 | 882 | • California: Camp Obamas as a launch point for neighborhood teams and volunteer leaders<br>• Volunteers can handle staff responsibilities |
| February 9–19 | 11 primaries/caucuses | 1,197.5 | 1,048.5 | |
| March 4–11 | 7 primaries/caucuses | 1,407.5 | 1,250.5 | • Texas two-step: with real accountability, volunteers can manage data |

(*continued*)

TABLE 3.1: **Continued**

| Date, 2008 | State | Pledged delegates *from election* (cumulative)* | | Key lessons for OFA field |
| --- | --- | --- | --- | --- |
| | | *Obama* | *Clinton* | |
| April 22 | Pennsylvania | 1,480.5 | 1,338.5 | • Large-scale pilot of the team model<br>• Volunteers can be trusted<br>• Staff respond well to empowerment, too |
| May 3–June 3 | 9 primaries and restored delegates from Michigan and Florida | 1,794.5 | 1,732.5 | |

*Delegate counts shown are those won by either candidate in electoral contests. The totals do not reflect superdelegate counts.

## 1. Respect, empower, and include volunteers

Since the Iowa caucuses were first instituted in 1972, the winner has gone on to become the nominee eight out of eleven times on the Democratic side, and six out of ten times on the Republican side. Almost all presidential campaigns pour enormous resources into Iowa in an attempt to deal an early blow to competitors. Obama's and Clinton's campaigns in 2008 were no exception.

As discussed in chapter 2, the 2004 Dean campaign had deployed nearly 3,500 "Deaniacs," the vast majority from out of state, to go door-to-door in the days before the caucus. Wearing orange hats to distinguish themselves, they called the operation the "Perfect Storm," a less-than-apt metaphor for the blizzard-prone Midwest. The influx of Deaniacs in the final days before the caucus was the culmination of the campaign hype surrounding the excitement that Dean had generated among youth, new voters, and the netroots. Despite all the enthusiasm, on January 19, 2004, Howard Dean took third place in the Iowa caucuses, trailing John Kerry by nearly 20 points. Many interpreted Dean's loss as a lesson about the danger of trusting youth and new voters to show up for a caucus. For early OFA field staff, the 2004 Dean campaign in Iowa was, in many ways, a cautionary tale.

Yet when Obama's campaign operatives hit the ground in Iowa, they quickly realized that they had to find a way to get new voters to the caucuses. They recognized that Clinton had a lock on most of the Democratic Party establishment in Iowa: Obama would never gain traction if the field program relied solely on the local Party. As Mitch Stewart recalled, campaign manager David Plouffe and Iowa state director Paul Tewes recognized early that they had to expand the base of caucus-goers in order to win. "If we had to rely on the normal universe—basically people who are Democratic Party activists—and not expand who participates, then [we'd] be in deep, deep trouble." To win, OFA would need to find new voters who would show up in January and persuade fellow Iowans to caucus in their corner. Second, only registered Iowa Democrats were permitted to enter the caucus arenas. Staff, many of whom were indeed from out-of-state, therefore had to identify and train a local caucus volunteer leader and what OFA would call a "math captain," whose job it would be to determine when Obama was getting 15 percent of the caucus attendees.[3]

Led by Tewes, Stewart, and field director Anne Filipic, the Obama team in Iowa needed a different strategy. How could they turn new voters into trustworthy volunteers? They knew their field program had to be far more disciplined and rooted in local communities than Dean's Iowa strategy had been in 2004. Dean's New Hampshire campaign had piloted a different ground game strategy, quite unlike his Iowa "Perfect Storm" debacle. According to Steve Hildebrand, OFA's deputy national campaign director, the Dean campaign in New Hampshire "presented an intriguing model," both because of its use of the netroots and in its novel use of organizing tactics.[4] Could OFA build a campaign that successfully borrowed from the community organizing canon?

It was in responding to this question that the Obama campaign mantra took root. Taking organizing lessons from the Dean campaign and the spirit of Obama's candidacy into account, "respect, empower, and include" became the refrain that defined OFA. Paul Tewes is credited with coining the phrase and the maxim was, as Bird put it, it "one-hundred percent, authentically Iowan." Under the aegis of respecting, empowering, and including local actors, the OFA team painstakingly built a field program that trained caucus volunteers to corral, count, and connect with Iowans, many of whom were disillusioned by the establishment, both right and left. "We started very grass-rootsy," said Stewart. "We would go to Java Joe's and we would steal their wifi." Four key innovations that would become part of the bedrock of OFA for years to come emerged in Iowa: enlisting volunteers early, focusing relentlessly on meaningful metrics, methodically expanding the campaign's roster of new supporters, and demystifying the rules of the democratic process.

From the start, the Iowa leadership decided to "bring in volunteers on the front end rather than on the back end," according to Stewart, who had worked as a regional director for John Edwards's campaign in 2003 and 2004. The Edwards ground game, as with most that came before it, "was very staff-heavy, meaning that there were only a few volunteers," Stewart said. Recruiting volunteers for the Iowa caucuses can be a "slog," regardless of the year or candidate. Unlike in the general election, "where you can just tap into a whole host of Democrats and just spend your time identifying volunteers," there are often half a dozen other viable candidates in this phase of the campaign. To address this challenge, the Iowa field leadership taught its organizers to do "one-on-ones with potential supporters," Stewart said, in order to make volunteers central to the campaign. By building relationships with Iowans and securing their commitment to Obama, the campaign could then "try to get them to take on a leadership role in the organization." Thus, although the Iowa campaign was flush with field staff, those staff were focused on empowering volunteers to lead their caucuses rather than turning out the voters on their own. Aiming to have as much "statewide coverage as humanly possible," OFA opened up nearly 40 field offices in Iowa and grew to 160 field staff before the caucuses, a number that Stewart said was unheard of at the time. "The scope of our footprint in the state was beyond anything we had seen before—a huge, huge staff."

To be sure, other campaigns recruit volunteers, but, as Stewart pointed out, the model is "usually one staffer as the center point of recruiting volunteers—so your growth is limited." Distributing leadership such that volunteers were recruiting other volunteers "is what was new both in Iowa in '07 and in applying that to the general election." He continued,

> Instead of having staffers split their time between calling voters, they spend all their time reaching out to volunteers, holding one-on-ones, and then using that as an angle for the volunteer contact [so that those volunteers become organizers recruiting new voters]. [The old model] might yield better early returns…but that plateaus really quickly and there is no room for growth. If you have folks that invest early in the volunteers, you start a bit slower, but the growth that you see in the end is explosive and much more so than what you could do if you had just staff-based activity.

Second, the centrality of metrics for which OFA became famous can also be traced, in part, to Iowa in 2007 and 2008. Plouffe decamped to Stewart and Filipic's office in Des Moines in the final weeks before the caucus. He would continually refresh and track the "number of supporters that we had identified, the number of precinct captains we'd recruited, and where they were, by county or precinct," Stewart remembered. On the afternoon of the caucus, the OFA field team and volunteers reached the goal of 100,000 identified supporters. The precincts were prioritized internally according to the number of delegates that they could apportion based on their population: in "tier one, I think we had 98% coverage, tier two it was like 80, tier three it was like 70%, and tier four was like 50%," Stewart said, referring to the quotas of committed Obama caucus-goers and local volunteer leaders in relation to OFA's internal ranking.

Third, in addition to the heightened focus on numbers, Stewart distilled what he repeatedly cited as OFA's Iowa primary strategy: "We had to expand the universe of people participating on caucus night. If we didn't we would lose." Two key demographics they targeted were new independents and young people. OFA launched "Barackstar" chapters at Iowa's 106 high schools, "because even if you're 17 you can still caucus if you will be 18 by the time of the general election," Stewart said. High school students, he continued, "were great at convincing their parents and even grandparents to caucus for [Obama]" too.

Finally, the influx of new voters meant that "there was a huge education gap on what a caucus actually was, so we came up with a program to demystify it," Stewart said. Cognizant that registering and identifying a supporter was necessary but insufficient, OFA empowered volunteers to "sit down and talk to people that had never caucused before, because [the local volunteers] are the best validators." This was one of the main tactics the campaign used to ensure what Stewart described as "everyone's fear: We know that there was the support there…but will they show up on caucus night?"

On January 3, 2008, at 7:00 p.m., Iowans poured into 1,781 precinct caucus sites across the state. The Obama campaign had an "organization established at each one of those precincts," Stewart said. A record 239,000 people turned out to caucus for the Democrats, compared with roughly half that (125,000) in 2004. For one winter evening, fire halls and school gymnasiums transformed into sites of direct democracy, where voters indicated their support for a candidate by standing in their candidate's designated area of the caucus site.

Zack Davis, then a pre-medical student at the University of Iowa, remembers walking in to his assigned caucus location and immediately leaving. "They told me that I had to register as a Democrat in order to caucus. I told them that wasn't going to happen." Davis had grown up in Kansas, where he said that the Republican Party was "the only political party I knew." He had volunteered on the Bush campaigns in both 2000 and 2004. He turned around and left the caucus, dismayed. Davis decided to talk to a friend about his dilemma: He was eager to participate in the historic election, but he recoiled at having to identify as a Democrat in order to do so. A friend convinced him that making his voice heard was more important than his political affiliation on the record books at the Board of Elections.

Davis returned and registered as a Democrat, but remained undecided about which candidate he would support. In part, he reflected, it was because he found the process overwhelming. "I didn't know what that entailed of me, what I had to do," he said. Yet, what most surprised

Davis was the "personalized" air that the supporters from Obama's corner exuded in the high school gymnasium:

> They were very welcoming and they just wanted to get to know me.... They weren't campaign staff. They were just other support-ers. And I think that opened me up to the fact that this is different than, you know, when I helped out organizing and just getting some other athletes on campus to vote for Bush in 2004. You did it because you were Republican and that was what they wanted you to do. It was what I felt was kind of expected of us, whereas this [the Iowa caucus] was like—it was a very personal touch. [The Obama volunteers] wanted to know my name. They wanted to know what I did. They wanted to know why I was there. And I think that is something that has always carried through, through all of the iterations of OFA.

Davis went on to become a regional field director for OFA, and the friend whose advice he sought that fateful night is now his wife.

The OFA team in Iowa delivered two important victories: not only did Obama win by almost a 10-point margin,[5] but staff leaders throughout the campaign began to believe that new voters and volunteers could be trusted when they were respected, empowered, and included by cam-paign staff. In his victory speech, Obama declared, "On this January night, at this defining moment in history, you have done what the cynics said we couldn't do."

A year earlier, Danny Johnson had taken time off from college to organize for Obama in Iowa. He recalled how the summer before the caucus, in 2007, "Clinton looked like she was going to just run away with the nomination." The outcome in Iowa, he reminisced, "was a 180-degree turn. We felt like we were a part of the most important political movement in a generation."

## 2. Avoid the "old school" command-and-control model

New Hampshire voters would go to the polls just five days after Iowa, on January 8, 2008. Ground staff in the Granite State had implemented a traditional command-and-control campaign model, in which staff were tasked with making hundreds of phone calls and door knocks a day. Dan Grandone moved to Manchester in the summer of 2007 to volunteer for Obama. He would go on to become a deputy field director in Wisconsin in 2008, and the OFA state director in 2010. Grandone observed that the field programs in the 2008 primaries "differed from one state to another depending on the leadership. The contrast between the state director and field director in New Hampshire versus, say, what Jeremy [Bird] set up in South Carolina and what Mitch [Stewart] set up in Iowa was like night and day."

Grandone remembers the New Hampshire leadership representing a "really old school style of machismo": The field director would pace the office with a baseball bat in hand, an intimidation tactic to keep the staff on the phone calling voters at all times. Rather than invest in volunteer capacity to reach voters, the field staff did all the voter contact themselves, including the persuasion phone calls and door knocks. "They ran an old school, fear-not-love, marketing operation," Ganz said, echoing Grandone.

After Iowa, Obama surged to a nearly 10-point lead in the polls in New Hampshire, and pundits declared that the Clinton campaign was all but finished. In a surprise reversal, however, Clinton won New Hampshire by 3 percentage points, a significant comeback victory after her third-place finish in Iowa. Numerous factors contributed to Obama's loss in New Hampshire. Many Obama field staff, however, interpreted the loss as a repudiation of the command-and-control model of staff-driven voter contact and a field program based on achieving voter contact without building capacity through investments in human capital. New Hampshire in 2008 was, according to Grandone and others, a missed opportunity to develop a new kind of people-powered field program, particularly given what the Dean campaign had built in the state in 2004.

## 3. Motivate people through relationships and neighborhood teams

Prior to joining OFA, Bird and Wicks worked for Wake Up Wal-Mart, a national campaign that built power among the workers of the world's largest private employer to fight the corporation's unfair labor practices.[6] Before that, as described in chapter 2, both had been part of the Dean campaign in 2004, Bird in New Hampshire and Wicks in Iowa. Hildebrand hired the duo for OFA in 2007, assigning Bird to lead the South Carolina field program, and Wicks the whole of the western United States, including Texas.

When Bird arrived in South Carolina, "there wasn't anybody really from Chicago telling us much," he said, "except for, 'wait 'til Iowa is over, and then we'll pay attention to you.'" The decision makers in Chicago had given the staff of the first four primary states—Iowa, New Hampshire, Nevada, and South Carolina—wide latitude to develop their own ground programs. Meanwhile, campaign manager David Plouffe was singularly focused on one number: the delegate count.

In designing the South Carolina field program, Bird knew that he wanted to get as local as possible. He was aware of the growing body of scholarly and anecdotal evidence demonstrating the importance of local contact. Research like Gerber and Green's GOTV studies, which, as described in chapter 2, began to gain popularity among practitioners in the 2000s, showed that personalized communication increased the likelihood of voter turnout.[7] Bush's 72-Hour GOTV Program and Dean's house meeting experiment in New Hampshire were further convincing examples of the value of face-to-face contact. But most important, Bird was a trained community organizer, and he believed that an empowered local citizenry could help the campaign win while bettering communities.

When Bird accepted the offer to be the field director in South Carolina, the campaign promised him 80 paid staff. When he hit the ground, they told him that he would actually receive only 30. Faced with what seemed like an impossible shortage of people, Bird asked, "How can you actually run [a volunteer-led program] when you don't even have enough staff to manage them? I was like, 'Well, I don't know how to do this.' I knew how to run a precinct captain program.... I didn't know how to run a volunteer-led, neighborhood team model program."

When they are understaffed, traditional campaigns often identify the parts of a state and precincts where they know they have a winning margin, called "base turf," and assign staff to those areas. This is precisely what the Kerry campaign did unsuccessfully in the 2004 general election. In South Carolina, by this strategy, Bird would concentrate his small field staff in Columbia and Charleston, press them to knock on hundreds of doors each day, and thereby garner as many votes as possible in Obama-friendly turf. Bird wanted more. He was eager to cover the whole state. In the past, Democratic field programs in the South were divided along racial lines: As Bird describes it, "a persuasion program, which means white people" and "a base program, which means black people."

Bird was eager to experiment with an alternate approach, and he had Ganz's guidance at his disposal. "Do you have any idea what you'd want me to support you with, when you'd want me to do it, etc.?" Ganz wrote in an email to Bird in June 17, 2007. "The key challenge seems to be to expand your trained leadership team," Ganz said, signing off with what would turn out to be a fateful post-postscript: "P.P.S. Did you have a chance to look at the Sierra Club stuff I sent you on leadership development, especially the material on the last session where we train people in coaching relationships, story, strategy, team design, and task design?"

In between the 2004 and 2008 elections, Ganz worked with organizational behavior scholar Ruth Wageman to develop a "team model" that could be used to organize volunteer activity within the Sierra Club. In this project, Ganz and Wageman were developing what Ganz now teaches as the "snowflake model" of leadership, which we detail in chapter 4. The model relies on leaders "accepting responsibility for enabling others to achieve purpose under conditions of uncertainty."[8] It creates a structure for a team of people to work interdependently together toward a shared goal.

Teams emerged as an alternate strategy to develop the organizational capacity Bird needed to win South Carolina. He faced the twin challenges of minimal staff and high vote goals, and he knew he needed a way to enable volunteers to do the work that paid field staff normally do. How do you motivate volunteers to take on great responsibility for no pay? How do you hold them accountable, particularly in a state that does not have the deep-seated primary and caucus traditions of New Hampshire and Iowa?

Bird was nervous. He had never developed, launched, and supported volunteer teams, let alone across an entire state. Bird recalls that even Ganz warned him away, arguing that it was too risky for him to try the team model without any experience. The first field plan that he drafted resembled the traditional precinct captain model and did not include many elements of community organizing. One of the campaign's political consultants, Craig Schirmer, called Bird when he saw the plan and said, "Where is the community organizing? That's why we hired you." So Bird went back to the drawing board.

In revising his field plan, Bird looked to the nascent team leadership model that was emerging in California. As further described below, Ganz, Wicks, and Sierra Club training director Liz Pallatto began to conduct leadership trainings first in California and later in Georgia, Missouri, and New York. These trainings organized volunteers into neighborhood teams. "I felt like [the team model being used in California] was the only way to do it at that point," Bird said. Bird was fortunate that his in-state bosses (the South Carolina state director and political director) supported his desire to experiment. He wrote in an email to Ganz that summer: "[They] believe in what I am trying to do and support it fully. I have the ability to do what I want to do so long as we continue to show others that it is working.... It will be a major test of my ability to teach and lead for sure."

Bird recruited Joy Cushman to help him. Cushman, who had also studied under Ganz, had a sister who lived in South Carolina. Whenever her job as a writing instructor at the University of Maine would allow, she traveled to the state headquarters in Columbia to visit her sister and help Bird develop the team strategy. Eventually, she quit her teaching job midsemester because, as she put it, "Teaching fifteen people how to write an essay did not compare to what they were trying to do.... I packed two bags and said, 'I'm going down.... We have to do this, I really believe in what's going on.'" Together, Bird and Cushman learned how to build a volunteer-led team program. "We had no idea what we were doing, to be honest," Bird said. Cushman agreed: "We were totally making shit up as we went, which is partly why I loved working with Jeremy.... We went from zero to sixty in no time at all because we invested so quickly in volunteers."

As Bird laid out the plan to Ganz in a June email exchange, the remaining eight weeks of summer would be used to "really build our volunteer base and to create volunteer precinct teams." The "Phase II program," he continued, "is leading up to a volunteer training on August 18—we will call it an Obama Organizing Convention (he [Obama] will be here for it). The next few months will really help me decide where we go with Phase III (strategy being a verb not a noun as you say)," he wrote to Ganz.

Cushman summarized all phases of the South Carolina approach in one, cascading sentence: "Tell your story, build relationships, learn to lead house meetings, build volunteer teams, and then teach people how to strategize to meet their own goals." These five elements would become the essence of the Obama campaign's neighborhood team program. The South Carolina program, as with Iowa's, began with the idea that you motivate volunteers by building relationships. Instead of the transactional interactions that characterize traditional canvassing operations, such as one-off leaflet drops or a ride to the polls, the OFA team in South Carolina built a structure for volunteers to get to know other people in their community and engage in purposeful action alongside one another. These relationships formed the motivational basis for volunteer commitment. Reliable volunteers were trained to be team leaders. Once formed, the team was then tasked with organizing its own neighborhood. This team would then perform the work that normally falls to field staff: dials, knocks, voter registration, and GOTV mobilization of targeted lists of voters.

Supporters who came from outside of South Carolina to canvass during the run-up to the primary in 2008 could scarcely perceive the difference between OFA employees and volunteer leaders. Greg Jackson, who went on to become field director in North Carolina in 2012, lived in Washington, DC, at the time. He was part of a group that traveled to the state to volunteer on weekends. Recalling those trips, he said, "I'll never forget... we went to some really rural areas outside of Columbia, and it was just amazing how excited folks were who had never really been engaged with presidential politics and how pumped they were for a primary." In addition to reaching voters in politically marginalized areas of the state, Jackson remembered getting off the bus from DC, receiving his canvass packet, and being trained to go door-to-door. "At the time, I just did whatever they told me to do, but later I found out that everybody instructing us and managing us were other volunteers."

Bird remembers a neighborhood team in Greenville, composed of "young white [high school] kids who were [on the same neighborhood team] with these older black women. They would talk about how cool that was, and how different it was. It just felt like we were doing something special, and it felt real."

## 4. Be people-focused but metrics-driven

In a campaign organization that would come to define itself by a secondary motto—"people-focused but metrics-driven"—the real test of the capacity of any field operation was the number of voters being reached on the phone and at the door. Were the neighborhood teams producing real results?

South Carolina staff were nervous about the effectiveness of their program. By its nature, organizing approaches take a long time to show results because they have to spend a great deal of time at the beginning developing relationships and training volunteers. Cushman remembers visiting Bird about a month after the tumultuous launch of the voter contact phase of the program. "It's not working," Bird said of the neighborhood team experiment. "'It had its moments of beauty, but then it was over.... We've got to blow this up. This just isn't working.'" Cushman counseled patience and remembers having a conversation with Bird during his crisis of confidence in the team approach. "Why did you do this in the first place, and what do you want out of this?" she recalls asking him. "And you know," Cushman said, "Jeremy was really in it to create a different type of politics, and give people a different experience in politics." In organizing parlance, Cushman and Bird had a recommitment one-on-one. The transformations Bird was seeking were not only about the way to run field campaigns, but also about reengaging people in the work of democracy.

Despite Chicago's laissez-faire attitude about their methods, Bird, Stewart, Filipic, and Wicks had to prove that their experiments in the field were enabling them to meet the voter contact goals set by Chicago.

According to Ganz, "Jeremy was under constant pressure from Chicago regarding numbers." In a midsummer email, Ganz alerted Bird:"I just wanted to give you a heads up that the 'word on the street' at the [Chicago] headquarters, at least among some who deal with administrative matters, is that SC is a big problem—I think the word was 'chaotic.'" Bird responded: "That is very unfortunate. Nothing better than administrative folks pushing paper in Chicago to talk about what is going on in SC without ever coming here." The campaign sent Schirmer, the seasoned political consultant who, along with Hildebrand, had hired Bird, to South Carolina to investigate.

Schirmer's intimidating reputation preceded him. Cushman remembers, "If you had a meeting with him he wanted you to have your numbers memorized: how many voter contacts, how many volunteers, how many [volunteer] shifts." Schirmer was known to cold call staff and inquire about their numbers, so all organizers "had to be on the ball," she said.

When Schirmer came to evaluate their work, Bird and his team scrambled to assess their neighborhood teams. Cushman says that this process was a blessing in disguise. She developed worksheets for each organizer to fill out with their volunteer leaders, including the names of those who assumed different responsibilities on the team, as well as granular data about the calls, knocks, and contact patterns from their turf. "Craig showed up, he loved it. He was like, 'Wow! I really know where you have capacity and where you don't,'" Cushman remembers. Schirmer had "a high level of expectation about clarity and planning ahead that really took us to the whole other level," according to Cushman. Once they had a way of assessing the strength of their teams, they knew where to invest their resources. The importance of taking time to audit and plan—first initiated in this last-minute frenzy in South Carolina—reverberated throughout OFA's entire campaign apparatus in both the 2008 and 2012 election cycles. Moreover, the numbers that Bird and Cushman were able to show Schirmer were beginning to show the payoff of an early investment in building local capacity.

In a July 17 email, Bird reported numbers: "We have had 46 house meetings thus far (20 this past weekend) and 517 one-on-one meetings.

We're averaging 12.2 people at the house meetings and pushing to get that number to 15. I am still working on ways to track the number of [commitments for house meetings] coming from [house meetings] but it is about 2 per meeting. The volunteers are making ID [candidate support identification] calls," he wrote. In a spreadsheet of statistics collected from VoteBuilder, Bird's team of 27 organizers had recruited 247 new volunteers in one week alone, nearly six months before the election.

South Carolina followed on the heels of a loss to Clinton in the Nevada primary. All eyes were on Bird's unproven field program. On January 26, the day of the South Carolina primary, Obama's neighborhood teams "blew the primary out of the water," Cushman said, beating Clinton by a more than two-to-one margin. Obama took 55 percent of the vote to Clinton's 27 and Edwards's 18. Although Obama had always been projected to win the state, the field team felt that it had done more than help secure 33 delegates to Clinton's 12. In addition to testing a version of the team model, they argued that they showed that "Barack Obama could come back," as Cushman put it, thereby reenergizing the campaign the week before the onslaught of primaries to be held on Super Tuesday.[9]

At 7:19 p.m. that night, Plouffe sent an email to the South Carolina campaign staff saying, "You guys hung the moon tonight—and picked up the whole campaign. And I would submit, the whole country. You built something people scoffed at—a real field organization—and dealt with as an intense week of politics as many of us will ever go through. Savor it—you just played an enormous role in shaping the future of our country and world."

## 5. Invest in training

While Bird and Cushman were experimenting with the neighborhood team program in South Carolina, Wicks was building a parallel operation in California throughout 2007 and early 2008. She faced the same challenge as Bird, but on a much bigger scale. She started with six paid organizers for the entire state of California and high expectations from the campaign about the voter contact numbers her ground game should produce.

A battle-tested organizer herself, Wicks realized that she would need to make staffers out of volunteers. "California really got what the team model was about," Cushman reflected, "because they didn't have tons of staff so they had to figure out how to structure volunteers to give them real goals." Wicks' commitment to figuring out a workable solution was rooted in her commitment to the campaign and to community organizing. She described what motivated her to get involved in political organizing in 2003:

> I was driving to work one day and one of my very good friends called me and said, "I tested positive for HIV, can you pick me up from the clinic?" So I drove to the clinic and I sat with him and the nurse. I learned about T-cell counts and viral loads and all kinds of other things related to HIV. We left and he got in the car and looked at me and said, "I don't have any health insurance." This is the week we started dropping bombs in Iraq. I got really angry about the direction our country was going, and I decided right then and there that I needed to get a lot more involved in electoral politics.

After working for Dean in 2004 and for Wake Up Wal-Mart for two years, Wicks told us that she "launched a campaign to get on the [Obama] campaign" in November 2006. She wrote an email to Hildebrand, who was Obama's senior adviser at the time. In the email, which she saved for posterity, she wrote that she needed to work for the campaign two reasons: "one, because I believe in him and two, I think he can win." The combination of those two, Wicks said, is exceedingly rare in progressive politics.

The process by which Wicks and her team of six paid organizers "figured it out" was both extraordinarily stressful and intensely creative. At times, she said, it felt like they were "drinking from a fire hose" in California: What they lacked in paid staff, they made up for a thousand-fold in an energized base of Obama supporters in the populous liberal state.

In the summer of 2007, Wicks pioneered what became institution-alized as Camp Obamas, the first of many innovations she would introduce in OFA. According to Ganz, these trainings were a response to pressure from donors:

> [D]onors in California and elsewhere who were pumping money into the campaign saw nothing from it, since all was focused on the four key states [Iowa, New Hampshire, South Carolina, and Nevada].
>
> They began raising enough hell that the campaign decided they needed to be thrown a bone, and Temo [Figueroa, OFA's national field director for the primary] called me up and asked if I could figure out how to do trainings or workshops to accomplish this purpose in California, St. Louis, New York, and Georgia. I got on the phone with Buffy [Wicks] and it seemed like an opportunity had presented itself.

Conceived as an organizing training, the Camp Obamas brought to-gether several hundred supporters over a period of three days. As Cush-man described it, they were faced with a dilemma: "You have a huge amount of volunteers, but what do you want them to learn? Just to tell the stories and do one-to-ones or do you want to actually set up a campaign structure?"

Wicks's response to this challenge was, "Well, let's set up a campaign structure, too." She knew that they had to formalize a program that would "produce the results that we needed to win."[10] Recalling Wicks's gumption, Cushman said, "I don't think Buffy knew what she was asking for" when she decided that they would tackle both organizing skills and the mechanics of the field program at the same time. The decision to do both at once was a departure from Bird's program in South Carolina, which moved gradually from the former to the latter.

As with Bird, Wicks was improvising with minimal oversight from Chicago. To prepare for the Camp Obamas, she organized a conference call with Cushman and Ganz, whom she had met through Bird. In less than two weeks, the three of them prepared 36 hours of content for the training. Ganz wrote to his Harvard and Sierra Club project colleague Wageman for advice:

> I've been asked to design a three-day training for volunteer com-
> mittees, beginning in LA, in 2.5 weeks. I'd like to come up with
> a condensed, focused version of our training, and since I've
> become a convert, I'd like to set it up as leadership team training
> rather than individual volunteer training.... I loved the way you
> formulated this work as creating the conditions (or structure)
> that can sustain calling, by the way.

In the days before, they stayed up "all night, every night," as Cushman said, preparing the participant guide. On the eve of the first Camp Obama in Burbank, it dawned on them that they didn't have any chairs for what would be three daylong sessions. Ever resourceful, Wicks sent out a final confirmation email to participants telling them that Camp Obama would be BYOC: Bring your own chair. Wicks, who had also charged all of the event's expenses to her personal credit card and run a 104-degree fever the day before the training, embraced what Ganz calls the "experimental spirit that makes for good organizing."[11] Wicks herself said that "that was just how we were organizing—with, like, duct tape and coat hanger. We were going to get through and we were going to be creative."

Ganz and eight other trainers led sections of the inaugural Camp Obama in Burbank, California on the last weekend of July in 2007—nearly six months before the first scheduled primary. On the second day, one participant, Susan Christopher, shared her personal story in front of the plenary. She opened by saying that she was a young working mom who arrived at Camp Obama "with a great deal of hesitation." She explained,

> I was afraid to believe in a candidate—again, and be disillu-
> sioned—again. I was afraid to pick a losing cause—again. Then
> Marshall [Ganz] started talking about working with Cesar
> Chavez, and marching in Mississippi. Then I sat down in my

group, and men wept who saw Bobby Kennedy shot, and felt that loss of hope, and a loss of everything he embodied in that generation. To have people like Marshall and those men sit there and say that for them, Barack Obama was the return of that hope—I began to have that hesitation melt away. I felt my heart softening again, I felt able to give a little bit more of me to this process. And then we shared our personal stories. And a Catholic, a Muslim, a Protestant, and a Jewish man shared their personal stories. We had just about every race encompassed in those personal stories, all within that faith difference. I could feel how special and how big what sits in this room was. I could feel that this campaign is about something really big, and really important. And it's the beginning of a healing for our nation. And a healing of generations. And the generations that came before that marched with King, and people who are just now graduating from high school were all working together, were mentoring each other, and were moving forward. And I realized that it doesn't matter if Barack actually fails me, and it doesn't matter if we win. It does—I'm in it to win it. But this campaign has made us win already.

Christopher could have justified her presence at Camp Obama by enumerating the planks of Obama's political platform with which she agreed. Instead, she sought to tell a story that resonated with her own emotional experience and those of the people in the room. The Camp Obamas began to teach volunteers how to build a movement by narrating a "story of self, a story of us, and a story of now," the craft of forging relationships with strangers through one-on-ones, how to recruit for and facilitate a house meeting, and how to build and lead effective volunteer teams.[12] By embedding these organizing practices within a campaign structure, the California Camp Obamas in Burbank and a second one in San Francisco launched 200 neighborhood teams over the course of just two weekends. Although not all of the teams endured through the election, many of these volunteer teams went on to open 25 field offices around the state, and turn California into a "voter contact powerhouse in the primary," as Cushman said. The brief but intensive training "combined the relational work of house meetings with the motivational force of public narrative with the structure of interdependent teams with the strategy based on accountable and measured action," Ganz reflected. Nobody knew it at the time, but the series of Camp Obamas that took place across the country in 2007 contained many of the OFA model's core leadership practices which we describe throughout this book.[13]

Jon Carson, the national field director for OFA in 2008, recounted his surprise when he saw what Wicks was able to do with teams of volunteers. As he told the story at a conference of OFA field organizers after the 2008 campaign, he paid little attention to Wicks throughout the primary season, periodically hearing that she was doing a "Camp this or Camp that" and not paying much attention. In one of their occasional check-ins, she told him that she wanted to give him a heads up that local volunteers were organizing a statewide phone bank on a Saturday. He barely registered the information, believing that a volunteer-run phone bank would not yield any results of note. On Saturday morning, however, he received a phone call from VAN (Voter Activation Network), the company that maintained OFA's voter database.[14] So many volunteers had been trying to access the platform from California that the entire system had crashed. Suddenly, Carson was paying attention to what Wicks was doing.

The Camp Obama experiment was distinct from the traditional ground game blueprint. The latter approach identifies the party faithful and charges them with activities like leafleting their assigned wards the night before the election and offering rides to the polls. Instead, Wicks and her team launched what became known as the snowflake structure, built on a scaffolding of interdependent teams with shared norms. "One of the reasons why the team model worked so well," Wicks observed, "is because there were so many people that wanted to be involved in this movement.... We needed to create avenues of engagement for people to be involved in a way that is beneficial and is taken very seriously by the campaign." The avenues they created equipped Camp Obama participants to run the campaign in their communities when they returned home from the training, all in the absence of paid staff.

OFA's California primary program had further long-term consequences. First, many of the people who later became leaders on the campaign were present in Burbank, including Cushman and Mary Jane Stevenson. Stevenson would become California's field director in 2008, and state director in 2012. Second, the participant guide that emerged from the first two Camp Obamas served as the primary source for the campaign's national field manual in the general elections.

Third, the California ground game was one of the first to leverage technology to bridge online and offline organizing, another hallmark of OFA. Wicks recognized an untapped resource in the Silicon Valley tech community: She knew that computer engineers could have a greater impact by developing useful software for the campaign rather than going door-to-door in three-hour shifts. Google volunteers built a call tool that supporters could log onto from home. It would serve as a prototype of the much-lauded voter contact technology OFA would use in subsequent years. Perhaps even more important, "The Burbank Camp Obama was the first time access to the VAN was opened up to the volunteer teams," Ganz said. That "was a very big deal at the time and took some real doing. Here's a campaign that trusts us, [the volunteers] thought."

Wicks worked for the Obama campaign and administration in a variety of roles for over six years, including in the White House's Office of Public Engagement. Yet, she reflected, those early days in 2007 were "the most crucial of my entire Obama experience," both in terms of what she personally learned and "what we learned as a movement." She enumerated the lessons from California:

> You have to really empower people to take ownership of the campaign. That means teaching them the technology. It means holding them accountable to the work that they're doing. It means creating an environment where they have support in the form of other people working with them and they feel like they are part of a broader movement.

What emerged from the first Camp Obamas in California was both an electoral-organizing model and a beta test of the team structure on a much larger scale, almost entirely dependent on unpaid volunteers. For that reason, "Buffy is a personal hero [for me] and one of the heroes of the OFA story," Cushman said.

As the returns trickled in the night of Super Tuesday, both candidates claimed victories. Clinton prevailed in large states like California and New York, winning 204 to Obama's 166 delegates and 139 to Obama's 93, respectively. Obama won in a string of smaller states, and the final tally at the end of the night was within a margin of 20 delegates: Obama's total count was 1,036 to Clinton's 1,056. Two weeks later, Obama narrowed this margin in the mid-February states, adding 287 delegates to his total compared to Clinton's 166. Although Wicks did not win California, OFA field leaders internally understood her work as significant. The outcomes she had achieved—both tangible and intangible—far outstripped what she should have done with the resources they had given her.

## 6. Be transparent with volunteers about data

Still in a dead heat, the two campaigns looked ahead to the March 4 primaries in Texas and Ohio, dubbed "mini Super Tuesday." Clinton was outpolling Obama in both large states, and she was decidedly the favorite in Ohio. As a result, Wicks said, all of OFA's field staff were "just sent to Texas...so you had people who were former field directors in other states who are now regional field directors in Texas." Wicks and Stewart, who were charged with leading the state, received this influx of a "really talented group of people." At the same time, they were under strict time constraints: "You have to build very, very, very quickly," she said of the "Texas two-step," a reference to its dual primary and caucus system.

For those who had deployed from California to Texas, it was clear that the field team needed to use technology to empower volunteers to contact voters at the local level. The state was simply too vast to do otherwise. "This was a big departure," Wicks said, for organizers who had come from Iowa, a smaller state that had hundreds of organizers building caucus teams for more than a year. In Texas, she said, they did not have the luxury of time or staff capacity, so they "really had to rely on the technology."

Wicks immediately put OFA's technologically savvy volunteers to work making a tool that would facilitate hyper-local organizing in

Texas. They launched the platform from a Howard Johnson motel in Dallas, where 300 organizers shared the bandwidth of a single wireless router. "It's so funny," she said, "when I think about how we utilize tools now versus how we did it then." Up to that point, the campaign had been using a platform called MyBO (MyBarackObama.com), which mobilized affinity communities rather than neighborhood-level teams. The new platform allowed supporters to type in their zip code, find the team in their area, and determine which of their neighbors were already involved. They could also download targeted lists of voters, make calls, and upload the data instantaneously. The new tools, in other words, gave volunteers the data they needed to help the campaign reach its voter contact goals.

Such mechanisms, Wicks said, seem self-evident today, "but back then," she said, "we really didn't have that kind of stuff." Giving volunteers access to databases with lists of voters was simply not done in prior campaigns. Doing so was further evidence of OFA's investment in giving volunteers the same responsibilities staff usually had, a feature of the Iowa, South Carolina, and California primary operations. In all three of those states, they learned that the campaign could trust volunteers to produce outcomes and that they could be motivated and held accountable through a network of neighborhood teams. Through the Camp Obamas, they developed a method for training volunteers on the skills they needed to organize their communities. In Texas, they learned that if they are going to ask volunteers to do the work of staff, they needed to empower volunteers with access to the data.

## 7. Get to scale, and fast

After South Carolina, Bird was dispatched to Maryland for the February 15 primary, and then on to Pennsylvania for the April 22 contest, again as field director. Reflecting on these transitions with hindsight that accompanied Obama's second inauguration, Bird said, "The great thing about a primary is people keep migrating to other states, and therefore learning together." Cushman remembers a slightly more chaotic situation in late February. During her primary "tour of duty," as early Obama staffers refer to their multiple deployments, Cushman had contracted such serious pneumonia that her doctor ordered her to "go home and rest, or you're going to die." Undeterred, she convalesced in Maine for one week before rejoining the team in Pennsylvania, five weeks out from its primary.

Bird—and all of the field staff—were "really quite tired" at that point, according to Cushman. Many OFA staffers who had been assigned to states scheduled to hold primaries after Ohio and Texas were confident that even if Obama didn't win the popular vote in both states, he would surely win enough delegates to be named the presumptive nominee, thus rendering irrelevant the rest of the primaries. According to Cushman, Bird was one such optimist. She remembers one day in late February when she and Pennsylvania political director, Nicole Price, "sat him down, you know, on the floor—we didn't have furniture in our Philly office at that point—and said: We cannot assume anything because it's possible that after Ohio and Texas, we're going to get a couple hundred organizers. If we don't have this structure set up then we're just screwed. We don't have time to turn this thing around."

Whereas the challenge in South Carolina, California, and Texas had been scarcity, the challenge in Pennsylvania was speed and scale. Bird and his team had to create a structure that would absorb the hundreds of organizers who would descend on the state, and make that structure productive in eight short weeks. In Pennsylvania, Bird, his staff, and his superiors gained important insights about how to make the team model work at scale.

The early Pennsylvania field leaders stayed up several nights in a row to map out the field structure. They divided the entire state into clusters of five to ten precincts. Each group of precincts—or "neighborhoods"—would become the purview of a volunteer-led team. Next, they allocated a handful of these teams to field organizer turfs, which would be assigned as staff came in from other primary states, should the party nomination remain inconclusive after the March 4 states. "We were so tired that I can't really remember the sequence of things," Cushman recalled of the consecutive all-nighters in which they demarcated turf and designed the training sequence.

Despite their delirium, they set up the field structure and conducted mass trainings under the cautious assumption that they should be ready for anything. Clinton won convincingly in Ohio and narrowly in Texas, bringing her delegate total to 1,427 to Obama's 1,533. Meanwhile, "Hillary and Bill were just camped out in Pennsylvania," Bird remembers, and ABC News began to air the controversial sermons of Obama's pastor, Reverend Wright, toward the end of March. The nomination still very much contested, the state received an influx of 250 organizers, eight times as many as Bird had started with in South Carolina. However, they had only a fraction of the time to implement the neighborhood team model. Because Bird and his team had invested time in creating a leadership structure, slicing up the states into neighborhoods, and training volunteers, staff that flowed in from other states received their marching orders to organize teams as soon as they arrived. As Wicks had done in California, they built an infrastructure that could productively absorb the staff and volunteers who poured in to Pennsylvania with just weeks to go until the election.

In this way, Pennsylvania served as another test of the team model. OFA staffers who had decamped from New Hampshire learned that instead of meeting their voter contact quotas through their own labor, their job was to empower local supporters. Rather than make persuasion phone calls, they were tasked with organizing local volunteers to talk to their own neighbors. Meanwhile, Bird and his deputies held the field organizers accountable for building relationships with strong Obama supporters like Shirley Bright, who remembers the 2008 primary well:

Right before the Pennsylvania primary in '08, [my mother and I] were watching the television news and the then-Senator came on. She wasn't really paying a lot of attention, but when she heard him, she sort of looks up and says, 'Who is that?' And I said, 'That's Senator Barack Obama.' And she wanted to know what he was doing. I said that he was running for President and she said, 'Of America?' And I said, 'Yes.'

And a little later on, shortly before the primary, she was in a nursing home and there had been an article in *Ebony* about the Senator and I just had it with me and she looked at the picture and said, 'I have seen him before.' And I said, 'Yes, that's Senator

Barack Obama." And she asked me to read the article to her and I did. And she closed the magazine and she held it close to her chest and this look just came on her face and I realized that she was thinking about all the things that we, as a people, had been through to get to the point to where the Senator was a viable candidate for the Presidency and she asked me if she could still vote. And I said, 'Yes, you can still vote by absentee ballot.' So, she said, 'Well, what are you waiting for? Go get me one.'

So I had to go get her an absentee ballot so that she could vote by absentee ballot in the Pennsylvania primary in '08. So my mom voted for the very last time exactly three weeks before her death at age 104.

Bright and her mother's story could have remained just that: a story that spoke to how Obama's candidacy had deeply personal resonance for two African American women from North Philly. Yet the organizers on the ground were trained not only to listen to stories like Bright's, but also to invite them to own a piece of "the movement to elect Barack Obama," as Ganz described that heady time.[15] Bright, who had never before been involved in electoral politics, remembers walking into a field office and asking what she could do to help. Instead of thrusting a get-out-the-vote script and a telephone upon her, the organizer asked her why she supported the president, shared his own story, and then asked her to take on a volunteer leadership role. After all, Bright knew the intricacies of her community far better than a 20-something staffer who had just arrived in Philadelphia, bleary-eyed from working nonstop in a slew of earlier primary states.

"It's urban," Bright said of her community. "It's in transition right now. It's been becoming gentrified, but a lot of the people still live here who lived there for 30, 40 years, or more. It has projects. It has newly redeveloped houses. It has row houses that have been on a block for many years, co-existing with blocks where houses have been torn down." Few out-of-state campaign staffers could have grasped these details and modified his or her canvass route accordingly in the handful of weeks before Election Day. Even if they could, the research surveyed in chapter 2 demonstrates that their appeals on behalf of Obama would not have been as effective as those of local residents. Bright was the phone bank captain for her team in 2008, and a neighborhood team leader in 2012. She devoted 20 to 30 hours a week to OFA on top of her full-time employment as a teacher. "Our constant goal," Bright said, was to make sure our team was "fired up and ready to go—we knew we had to fire each other up" to "turn North Philly out." Bright's story is a microcosm of what was taking place across the state: the Obama campaign was learning to create structures that would harness personal commitments and translate them into real civic capacity.

Bird knew that because of the condensed time period and large scale of the operation, not every volunteer leader would be as competent or invested as Bright. At times, he said, "We just nominated people as team leaders. We only had eight weeks, so if Jane said she wants to be a team leader, great—you got it." The field staff quickly learned that often "the people who say they want to be leaders are probably the worst leaders; the last people in the room are the worst leaders," Bird said candidly. This critical reflection gave rise to a volunteer testing system, which OFA would later institutionalize. Despite the team model's imperfections in the Pennsylvania primary, Bird said that it "worked in a lot of places in the state...people bought into it—all the organizers were, like, 'hey, this is cool.'"

Obama lost the Pennsylvania primary to Clinton by 9 points, but the polls had had him down by 22 points. Clinton had considered the state a must-win in order to remain viable, but took only 12 delegates more than Obama. The OFA teams had registered over 100,000 voters in less than three weeks in the lead-up to the primary and knocked on a million doors before noon on Election Day. From Carson on down, the OFA field staff saw the electoral outcome in Pennsylvania as another indication of the promise of the neighborhood team model. They believed that Pennsylvania's field program would only have achieved a fraction of those numbers had they favored voter contact in lieu of capacity building and training in the two months they were deployed on the ground. Thus, in Pennsylvania, the campaign began to see how the neighborhood team model could be run at scale.

## 8. Convene and reflect

Obama did not clinch the nomination until June 4, 2008, but was considered to have an insurmountable lead in the delegate and superdelegate count weeks before. In response to the Wright controversy, Obama had delivered what is considered to be one of his most historic speeches, called "A More Perfect Union," colloquially known as "the race speech." One of his most memorable lines, that "we are not a collection of red states and blue states; we are the United States of America," was repeated verbatim by no fewer than five of our interview subjects. Obama reminded Americans "that we cannot solve the challenges of our time unless we solve them together." Solving these problems would be impossible, he continued,

> Unless we perfect our union by understanding that we may have different stories, but we hold common hopes; that we may not look the same and we may not have come from the same place, but we all want to move in the same direction.

The field arm of OFA had revealed similar fissures, albeit along much more technocratic lines. Throughout the 2008 primary, Berman observed, "the [Obama] campaign was often an internal battle between tradition and innovation, decorum and experimentation, a few early states versus the rest of the map."[16] Because OFA had implemented a variety of full-fledged field programs in over a dozen primary states, they had the opportunity to test how various tactics were resonating with staff and volunteers against electoral results. "The campaign celebrated outcomes," according to Cushman. More important, "it had a curiosity around, like, how do you get those outcomes?" she said.

Carson, the national field director, was well aware of the divergent strategies on the ground. Tasked with writing a field plan for the general election and hiring field directors for each battleground state, he did exactly what OFA organizers would do with great success at the local level: empower other leaders. Carson convened the primary's key players in Chicago, including Bird, Wicks, Stewart, Cushman, and two field leaders from Nevada, Mike Moffo, a creative type, and Mark Beatty, the group's expert on structure and planning. Bird remembers Carson saying to the group, "I like what you did in the primary. Figure out what common stuff is happening, and let's try to plan around that." Wicks expressed gratitude for Carson's foresight: "Thank God for Jon Carson, who understood that was what was going on and said, 'Let's get everyone together who does field and figure out how best to organize.'" In this way, the chief architects of the caucus teams in Iowa, the neighborhood teams in South Carolina and Pennsylvania, and the tech-savvy volunteer teams in California and Texas were invited to create a unified structure for the general election.

How could Obama's high-level field staffers translate what they had learned about organizing and electioneering into a national strategy for the general election? Ganz, who had significant but indirect influence on the convening, wrote to Hildebrand, "One challenge this campaign faces is to 'walk' Barack's 'talk.' This campaign is different in that the level of volunteer motivation is very, very high. To miss the opportunity to recruit, train, and develop this volunteer capacity is to miss the comparative advantage of this campaign—and to run just like every other campaign that has a hard time recruiting volunteers."[17]

How could OFA make relational organizing and voter contact—the singular metric by which traditional field campaigns measure their success—symbiotic? Funding, technology, targeting, and a strict timeline provided further nonnegotiable parameters for the drafting of the field plan. After much deliberation, the group decided that the neighborhood team model would be the most effective, scalable, and philosophically coherent field plan for the general election. There was some internal debate about how rigid the model would be in each state. "Do teams need to have specific titles and roles, or do you just let people figure it out as a team?" Bird remembers them discussing. "We all kind-of agreed that there are certain things that need to be done, like the way they did in Iowa with the math captain," a role that evolved into the "data captain," which we describe in further detail in the next section.

The meeting in Chicago was "the biggest culture shift," Cushman said, "because in the primary there had been all these competing organizing models, and then on that weekend all the field directors and deputies got trained on a unified field program." They were told, "This is the organizing model for the general election." The organizing manual that the team of top field staff assembled incorporated field tactics that had been used in Iowa, South Carolina, California, Pennsylvania, and Texas, including one-on-ones, house meetings, planning and auditing action, and building teams. It outlined "every single thing, from how to run a house meeting, to how to run a volunteer training, to how to set a vote goal. It had sample volunteer packets, the whole thing," Cushman said. Additionally, the regional field directors from Iowa collaborated on a draft of a document titled "OFA Principles of Organizing," which enshrined "respect, empower, include" as the campaign's central maxim.

Despite the seemingly exhaustive list of instructions in the manual, Carson allowed the field directors to tailor their state's strategy within the framework. According to Grandone, Carson left "a lot of space for each state to develop its own program." The campaign could have, for example, defined and enforced national days of action throughout the summer. Instead, Chicago gave field leaders the autonomy to write their own field plan within the volunteer-led structure and specify their own timelines, so long as they were producing results in the form of voter contact. Modeling such behavior—trusting leaders to abide by shared norms while permitting on-the-ground innovation—engendered a creative culture that permeated most levels of the 2008 field campaign. As we will see in the next section, many organizers and teams embraced OFA's guidelines while adapting them to the needs of their particular turf or team. As Cushman points out, "If you write a field plan, there's no excuse if you don't meet the field plan. So it is different than saying, "Here's your field goal, you have to meet it," a grievance that some field organizers cited about the 2012 campaign, as we discuss in later chapters.

In 2008, Chicago gave each field director clear, consequential, and meaningful goals to which they were held accountable; that is, the number of new voters the state needed to register to expand the electorate or the number of votes it would take to win. These goals contrasted with traditional ground games, including OFA's primary incarnation in New Hampshire, which tend to specify tactical goals, such as the number of door knocks, phone calls, and registration forms each staff member had to collect in order to meet his or her daily quota.

Carson's convening and the deliberative way in which the top field staff drew up OFA's general election battle plan thus tried to negotiate a delicate balance between national purpose and local action. Often, people see campaigns as "being either top-down or bottom-up."[18] Both extremes have their flaws: The former concentrates decision-making power in the hands of professional politicos who are far removed from the ground; the latter can lack direction, organization, and transparency. In designing a field plan that would institutionalize principles of community organizing in an electoral context, OFA tried to resist the top-down versus bottom-up dichotomy. While the framework provided a clear hierarchy of goals and responsibilities, it also left considerable room for interpretation at the local level. As OFA headed into the summer, the field team in Chicago sought to create a strategy that bore greater resemblance to a movement than any other presidential campaign they had known.

## 9. Keep building your capacity pipeline

The field strategy outlined in the Chicago summit depended on hiring an unprecedented number of organizing staff. In order to maintain a ratio of five to ten precincts per neighborhood team (contingent on whether the turf type was classified as rural, urban, or suburban), the model would require nearly 500 paid field organizers in Ohio alone. At the same time, even though Obama held a considerable lead in pledged delegates at the end of March, he was not officially named the nominee until the beginning of June. Wicks remembers struggling with the question of how to transition OFA into a general election mode while respecting the fact that Clinton, who won 18 million votes during the 16-month-long primary battle, had not yet conceded. "We couldn't really publicly be out there kind of building our general election strategy while we were still in the primary. So we had a handful of staff, about a dozen or so people who were trained field operatives who were deployed to all the battleground states," Wicks said, "to start laying the groundwork for what our general election infrastructure would look like in those states, kind of quietly."

Additionally, the primary battle had generated a large number of "really talented field staff who had been with us for a long time at that point," Wicks recalled, all of whom were eager to be assigned to their final posts. With the election just five months away, Carson knew that they "would have to put the pieces in place very quickly," to be "ready to get out into the field and start building and hiring," according to Wicks. The staffing questions were two-fold: First, who would be hired for the state leadership positions? Second, how would OFA fill the thousands of field organizer positions needed to successfully execute the hyper-local field plan?

To the first question, Wicks said that it was similar to assembling a puzzle, in terms of which veteran field staff would deploy to the top three state posts: field director, state director, and general election director. Carson and his confidants knew that "those were very key and important decisions," Wicks said, particularly in light of how the diversity of leadership throughout the primary had generated different kinds of field programs. Four years later, when Bird assumed the post of national field director, he confronted the same task for the reelection. His top priority, he recalled, was to find field directors who understood the OFA electoral-organizing model. Bird knew that otherwise, once field directors got on the ground, they might deviate from the model by holding organizers accountable for voter contact early on, rather than for relationship-building metrics. The staff production method, consistent with the field strategies used on traditional campaigns, would yield more knock and call attempts at the outset but fail to build the foundation necessary to absorb the influx of volunteers that inevitably appear closer to November.

OFA's second daunting task would be to recruit, hire, and train an army of field organizers to implement the neighborhood team model. Because of the demanding nature of the job and Obama's base of support among young people, Chicago knew that the vast majority of these positions would be filled by college-aged students who had no prior campaign experience. Faced with this challenge, Wicks had yet another stroke of insight: "Jon Carson and I got together in the kitchen of the headquarters and we talked about the idea of rolling out a fellows program.... We have all these people who want to get involved," she reasoned, and "if we launch a fellows program, we can recruit all these people and have 200 or 300 people per state signed up to a six- to eight-week program."

Although they were aware of how enthusiastic young people were about Obama's candidacy, they didn't know how many would be willing to commit their summer to the campaign, unpaid, working 50 hours a week. Their initial call for applications generated 10,000 resumes. Wicks spearheaded a "phone bank interview process" to filter the applicants and assign the fellows to a state. The collateral effect of this process "forced the hand of leadership" to make decisions about who would fill the senior staff positions, "because you have 300 people showing up in your state on June 1st," Wicks said, and they would need to be trained on how to execute the neighborhood team model. "We better have our leadership in place for managing that," she said.

The Obama Summer Fellows program made the field program materialize in the general election battleground states. It served as another example of how OFA channeled its enthusiastic but atomized mass of support into an organized field program that, based on experience in the primary, had the potential to yield substantive results. Moreover, Wicks reflected, "the investment that the campaign put into hiring organizers to really develop out the strategy locally I think was a testament to the President and the leadership of the campaign."

## 10. Balance national purpose with local action

Each battleground state ran a different version of the field program in 2008; there was "mixed implementation [of the neighborhood team model] across the board," said Cushman. For example, according to Bird, there was "no standardization of what [being a neighborhood team leader] meant." One indicator came from Florida, which had logged over 20,000 neighborhood team leaders in the VoterFile by November 2008, while the rest of the map—over a dozen other battleground states in all—had a combined total of just under 50,000. Yohannes Abraham, the field director in Virginia, told Bird and Stewart that his team ran "a hybrid model," of the Iowa and South Carolina programs from the primary. Pennsylvania, Ohio, Missouri, and Colorado ran stricter versions of the team model; New Hampshire and Nevada did not.

Cushman, who was originally assigned to a national role, only lasted two weeks in headquarters. She "knew she was going to go crazy in Chicago," that she needed to be "in the field, coaching organizers and organizing." She remembers asking senior staff, "What was one of the hardest things that had to get done?" Their reply was, "We don't know if Georgia's possible or not, but we have to register 200,000 voters there. So I was like, all right. I want to do that."

Cushman deployed to Atlanta in the beginning of July to work alongside Alex Lofton, Aharon Wasserman, and Charlie Anderson. It was, Cushman said, "the best team, to date, in my life…just the sense of like, 'This is new,' and figuring it out. There was not an ideology around it, which I think started to happen a little bit more later." Perhaps subconsciously, Cushman, Lofton, Wasserman, and Anderson would run the state headquarters as though it were a neighborhood team, with a shared overarching goal but clearly delineated, interdependent responsibilities. "We were all committed to volunteer organizing, but we had really different strengths," said Cushman, who was the obvious choice for leading Georgia's training program.

Wasserman took the lead on determining how data from the field would be compiled and reported up and down the chain of command. Up to that point, field organizers would call in their daily metrics or input them in an unsystematized array of spreadsheets. In an interview years later with *TechPresident*, Wasserman said that it dawned on him that he "was spending five hours every day doing spreadsheets, but in the end I had no idea what had actually happened because all I had been doing was cutting and pasting."[19] In an effort to streamline the process and make it more transparent, Wasserman and another staffer, Justin Lewis, built the platform that would become NationalField, which later launched as a social data company that is used by private companies and public advocacy groups, as well as on progressive campaigns.[20]

Faced with a monumental voter registration goal, the Georgia team started at a sprint, collecting forms with the brute labor power of their paid staff. They quickly realized that the organizers could not exceed a certain threshold of production—at best 40 forms per staffer, per day—even if they spent all of their waking hours registering voters. "So," Cushman said, we had them stop, slow down their voter reg[istration], and really focus on [volunteer] recruitment." They conducted trainings across the state, including retraining their field staff on the tenets and practices of organizing. In these weekend-long trainings similar to the early Camp Obamas, they trained more than 2,000 Georgians, arranged them into volunteer teams, and provided them with clear voter registration goals. After these trainings, the Georgia field team registered 210,000 voters. "One of the biggest accomplishments, I felt, on the whole Obama campaign was registering people in their 50s, 60s, 70s in rural Georgia who'd never registered to vote," Cushman said. "So we had convinced ourselves that we were going to win," she added.

On August 30, the Friday before the Georgia field team enfranchised 34,000 people over Labor Day weekend, Sarah Palin was named the vice-presidential nominee on the Republican ticket. "No one knew what that meant," Cushman remembered, describing OFA staff and the country's shock at McCain's choice of the unknown female governor of Alaska. Georgia was one of the reddest states with a sizeable OFA field staff, and Chicago expected that Palin would galvanize the Republicans to turn out in greater force there. As a result, Chicago sent Hildebrand to Atlanta, Cushman remembers, to tell them "you guys are all shipping out." Cushman, who was redirected to Florida to help run the GOTV phase of the campaign, was devastated that they "wouldn't get to see [the team model] through" in Georgia. In the days before the Georgia staffers left for other states, "we trained our volunteer teams to take the reins, and they really did," she said.

The *Almanac of American Politics* reports that turnout increased by 7 points nationally in 2008 as compared to 2004. Of the 131 million Americans who cast ballots, about 14.5 million were first-time voters. Obama won a nearly 70 percent share of them.[21] In Georgia, turnout among black voters increased 7.5 percent between 2004 and 2008, to a historic high.

## FURTHER LESSONS FROM 2008

OFA's 2008 field program combined some of the most successful elements of the grassroots and electoral campaigns that preceded it, while wholly innovating on others. Consistent with Dean's DNC philosophy, exemplified by the 50-state strategy, OFA was committed to organizing everywhere. It did so, however, by focusing on the states that could deliver the necessary 270 electoral college votes. In 2000, Gore had bet everything on Florida; in 2004, for Kerry, it was Ohio. Obama's team expanded the list of battleground states in which they would run a robust ground campaign, and within those states, OFA engaged volunteers in both urban strongholds and rural, Republican counties—something Democratic candidates rarely did. OFA also pursued a field strategy that they believed was at once efficacious and empowering, a delicate balance that was, according to some of our interview subjects, not always struck.

As demonstrated throughout this chapter, OFA's field model emerged through a combination of its leadership's resourcefulness and risks. Many significant innovations, including the neighborhood team model, Camp Obamas, the Summer Fellows Academy, NationalField, and Carson's summit in Chicago, were the result of senior staff exemplifying the behavior they were asking of their volunteers—that is, taking responsibility for one's turf or territory, working interdependently with others, adapting the model as necessary, tracking results, and refining their tactics. The tenor of the campaign throughout those early months was one of hope and enthusiasm. And, writes Ganz, "If you're up in hope or enthusiasm, you're more likely to ask questions and learn what you need to learn to deal with the unexpected."[22]

In addition, OFA's field strategy stemmed from the commitment shown by leaders throughout the campaign, many of whom, quoted at length in this chapter, left steady jobs, school, and their family to work for OFA. "We had a little movement to build, you know?" said Grandone. When Cushman quit her teaching job at the University of Maine, she said, "It was just the spirit of, like, we're in this crazy moment, we don't know how to do this, we're going to figure it out." Wicks and Bird, who proved to be formidable organizing partners in crime, were central champions of the electoral-organizing model. Their willingness to take risks on untested strategies and invest countless hours in operationalizing and scaling a model was what enabled OFA to work toward "creat[ing] a different kind of politics," as Cushman said of Bird's aims.

"It's not like we came up with this whole new way of organizing," Bird said. "It's just that it's able to be much, much more local." He noted that OFA "could have gone with a lot of different models, but none would have left the legacy we're leaving." "And," he added, "I don't think [other models] would have been as effective." Indeed, for dozens of the staff and volunteers interviewed for this book, the process by which OFA conducted the campaign was as important as the victory, as Susan Christopher said to early supporters at Camp Obama. Obama's primary staff were eager to "pull people into this campaign, into this movement and give them ownership of it" in a systematized way, Wicks said. "They are as important a part of the strategy as a television ad and a direct mail piece."

In part II of the book, we describe the nuts and bolts of the OFA field model in greater detail, drawing on interviews with members of OFA's grassroots army and highlighting the subjective but nonetheless telling experiences of the leaders who toiled in relative obscurity on both of Obama's campaigns for the presidency.

**PART TWO**

# THE NUTS AND BOLTS OF THE OBAMA GROUND GAME

# 4.

# BUILDING DEPTH BY INVESTING IN RELATIONSHIPS

If [an organizer] can't build relationships, they're not going to be successful no matter how many calls they make or how many doors they knock. They're not going to be a successful field organizer with the Obama campaign if they can't go out and build those relationships.

—*Alex Steele, Field Organizer 2008, Deputy Field Director 2012*

Prior to 2007, Alex Steele had never been involved in a political campaign. "Neither of my parents were political or activists in any sense of the word. We come from a very rural area outside of Fresno [California] and pretty humble beginnings, so there wasn't a lot of political talk or activism in our household. But I was lucky enough to go to college, to be the first in my family to do so." In late 2007, Steele's friend James gave him a call to say,

"Guess where I'm at? I'm in rural Iowa working for Barack Obama and they just made me a field organizer and I need some help, and you're the only guy I know who wears cowboy boots. So why don't you come out and help me because I'm in the most rural area in all of Iowa and I could use some help." So I said, 'Yeah, absolutely.' I was lucky enough that I didn't have a car payment or anything really holding me down at the time. I have a twin brother—identical twin brother, by the way—and he did have a truck payment that he had to make so he couldn't go. So I went.

To that point, Steele had never traveled outside of California, except to Nevada and Oregon. His family's impression of his assignment, he said, "was like, 'Oh wow, you're going to Iowa!'" Steele remembers thinking, "This is going out East. I'm going to go out there and see the sights in Iowa!" He was assigned to Allamakee County, an area so rural that he was unable to book a plane, train, or bus ticket to his post. "I had to stop in Wisconsin," Steele said, and James, the OFA field organizer who had recruited him, drove across the state line to pick him up. Steele moved in with a host family in Waukon, a town with a population just shy of 4,000. "They had the one stoplight in the whole county, and they were really proud of it," Steele said. During the 2008 primary season, he remembers that a John Edwards staffer came to Waukon once, and that "the Hillary people came, but they weren't centered there," as was Steele.

Steele began knocking on doors in Waukon as soon as he arrived, trying to build relationships with people in the town. He described his first canvass shifts as "the beginning of one of the most transformational times in my life, where [behind] a lot of those doors were a lot of the same struggles and hardships that my family had gone through growing up." In every corner of each one of Iowa's 99 counties, OFA organizers like Steele began to build personal relationships with volunteers and voters. "People would know me," he said.

> We were in those counties 24-7 living in them, eating there, really being part of them. When I'd call people, I'd say "I'm right here in Waukon." They'd say "Where are you from?" "Well, I'm here in Waukon. I live right there. I live on such-and-such a street" and they'd be like, "Oh yeah, so-and-so used to live down there and we went to school [together]"...just sharing your story and having them share theirs. So when you got time to caucus, it's not some Obama staffer calling them. It's Alex. They'd be like, "Yes, Alex. I'm ready."

After Iowa, Steele's primary tour of duty took him through Nevada, California, Texas, Indiana, South Dakota, and then Colorado for the general election as a field organizer. His regional field director asked him to come back to help with OFA 2.0, after which he was hired as one of the state's deputy field directors for the 2012 general election. "Those three letters O-F-A have defined me for so long," he said. "It's consumed most of my twenties."

Reflecting on what he learned as an unlikely campaign volunteer who then made a career of "organizing to expand the electorate," Steele said that "more than anything, us being on the ground for as long as we were and using real community organizing tactics and strategies, those relationships that we built in the community were just invaluable." The relationships, many of our interviewees said, took time to forge but became the foundation of the field campaign.

Our interviews suggest that OFA's ability to motivate volunteers and persuade and turn out voters depended in large part on the strength of interpersonal connections at three levels: among the field staff themselves, between the field organizer and the volunteer, and between the volunteer who performed voter contact and his or her neighbor. People may have joined the campaign because of Obama's opposition to the war in Iraq or his stance on gender equality, but, as many of our interviewees told us, they put long, thankless hours into the field because of their relationships with others.

OFA's philosophy was one that sought to recognize the humanity of both its staff and the volunteers. Instead of treating them as interchangeable phone-calling or door-knocking machines, OFA sought to get to know them as people from the moment they made contact with the campaign. Jenni Boyle-Smith, a field organizer in Ohio, describes the way the campaign trained its staff to use relationships as a conduit for investing in people:

It's about the human element, and so when we talk about issues is it health reform, is it the war, is it birth control? Whatever it is, when you talk about the issues then people can connect on a real level versus just repeating talking points and quoting commercials. So it was really asking those probing questions to figure out what the person on the other end of the phone or on the other side of the door, what was going on in their life and how the issues of the campaign were affecting them personally.

Seventy-five percent of our interview subjects attributed the vast amount of time and energy they dedicated to OFA to the campaign's human presence in their communities—either a personal relationship with someone on the campaign or recognition of OFA's attempt to make a long-term investment in their community.

Relationships were thus central to OFA's decision to "respect, empower, and include" volunteers in its ground game. They became the means by which the campaign motivated the staff, the staff motivated and invested in building the capacity of volunteers and, in turn, the way volunteers motivated the voters they were mobilizing. Steele did not just spend his time knocking anonymously on doors in Waukon; he sought to get to know the people living in those homes, by "just sharing [his] story and having [the volunteer] share theirs" in order to understand each other's "struggles and hardships." By getting to know people as human beings, and valuing their whole person, staff and volunteers sought to create a new source of motivation and capacity. Staff, volunteers, and voters told us that they took action with the campaign not only because they supported Obama, but also because they supported each other.

This chapter describes the tactics OFA used to invest in its people and to build and maintain relationships throughout all layers of its field operation. Using relationships to organize and build power is a strategy that comes straight from community organizing.[1] We begin by describing the way community organizers use relationships to motivate and build capacity in others. Next, we describe the way OFA invested in its staff, recognizing the importance of its human resources at every level. Finally, we show how the staff built relationships with volunteers—and later, the volunteers with voters—as a way of asking them to commit to leadership roles and sustain their motivation throughout the multi-year campaigns.

## BUILDING RELATIONSHIPS TO DEVELOP LEADERS

In his book *Dry Bones Rattling,* Mark Warren describes the work of the Industrial Areas Foundation (IAF), an organization founded by Saul

Alinsky to bring economic empowerment to poorer neighborhoods in Chicago. Warren turns his attention to the Southwest IAF, a branch based in Texas that focuses on organizing low-income Hispanic communities. Founded by Ernesto Cortes, the Southwest IAF originally began as Communities Organized for Public Service (COPS). Over the two decades that Warren examines, COPS and IAF generated considerable political clout, bringing over $1 billion in service and infrastructure improvements to San Antonio's low-income neighborhoods. In doing so, this low-income Hispanic constituency—traditionally marginalized in Texas politics—achieved victories far beyond what most outside observers expected. Warren argues that they accomplished these wins through relational organizing.

A core principle of both IAF and OFA was that organizers should never do for people what they can do for themselves.[2] Instead, the job of an organizer is to empower others to become agents of change themselves. When adapted to OFA, this meant that field staff were not responsible for making phone calls, knocking on doors, and engaging in voter contact. Instead, their job was to develop the capacity of a team of volunteers to run the voter contact program in the communities in which they lived.

Empowering neighborhood teams meant OFA staff had to turn volunteers into leaders. Leadership, as defined by a 2008 Camp Obama training manual, was "enabling others to achieve purpose in the face of uncertainty by focusing on one's own calling, the calling of one's community, and the call to action."[3] This definition of leadership, which originated in Ganz's teaching materials, aligns with the IAF philosophy that organizers should organize themselves out of a job. Austin Brookley, a field organizer in Boca Raton, Florida, summed up this outlook, consistent across the majority of our interviews, in one phrase: "Everyone can be a leader in a democracy."

In some places, volunteer leaders took the place of staff. Dan Grandone observed that,

> Where we had an organizer having to cover, in some cases, hundreds of miles of turf,... the organizers by and large had no choice because... it wasn't humanly possible to be at all these places in

the northern part of the state with all their leaders for the teams and all the meetings. So they were forced out of just pure necessity to figure out how they were going to give someone what they needed, to bring the right leader on board who could ultimately, from pretty early on, run their own meetings and think strategically and be able to coach others and run an arm of the campaign without an organizer being right there as the crutch.

For organizers, developing leaders begins with developing relationships. Warren argues that in the IAF, leadership development happened primarily within the relationship between the professional organizer and the grassroots leader—the organizer's job is to teach the "art of politics" to the local volunteer through their relationship.[4] "Moreover, in the IAF's view, the 'arts of politics' can only be learned by someone who has acquired the ability for critical self-examination and personal growth."[5] In organizing, relationships become the locus of learning and motivation.

> IAF trainers stress that the Latin root of the word interest is *interesse*, which means "to be among or between." The IAF suggests participants should take a relational, not individual, understanding of self-interest, since a person's interests develop in the context of their relationships with others.[6]

As with community organizers, OFA organizers sought to create a relational basis from which they could motivate their volunteers, and cultivate their capacity for action over time.

Michelle Kleppe, the 2012 field director in Wisconsin, highlighted the distinction between OFA's focus on capacity building and more traditional campaigns:[7]

> One of the first conversations or group discussions that we would have with new staff coming on was around the difference between organizing and mobilizing. And the idea that most electoral campaigns are focused on mobilizing voters—you need to get them to turn out. One of the unique things about our organi-

zation and the Obama campaign back in 2008 was the focus on actual organizing [to develop the capacities of people and their communities] instead of just slash-and-burn mobilizing [to generate votes]. And so, I think it helped organizers to clarify the difference between those, and then we talked through a calendar, saying, there are going to be points in the campaign where you're going to have to mobilize. This makes the space in between much more important for the real organizing work.

Kleppe went on to point out that there were periods in which OFA did indeed engage in "slash-and-burn" mobilizing. In the waning weeks of October, many organizers and their teams were tasked with recruiting 70 volunteer shifts per day, a testament to both the intensity and scale of the final phase of the campaign. It was, however, during what Kleppe referred to as the "space in between" in which, ideally, the organizers engaged in the "real organizing work": identifying, recruiting, and developing volunteers as leaders by building relationships with them. Staff who had successfully recruited and trained volunteer leaders in the organization-building phase of the campaign (for OFA, this meant prior to October) could step back in the final weeks. By that time, the volunteer leaders were seasoned trainers and motivators themselves and were thus entrusted to staff the GOTV staging locations themselves.

Bird recognized the value of relationship building for leadership development and growing OFA's ground capacity. Without the relationships undergirding the voter contact numbers, "then it's just a number in a spreadsheet" and the longer-term outcome is "not as good," he observed. Bird and the field directors he hired sought to get as many organizers into their turf as early as the budget would allow to give them time to establish a relational basis for their work. "It takes time to get somebody—as eager and bright and energetic as they may be—to understand what it means to develop a [volunteer] leader who can ultimately go out there and run their own meeting and can agitate a group of other people when they need to," Grandone said.

To make the relational organizing model work, the campaign's field directors had to start by modeling this approach and thus building capacity among their own staff. By carefully hiring and training its paid workers, OFA laid the foundation for a relational organizing program that would enable it to empower volunteers.

## INVESTING IN STAFF

When Bird assumed his position as the national field director of the 2012 campaign, his first task was finding and supporting the right people. The national field plan for the reelection effort was all but written by the time Bird assumed the post. Having developed the model in the 2008 primary, piloted it at a national scale during the 2008 general election, and further fine-tuned it during Obama's first term alongside Mitch Stewart at Organizing for America, Bird stepped into his new role in OFA 2012 with a much clearer sense of how to run the field program. "It was done," he said. "Mitch and I, now, at this point had worked on it for four years. We were given the autonomy to run our program, however we wanted to run it, and no one objected to running a team program."

Bird knew that deciding who to hire would be one of the most important choices he would make. The neighborhood team model was predicated on the idea that success depended on the quality and quantity of the campaign's human capital. The 2008 primaries were all about figuring out ways to make the investment in volunteers work. To run the team program in 2012, Bird had to invest in his staff.

At the outset, Bird looked for field directors who believed in or had experience implementing the neighborhood team model. "You have to believe in it...nothing was more important," Bird said. He explained his reasoning by pointing out how deliberately slow the first 13 months of the campaign were in terms of voter contact numbers. Unless field directors believed in building capacity by forming relationships with volunteers, Bird cautioned, they could be tempted to "take shortcuts" in the early phases, producing inflated numbers that reflect knocks and calls made by staff instead of volunteers. Then, when it came time to position field staff in their GOTV bunkers—where their singular job was to receive and report shift numbers up the chain of command—Bird worried that their ground capacity would disappear, having never been built in the first place. Without this pipeline of trained volunteers, the campaign believed it would be leaving votes on the table. Furthermore, without strong relationships with neighborhood team leaders who knew how to autonomously run staging locations, not only would production dramatically decrease, but OFA field leaders feared that they would fail in their larger, stated goal of resurrecting a stronger and more inclusive civic infrastructure.

For this reason, Bird wanted to hire field directors who were confident enough in the model that they would train and incentivize organizers to build the capacity of the neighborhood teams, who would later account for the growth of OFA's voter contact numbers in the run-up to the election. "It's not a big group of people" who had the experience Bird wanted in his state field directors. So he hired people who had experience using this organizing model. "I had a very close relationship with the Ohio field director, the Florida field director, the North Carolina field director, the Virginia field director. I'm friends with—or knew very closely—almost every field director in the country, and those relationships were really important." All but one of the 2012 field directors had cut their teeth on the Obama electoral-organizing model four years prior. Jenn Brown, Ohio's field director, had been a regional field director in the state in 2008, as had Meagan Gardner, who went on to be the Iowa field director. Gabe Lifton-Zoline was a regional field director in 2008 and field director in 2012 in his home state of Colorado. Allison Zelman walked into the Obama office in Oakland, California, on a whim in 2007 and was invited to participate in, and later organize, Camp Obamas. She went on to become a regional field director in New Mexico in 2008 before assuming the role of Pennsylvania field director in 2012.

All of these field directors worked closely with Marlon Marshall, the deputy national field director. As the national field director in 2012, Bird spent the majority of his time wrangling the complex interrelationships of OFA's dozen departments that occupied over 50,000 square feet in a downtown Chicago high-rise, which, at its peak, housed over 650 staff.[8] Bird compared it to the "kind of matrix-model of big companies," managing many of the operations, analytics, digital, communications, data, finance, political, policy and research, voter protection, GOTV, and sur-rogate scheduling teams so that they were "actually serving the states in a way that got them to the votes they needed—and telling that story to headquarters," he added. The person closer to the ground, who man-aged the field more directly, Bird said, was his deputy, Marshall, who was named the deputy director of the White House's Office of Public Engagement shortly after Obama's second inauguration.

As Marshall tells it, his journey toward the Obama campaign began during his student years at the University of Kansas. While an undergrad, he served as vice president of KU'S student body and initiated an orga-nizing drive to pressure the university's administration to recruit more students of color. As a consequence of that experience, "organizing, com-bined with a quality education," Marshall said, "drove [his] passions" and piqued his interest in political campaigning. After graduating, he worked for the Kerry campaign in 2004, and in 2007, he joined the Clinton cam-paign as the field director in the Nevada, Ohio, and Indiana primaries.

In those states, he said, "[we] used a lot of similar organizing tactics," due in large part to coaching from Karen Hicks, Clinton's national field director. As mentioned in chapter 2, Hicks had run Dean's 2004 pri-mary campaign in New Hampshire. With Hicks's mentorship, Marshall developed a volunteer-rich field program in the primary states he led. When Clinton conceded, Marshall was one of a handful of high-level field staffers from her campaign who went on to work for OFA; he di-rected Missouri's field effort for the 2008 general election.

As the deputy national field director in 2012, Marshall's job was to manage what the campaign referred to as "regional desks." Chicago divided up the country into five regions: Great Lakes/Mid-Atlantic, Northeast, Southern, Midwest, and West. Each regional desk had one director and approximately 12 headquarters staff who worked beneath them to sup-port the states, including at least one representative from each of the departments mentioned above. OFA ran parallel "battleground" and "border states" programs, both of which had a national-level director. Border states were places like California and New York, which would export volunteers to swing states to supplement local teams' canvassing capacity, or make calls into neighboring states like Nevada and Pennsylvania. Alongside the regional desks and battleground and border-states programs, OFA ran a constituency-based program called Operation Vote. This program was yet another field-based program that sought to mobilize "core constituencies" like African American, Latino, LGBT, faith, military, Jewish, women, and youth populations to the polls. Buffy Wicks spearheaded Operation Vote.

Simply hiring the right people who were loyal to the program was not all the campaign did. In an unusual move for an electoral campaign, Bird also found executive coaches for all the field directors, and for some of the other key leaders of the Obama ground game. Forty professional executive coaches did pro bono work for OFA, developing one-on-one relationships with field directors to help them think about how they manage and develop the leadership potential of their deputies and the hundreds of paid organizers who deployed to their state.

The idea to offer the field staff executive coaching began when Bird himself developed a relationship with Robert Gass of the Rockwood Leadership Institute, who began coaching Bird in the beginning of 2011. Bird says, "I just thought it was awesome, and it really helped me. . . . And I was trickling down what he was teaching me to the people I was managing. I was saying, 'Hey, you're now managing other people. I go to this guy who taught me some of these things you should think about this as you go along.'" To ensure that all of his staff could have the same kind of learning opportunities, Bird made sure that coaching relationships were built into the field staff hierarchy.

### The Battleground States

Once Bird hired the field directors in each state, the field directors themselves had to hire their own state's staff. While the neighborhood team model, which we describe in the next section, had locally adapted versions, the staff structure (depicted in Figure 4.1) was nearly identical in all the battleground states and throughout both election cycles.

As shown in Figure 4.1, each state's field director managed from two to seven deputy field directors (DFDs), depending on the size of the swing state. Each DFD managed a region of three to eight regional field directors (RFDs) who, in turn, managed between five and ten field organizers

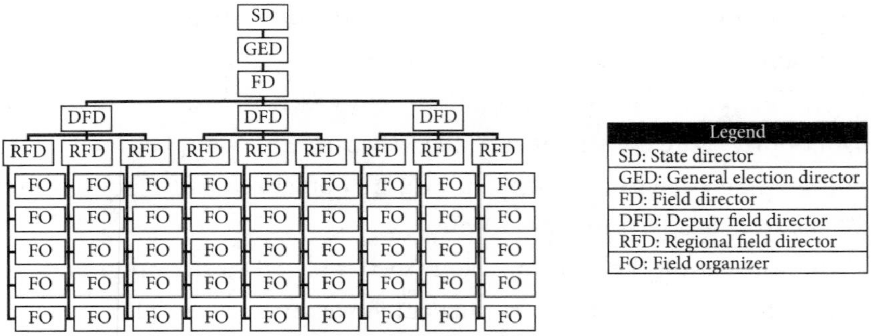

FIGURE 4.1: **Structure of field staff at the state level**

*The number of deputy field directors, regional field directors, and field directors varied depending on the size of the state. Some states had as few as two DFD regions, others as many as seven.*

(FOs). Often, people were hired and promoted through this hierarchy "just because they were good at their last job," said Bird. But "being a good field organizer doesn't necessarily mean they're going to be a good regional field director. In fact, some of the best organizers are terrible at that," Bird said, because they want to be executing, rather than training and coaching other organizers.

One 2012 field director said that the majority of her state's RFDs had been promoted after excelling in their previous role as FO. By contrast, field leadership in Florida rarely practiced promotions. "I think there was a desire to keep good organizers as field organizers, because we had already developed such close relationships with our volunteers," one Florida staffer said. This organizer knew of only one case where an RFD came up through the FO ranks in the state, and that was under extenuating circumstances: just two months before Election Day an RFD had resigned, and "state leadership wanted the replacement to be familiar with the turf." In many cases, especially in Colorado and Ohio, many 2012 RFDs had worked as field organizers in the 2008 campaign.

The colossal staffing task that OFA faced, however, was to recruit, hire, and train 2,500 field organizers, over half of whom were brought on board in the final four months of the campaign. Some of this talent came from the Summer Organizing and Fall Fellows programs, offspring of the initiative that Wicks, Carson, and Cushman had spearheaded in

2008. In 2011 and 2012, California, New York, and Illinois ran what were called Field Organizer Academies, the graduates of which Bird said they hired by the hundreds because they "knew what it was like to work in a place with no resources, and had gone through the training program." The Fellows programs and Academies attracted thousands of resumes, which, once culled into cohorts, became OFA's primary hiring pool to fill FO positions in battleground states. Fellows programs were 12 weeks long, and Academies were two-week boot camps. Both used much of the original material from the 2007 Camp Obamas to train would-be staff on basic organizing principles and skills, a day-in-the-life of an FO, and techniques for building neighborhood teams.[9]

Despite these built-in talent pipelines, upper-level field staff told us that they spent inordinate amounts of time recruiting for these roles—a reflection of the value OFA attached to finding a good organizer instead of just another warm body to knock on doors and register voters. Sometimes this was taken to extremes: one field organizer, Shenelle Fabio, remembers being interviewed six times by five different people for a field organizer role. She had graduated from law school at the Ohio State University in May, and the interview process lasted so long that she had returned to her home state of Florida in July when she received the job offer for a position in Columbus.

Many states would not extend an offer to a field organizer without having the field director or the general election director first "sign off on" or personally interview the candidate. Pennsylvania field director Zelman said, "I am the kind of person who works till 3:00 am every night and I expect, honestly, the same of my staff," she said, only half-jokingly. "And it is crazy, but to me you have to be that determined and that willing to do anything and work that hard to get this kind of job done." Zelman said that regardless of the time pressure she and her staff were under to fill FO slots, "we always did double interviews, and we always checked all three references."

The Colorado field director, Gabe Lifton-Zoline, admitted that he and his staff "got a little carried away" in their hiring process. "We wanted the nicest people we could find, the smartest people we could find, who were willing to work really hard. Political experience or campaign experience mattered less, as we saw it, than their ability to want to work hard with a bunch of people who had similar ambitions." Whenever Lifton-Zoline would receive a promising resume, he sent it to all of his DFDs at the same time. "They had to claim whose it was and they had to call [the candidate] within ten minutes, and if they didn't call them within ten minutes, it went back out to the general pool and anyone could have them.... They would go nuts; it was an amazing thing to watch."

Just as the campaign offered executive coaching to the field directors, they wanted to make sure the DFDs, RFDs, and FOs also had appropriate training and coaching. The campaign gave all the field directors a budget to hire a state-level trainer, who often had one or two deputies to aid in the monumental task of training hundreds of organizers and, indirectly, thousands of volunteers. Bird says, "If you ask the field directors, 'What was one of the best things the campaign did?' 'Hiring a training director,'" they would respond immediately. As he puts it, in 2008, the campaign "did trainings" but "did not have a training program, which is where we started to get [in 2012]. And we got pretty damn good—way better than any campaign I've ever been around. [In a longitudinal training program], you do initial trainings, but there's an actual program [where there are] multiple opportunities for them to keep learning data, keep learning digital. [W]e trained them throughout the process."

In addition to OFA's intensive hiring process and training program, there was an ongoing coaching system embedded into the field structure itself. The majority of field organizers whom we interviewed reported having highly productive relationships with their regional field directors; the findings were similar up the chain: RFDs to DFDs, DFDs to FDs, and FDs to staff in Chicago. Because this study's sampling method may have overrepresented the star organizers, we suspect that positive assessments of working relationships were also oversampled. Nevertheless, for a relationship-based field campaign to work, "communication has got to go both ways," said Bird. In order for FOs to absorb and transmit what they're hearing and seeing on the ground, they had to have real relationships with both their volunteers and their RFDs, who, in turn, had to have productive relationships with their DFDs and so on.

Thus, OFA encouraged its field staff to act as coaches instead of managers. Matt Caffrey described how his regional field director, Ethan Frey, was "invested in us personally as human beings and not just workers," just as Caffrey was in his volunteers. Frey had worked in Toledo on the 2008 campaign and as a labor organizer with a hotel workers union in Miami before returning to the campaign in 2012. He often assembled reports that would show his organizers where there might be undiscovered volunteer leadership in their turf, and worked with them one-on-one to devise tactics for building their teams. "He would give us that sort of information to help us not only hit our goals, but to then make the work we were doing to hit our goals have a bigger impact," Caffrey said.

## OFA'S RELATIONAL STRATEGY FOR ORGANIZING VOLUNTEERS: AN OVERVIEW

If relationships reinforced capacity at the staff level, how did this approach operate at the level of volunteers? How did OFA organizers like Caffrey develop relationships with Obama supporters in ways that cultivated the leadership capacity of ordinary people? OFA employed a host of classic relational-organizing tactics: one-on-ones, personal stories, public narrative, the art of a "hard ask," house meetings, leadership training, and relentless relationship maintenance and follow-up. Figure 4.2 indicates how these tactics were cyclically related. As depicted, organizers constantly sought to identify prospective volunteers, nurture relationships with them, generate commitments, test their ability to produce outcomes for the campaign, and, ultimately, accept a leadership role. If the volunteer committed to this role, she became an organizer charged with identifying prospective volunteers, and repeating the organizing cycle to develop more leaders.

When field organizers first arrived in their turf, their first job was to get to know the community in which they were stationed, as Steele had done in Waukon. How were social relationships within the county, town, or neighborhood structured? Where did people gather? Who were key leaders? The initiation process Steele described in Allamakee County was not atypical. Written training documents instructed OFA organizers

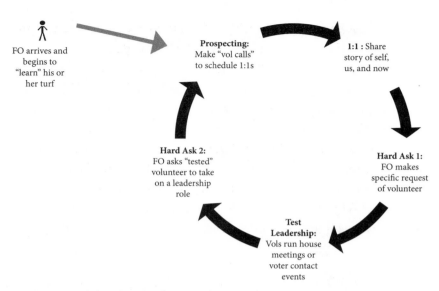

FIGURE 4.2: The OFA relational-organizing cycle

*A version of the process that OFA field organizers used to identify, recruit, and empower volunteer leaders in their turf.*

that the "first job of any organizer is to get to know the ins and outs of the community you'll be working in. This is your turf. You must own it."[10] The organizers also lived in "supporter housing," which often meant an extra futon or spare bedroom at a local volunteer's home. Many staff learned by osmosis where people worship, shop, study, and celebrate simply by living in the community in which they were organizing. OFA took pains to alert their new organizers to first, learn "proper pronunciation of your town/area," and second, to map out the places potential volunteer recruits gather: "libraries, senior centers, schools, places of worship, union locals, major community groups (PTA, Sierra Club, etc.), late night places to get food, closest coffee shops to field office, sites that can hold 100–200 people, gated communities (and ways to reach these people) and other major attractions and 'hot spots.'"[11]

After mapping out their turf in this way, organizers would call volunteers that the campaign's database had identified as Obama supporters in order to schedule one-on-one meetings. Here, they could draw on the campaign's extensive data and analytic expertise to call only the most promising volunteers in the database. Before a field organizer received his or her official campaign phone—and sometimes within their first few hours on the job—their campaign bosses handed them a list of the organizing goals to which they would be held accountable, and instructed them to "pull a list" of MyCampaign volunteers from VAN. In the campaign's database, organizers could access presorted tiers of volunteer leads, though they were not informed how Chicago's data modeled the hierarchical categories into which the potential volunteers fell. This process of increasing the pool of prospective volunteers speaks to the symbiotic relationship between data and field. The prospect pool began with the campaign's database, but once the organizer had a network of relationships in the community, he would use those networks to identify other prospective volunteers and leaders and to eliminate erroneously identified supporters and those unwilling to volunteer for OFA. The two best indicators of whether or not a new field organizer was starting to build capacity, we learned, were the number of volunteer recruitment calls he or she made—not dials or knocks to persuadable voters—and how many of those calls were converted into one-on-one meetings with supporters.

After identifying prospective volunteers, the organizer had to cultivate the commitment and skills of these prospects through relationships. In a one-on-one meeting, organizers would meet with volunteers in person to get to know them, identify what values they had in common, and ask the supporter to commit to taking on responsibilities within the campaign. While they took on many forms and struck a variety of tones, one-on-ones were intentional and structured conversations. Organizers were trained to use personal stories as a way of getting to know the volunteers and communicating about shared values. Once they found volunteers willing to commit to taking on responsibility, organizers would support those volunteers in hosting house meetings or leading voter contact events. These volunteer-led events were opportunities to test potential leaders to see who followed through and also identify additional potential volunteers. Once someone successfully led a voter contact event, the organizer would, ultimately, ask them to commit to a leadership role.

The process did not always follow this precise sequence. For instance, some supporters were eager and receptive and only needed the softest of asks to take on a leadership role. Howard Dolginoff, a team leader from Palm Beach County, Florida, was one such recruit. He said he was a "lifelong Republican up until about halfway through George H. W. Bush's term of office." He crossed party lines and dabbled in activism in the 2000 and 2004 elections, and volunteered for OFA in 2008. In 2011, he explains, a field organizer called and asked him, " 'You want to volunteer?' And I said, 'What took you so long?' " After his one-on-one with the organizer, he started to come in to phone bank at "three hours a pop, two to three times a week, for about two months." Recognizing his dedication, the organizer said, " 'You know, I need somebody to step up, and run the phone bank, would you be willing to do that?' And I said, 'Sure, no problem.' "

Even though Dolginoff was easier to recruit than others, the OFA staffer went through the same organizing process with him that is depicted in Figure 4.2: holding a one-on-one meeting, testing him for his commitment, and then asking him to assume a leadership position. Thereafter, Dolginoff was taught to repeat the cycle with other supporters in his community, expanding the campaign's organization through his own efforts and local expertise. In the process, Dolginoff developed a relationship of trust and respect with the OFA organizer, which, in turn, facilitated his commitment to the campaign. Dolginoff says, "[B]y then I was comfortable training other people, and Stan [the field organizer]— he was a great leader. I really enjoyed working with Stan, a nice, nice guy, well organized, knew how to make the hard ask, knew how to get you enthusiastic about whatever the mission of the day was."

## THE MECHANICS OF RELATIONAL ORGANIZING IN OFA

Organizers began their work by building relationships with local Obama supporters. Their aim was to grow the ranks of volunteer leaders who would take responsibility for executing the voter contact work of OFA's ground game. Dolginoff is a prime example of how data targeting facilitated OFA's field program by identifying the people who needed only to be given the opportunity to join the campaign. If they were lucky, field organizers might find a handful of volunteers who, like Dolginoff, were willing to accept leadership responsibilities the moment they were asked. According to our interviews, however, far more common in 2012 was the sense that organizers were building a volunteer infrastructure with very little preexisting capacity, and with a smaller and less enthusiastic pool of volunteers than in 2008. To overcome these shortcomings, organizers needed to invest heavily in building relationships. In 2012, Kate Malloy described her first month on the ground as, "building from scratch all of the relationships that I had. So in the beginning, it was pretty challenging because there really wasn't any legacy."

## *"You've got to sit down and talk to them face to face"*

In the OFA model, the voter contact capacity of any field organizer's turf or neighborhood team began with a single conversation, called the one-on-one. Recounting how her team grew from three to fifteen, neighborhood team leader Pat Bruner of Colorado said that she and her fellow volunteers "were [holding one-on-ones] with eight to ten people a week." She recalled being told that these conversations might take 30 minutes each, "but when you live in an area where there are a lot of Republicans and people who are more progressive feel sort of isolated, our one-on-ones were going anywhere from one to two hours. I had one that was four hours long."

What makes a one-on-one different from an everyday conversation one might have with a neighbor, colleague, or friend? In addition to being "very personal, at times" as Bruner put it, one-on-ones are also directed and disciplined conversations. They build public relationships and are therefore the most basic tool of organizing. As OFA taught them, one-on-one meetings have agendas: first, both parties exchange their personal stories, often incorporating how they came to the campaign, what inspires them, and whether anything in Obama's story resonated with them.

Second, the organizer or volunteer leader described the strategy of the campaign, emphasizing the ways in which local leadership would be key to OFA's success. Third, the organizer or volunteer makes an ask.[12] The organizer is taught to remain attuned throughout the conversation to the person's talents, strengths, motivations, interests, and social connections so that she could formulate an appropriate request. Critically, however, the one-on-one is not about "extracting resources from people—money, time, whatever," as Ganz taught at a 2007 Camp Obama in Colorado. Only when the supporters' "real interests are on the table" will an organizer be able to make an ask that will "lead to action, to storefront offices, to house meetings, to commitments to *do something*."[13] If the person runs a ministry, for example, the organizer might ask her to host a house meeting at the church. If the supporter is part of a Thursday evening bridge group, the organizer might ask the volunteer to run a postgame phone bank. At its core, relational organizing is about interacting as human beings.

In other cases, the ask might be less obvious, as in the case of Mary Pizzariello, a full-time working mom who lives on an acre of land in rural Nevada. An organizer called her "out of the blue" and asked her to come in for a one-on-one. A self-described proponent of "family values," Pizzariello doesn't "believe in divorce—you are married through thick and thin 'til death do you part." Strongly opposed to the Iraq war, Pizzariello said she thought "we should have dropped a nuclear bomb on Afghanistan and gone after Bin Laden; that's how strong I felt." Pizzariello had never done political volunteer work before but had an aptitude for computers, and given her job and family constraints, she may not have seemed like an obvious candidate for becoming a core volunteer. However, as Pizzariello herself said, she was "spouting that [she] supported Obama," so she "wanted to put [her] time where her mouth was." With this constellation of facts, the organizer asked her to become the data captain on her neighborhood team. She was given a login to VoteBuilder and charged with entering her team's data after each phone bank, canvass, or voter registration event.

For Bruner, and nearly all of the OFA organizers we interviewed who successfully organized their turf, "the best way to recruit people is you've got to sit down and talk with them face-to-face. The phone does not work." Bruner's team's conversion rate spoke for itself: "From all of the one-on-ones we did, almost every person we talked to ended up volunteering with the campaign in some way and some of them committed to being almost full-time volunteers." She marveled at how "people wanted to talk about [the election], that they were actually glad to be asked the questions and they really enjoyed sharing their opinions."

Organizers were instructed to have one-on-ones both with volunteers who had dedicated time to the campaign, and with individuals who have the "potential to become leaders," as one training document read. Yet, as some of the stories we collected attest, often it was only after an organizer had a conversation with someone who, at face value, may have seemed an unlikely leader that they discovered that person's potential to take on great responsibility. The same was true for hiring organizers, as in the case of Zack Davis and Alex Watters, a story we revisit below.

## A Story of Self, Us, and Now

OFA used stories to facilitate relationship building and to mobilize teams to act. In trainings and one-on-one meetings, organizers and leaders taught new volunteers to tell their own story as a way of asking others to join the campaign. Developed and codified by Ganz, this approach, called public narrative, draws on stories about oneself, one's constituency, and the urgent challenges the constituency faces. Instead of a policy script, Ganz teaches public narrative as a way of communicating the values that call people to action, and, finally, moving them to action. The method, Ganz said, "emerged out of the 'story of hope' element of the 'story, strategy, structure' framework I've used since California campaigns in the 1980s." As described in chapter 3, "it became 'self, us, now' during the Sierra Club project in 2006, was introduced in a class I first taught at the Harvard Kennedy School that year, and then [brought] to the campaign in July 2007 at Camp Obama in Burbank," Ganz recalled.

The use of stories resonated with OFA staff and volunteers in part because many of them felt called to the campaign by the powerful stories Obama himself told. When Obama delivered the keynote address at the Democratic National Convention in 2004, he opened with the improbable trajectory that brought him to that stage: "My father was a foreign student, born and raised in a small village in Kenya. He grew up herding goats, went to school in a tin-roof shack. His father, my grandfather, was a cook, a domestic servant to the British." Throughout the speech, Obama communicated the belief his family had in America, and the American dream, through the choices they made—to immigrate to America, to enlist in the military, to name their son Barack, "believing that in a tolerant America your name is no barrier to success." He connects his own story to the experience of millions Americans around the country, who also believed that "all men are created equal" and harbored "a faith in simple dreams."

Nearly a decade after this speech, fourteen of the staff and volunteers whom we interviewed identified it as the precise moment at which they decided not only to vote for, but to work for, Obama, should he ever run for president. Volunteers of all ages spoke of feeling called to action by the story he told. Jyoti Jasrasaria, a field organizer and deputy regional field director in Florida, had "holed herself up in her parent's family room" to watch "the whole DNC and the whole RNC...to make sure that I [knew] what party I'm in." She was 14 at the time and remembers being riveted by the speech, threads of which she wove into telling her own family's immigrant story when she later worked for OFA. Ohio volunteer leader Nancy Beadle, 82, reflected, "Ever since I heard Obama speak at the Democratic National Convention, I thought, 'Wow, he can really lead!'" Dolginoff, 66, the "easy recruit" described above, said he was "mildly involved in the 2000 [election], and was very disappointed, and got more involved in 2004, and was even more disappointed, and I never got involved in any midterms, but in 2004 I saw Barack speak at the Democratic National Convention, and he had me. I knew he was going to run for president, and I knew I was going to work for him." Blanca O'Leary, age 54, put it this way: "Most of my life I've been waiting for somebody to give me the gleam in my eye of the people that I used to see that worked in Bobby Kennedy's campaign." Harlan Kutscher, a neighborhood team leader from Pennsylvania, described the effect the speech had on him as though it were the self-evident response of anyone watching: "I obviously had been really impressed with him in the 2004 keynote speech that he gave at the convention."

Even those who did not tune in to the DNC speech that year remembered how Obama's story reverberated throughout the progressive community. Joy Cushman was returning from graduate school in Scotland in the fall of 2004 and had not seen the speech, but "everybody was talking about it when I got back to the States." Cushman had just started a new job as a community organizer in Massachusetts and immediately purchased a copy of Obama's autobiography. She said to her boss, "If this guy ever runs for president, I have to tell you I'm going to take off." Seven other respondents made similarly public declarations. Bobbie Gustine, who lived in Oklahoma at the time, announced to her husband, "If he ever runs for president I am going to go volunteer for him," because it was the first time I felt, as a U.S. citizen, inspired by somebody."

OFA trained its staff and volunteers to tell stories as Obama had done at the DNC as a way of encouraging people to take action with the campaign. This kind of storytelling became part of the campaign's DNA. "All of us walk around with a text from which to teach, the text of our own lives,"[14] Ganz writes. Many of the organizers and volunteers we interviewed were so practiced at this art that they narrated their personal stories at the outset of each interview. Most organizers told their story on a daily basis: at one-on-ones, at volunteer trainings, at house meetings, at organizational meetings, and when speaking to persuadable voters.

The theory behind public narrative is that stories are a way of communicating values that tell people *why* they should take action.[15] Traditionally, when campaigns talk about why someone should support a candidate, they focus on policy positions: Vote for my candidate because she shares your views on health, the war in Iraq, or the economy. Research shows, however, that these kind of cognitive appeals to taking action are not nearly as powerful as appeals to the underlying values that people hold.[16] Sociologist Katherine Chen, for example, studies how organizations can manage volunteers through narrative, using stories as tools "that help members contemplate alternative avenues of action, rather than just promoting elite interests or organizational maintenance."[17]

Yet, how can people communicate their belief in abstract ideals like social justice, equality, or the American Dream? By telling stories about specific choices that individuals and groups of people make, Ganz argues that organizers convey their values in ways that call people to action. Obama's speech at the 2004 Democratic National Convention—which Ganz and his team used to teach public narrative at the Camp Obamas— would not have been nearly as powerful if he simply said, "I believe in the American Dream." Instead, he illustrated it for people describing the choices his ancestors had made that attest to their belief in this dream. Telling one's story in a way that moves others to action requires great skill. "Simply saying 'follow me,' is not enough," OFA trainers would warn new organizers.[18] To learn to tell one's personal story, OFA taught its organizers and volunteers to reflect on times in their lives when they first realized the importance of being heard, refused to be complacent about abuses of power, and above all, the circumstances that led to their shift from inaction to action.

As a result of this training, the staff and volunteers we interviewed could tell powerful stories about the choices they made to join OFA. Watters, the quadriplegic staffer introduced in this book's first chapter, told the story of his choice to become an organizer after his accident. "Ever since ... my accident, I was always looking for a career where I could give back." For Jasrasaria, it was the connection between her family's immigrant story and that of Barack Obama's: "The United States is a country that has always supported people when they're at their lowest points— and provided both stability and mobility ... for my parents, the American Dream was a real thing. They took a lot of risks, but then they found success and a home here."

Lodro Rinzler, a field organizer in Ohio, found his call to action when his friend Alex Okrent, a long-time Obama staffer, died suddenly and tragically in the midst of the campaign. A friend of Rinzler's from college, Okrent took time off from college first to work for Obama's 2004 Senate campaign, and later the 2008 and 2012 campaigns. On July 13, 2012, with fewer than four months to go until the election, Rinzler received a call from a friend telling him that Okrent had collapsed at work in OFA's Chicago headquarters. Devastated, Rinzler made the choice to "live [his] life doing anything I can for Alex." Rinzler packed up his apartment and deployed to Ohio to "enter Alex's world, one of tremendous hard work and devotion," serving as a field organizer on the campaign. Okrent's girlfriend, Miranda Stone, came to Ohio a few weeks later, serving as Rinzler's deputy field organizer. By describing these choices, the organizers could communicate to volunteers why they were working for OFA.

Personal stories became the basis of the relationships organizers built in one-on-ones and at public gatherings large and small. Jenni Boyle-Smith, the organizer in a 73-percent Republican part of southern Ohio described her approach to relationship building:

> When you meet people and you figure out their personal story of what is going on in their life, how are they going to be affected— then you can connect with them. You find something that you have in common. And people have way more in common than you would ever think. It just is a matter of taking the time and asking the right questions in order to connect with them. It's your personal story, their personal story, and having that meet with the president's agenda. That's how you do grassroots organizing. You have to connect with people because it is not just a transaction. If I need someone to go persuade a stranger, they need to know why they are out there—and it is not just because their parents voted Democrat.

Exchanging stories allowed organizers to express, articulate, and share the values and underlying ideals that connected people to the campaign. It enabled them to move beyond transactional mobilizing, in which interactions with people are treated like business dealings, and into relationships in which people become connected to each other.

Personal stories may have been particularly powerful in more conservative areas of battleground states, where appealing to people on policy grounds would have been nearly impossible. Staci O'Brien got her start with OFA as a neighborhood team leader in the "reddest county in Wisconsin," where "people would whisper" when they talked about "liberal" politics.[19] Erin Roediger, age 30, was organizing in the most conservative congressional district in Colorado, home of Christian groups like

Focus on the Family as well as three military installations. The training she and her volunteers received on using stories, Roediger said, was,

> one of the best things that we learned, because it really did give a chance for people in Colorado Springs—where you don't really necessarily go around talking about their liberal views—to feel safe to talk. And a lot of people would be quiet and whisper when we were in coffee shops because we were in public. So it just gave them that opportunity to speak and be heard, and that their ideas weren't crazy and their ideas weren't wrong.

Stories provided a way to break through traditional party divides. Laura Diviney, a volunteer from Charlotte, North Carolina, noted that her family is "loaded to the brim with Tea Party people." Her husband's family, she said, can be characterized as "staunchly Republican." But, when Diviney's husband described his reasons for supporting Obama at a family reunion in 2012, "everybody supported him in his remarks" because he told a "tender and heartfelt" story that "described his morality, not...his politics."

The stories also afforded staff and volunteers a means for describing to others the feelings of enfranchisement, voice, and solidarity they felt by working on the campaign. Many interviewees acknowledged feeling frustrated and alienated by American politics, as Susan Christopher had done while sharing her personal story at the first Camp Obama. Through their work on the campaign, however, staff and volunteers said their disillusionment transformed into a sense that they could do something real to make a difference.

In many cases, the staff and volunteers with whom we spoke felt like other political actions they had taken before the campaign did not matter. Bruner, the volunteer who had a four-hour one-on-one, said, "I found myself getting really frustrated obviously with the Bush administration, and I didn't really have any way to act that out, I guess is the best way to put it. So I started getting on blogs and reading and then communicating with other people over the Internet and getting hooked again on politics." But venting into the abyss of the Internet, Bruner continued, did not unburden her: "I found that rather than being an outlet, it made me even more frustrated because you're just typing, and it felt like it was making everything more aggravating. I felt maybe it's time I actually start doing something."

Volunteering in the relational context that OFA created, by contrast, gave interviewees an expanded sense of how they could be involved in the political process in a tangible way. Instead of just "go[ing] to the election booth to pull a lever," Terrell Martin, a volunteer leader in Wisconsin, said, "I could be a part of this campaign." Ann Cherry of Beaufort County, North Carolina, echoed Martin:

> Instead of just being a voter, I could be a participant in electing the candidate I wanted to win. So, the first thing I did was show up at my precinct meeting, which was announced in the paper, to which no one came. So, I went back home, thinking I had mistaken the place or the time, and discovered I had it right. I called the county chair—and I had never done anything but vote. I had never been to a Democratic Party meeting or worked on a campaign or anything. I was just a voter. He told me my precinct was unorganized, so I asked him how you go about doing that [organizing it]. When the Obama campaign came to eastern North Carolina, I volunteered, and I just never quit.

By telling these stories about the choices they and others in the campaign made, OFA staff and volunteers strived to communicate the values that moved them to action. In doing so, they created a relational basis for asking others to work alongside them to write a "story of us," which served as a source of ongoing motivation throughout the campaign.

### Making the "Hard Ask"

By choosing to assemble a ground game founded on relationships, organizers and team leaders created a context that made it possible for them to ask volunteers to commit to specific, ambitious outcomes. This type of request was dubbed the "hard ask" because it was concrete and clear, but also because it could be uncomfortable to ask people to commit to quantifiable results. Boyle-Smith, the organizer from southern Ohio, contrasted it with a "soft" or "easy" ask: "You learn over the hundreds and hundreds of calls…how to make your hard ask…[which is] when we actually ask somebody [to give up their free time to come volunteer for OFA]. An easy ask is, 'We know you support the president. Is that correct?' And we already know that, so that's an easy thing to ask people."

Yet, the urgency of the election demanded that organizers ask for real commitments. Most OFA field offices featured a large backward counter, which tracked the number of days remaining until November 4, 2008, or November 6, 2012. Every morning, field directors would send a daily update email to all organizers with the diminishing count toward "E-Day" in the topline. Some staff preferred the scare tactic approach: "Remember, when you're not working, the McCain [or Romney] campaign is," or "every day we don't contact voters is a day when only our opposition is getting their message out." Through such reminders, organizers sought to summon what Martin Luther King Jr. called "the fierce urgency of now," that is, the need to take immediate action. The most effective organizers and volunteer leaders could channel the relational capital they built to mobilize action by making the "hard ask."

One field director remembered, "If [organizers and volunteers] were worried or nervous, we would help by giving them hard ask trainings, which they loved. When we trained people and gave them opportunity to practice and to see other people give hard, specific asks and be successful, they were less nervous and more confident and then they felt they could take on anything." OFA's hard ask training had seven components:

1. Build urgency (give context about why the commitment you are asking of the supporter is important to do *now*).
2. Use strong language (avoid questions that could elicit one-word or yes/no responses, such as "Is this a good time to talk?" "How are you today?" or "Can you…?").
3. Know your audience (tailor your ask to the information you have about the potential volunteer).
4. Ask for something specific.

5. Ask and shut up (wait as long as long as 20 seconds for a reply).
6. Be persistent.
   a. Ask #1: Can we meet between 2 and 4 p.m. on Thursday?
   b. Ask #2: When on Thursday works better for you?
   c. Ask #3: When in the next three days can we get together?
   d. Ask #4: What day and time does work for you?
7. Take notes and reflect on your ask to improve the next one.[20]

To become comfortable making these asks, people needed practice. The field director quoted above continued, "If you train people, and have them see other people do it, then they're less nervous and then they take it on." Moreover, no organizer could do this well without a great deal of practice. Nicholas LaCava, an organizer in New Hampshire, called it "one of the biggest skills you get used to [refining]."

The hard ask had to be both precise and persuasive, so Boyle-Smith's regional field director, Anna Gilbert, had her organizers practice their hard asks on their morning conference calls "to get that down, to be quick, to connect with people, and [to] get everything out you need to say concisely and effectively. It takes a lot of practice," Boyle-Smith said. A weak ask might sound something like, "It would be great if you showed up at one of our canvasses." A stronger version of this ask, organizers were taught, could instead be, "Can I count on you to join us at our canvass on Saturday at 10 a.m.?" According to OFA's received wisdom, the most effective time to schedule volunteers is within 72 hours of the conversation—further reinforcing the campaign's sense of urgency.

The hard ask, like the organizing cycle abstracted above, did not always work as prescribed. What made the hard ask elicit a firm commitment was the strength of the relationship the organizer had built with the supporter, such that the organizer could make an appropriate request suited to each volunteer. Stephanie Monahon, who oversaw organizers working with Puerto Rican and Dominican diasporas in Pennsylvania, observed,

One thing that we noticed, in the Latino community in particular—we get used to: you go, you sit down, you have a one-on-one, you make the hard ask, somebody says "yes," and then you move forward, right? That is actually not the way it works in the Latino community at all. You go, you sit down, you get to know them, and then maybe they agree to meet with you again, or introduce you to the next person that you need to talk to. And we found in general it would take about three meetings, three one-on-ones, before we would get to a place where we could actually make an ask.

The hard ask in practice, then, was rarely how it looked in theory. Nevertheless, OFA volunteers and staff agreed that the ability to convey a sense of urgency that generates commitment was indeed based in relationships. Watters said, "I like to think that I'm good at talking to people and good at relating, but it's very different... talking in front of a group to actually inspiring them to do something for you." The "anatomy of the hard ask," as he referred to the seven steps above, was a concept he had to study and try repeatedly in order to "get from, you know, tell me your story, let's talk about who you are to okay, this is what I need from you."

What were the commitments that the organizers sought through their hard asks? The first was, of course, the one-on-one. Once the OFA staffer and potential volunteer leaders met in person and began to build a public relationship, organizers relayed the campaign's strategy by explaining the neighborhood team (or "snowflake") model, which we detail in the next chapter. They also outlined the role the potential recruit could have in helping the campaign reach its destination: the election (or reelection) of Obama. In transparently describing where the campaign was headed and how integral volunteers were to the execution of its strategy, OFA wanted to do more than increase turnout through shoe-leather politics. The campaign worked toward a much bigger and more difficult ask, that is, for the supporter to accept responsibility for a local leadership role: to do the job of a field organizer. This was, our respondents noted, the hardest ask of all and part of what differentiated OFA from many presidential electoral campaigns that preceded it.

By October of the election year, OFA staff and volunteer leaders' had a singular, transactional ask to make: Will you ommit to door-to-door shifts for GOTV? The field operation's proximate tactic for turning out as many Obama votes as possible was straightforward: to speak directly to as many of the right voters as possible just before they went to the polls. With just weeks to go, GOTV shift recruitment did not allow time to sit down with a volunteer, ask them to make a considered choice about his or her values, and test them for a leadership role. Toward the end of October, Malloy remembers, "we had daily goals of recruiting 70 shifts [per field organizer]. That was our daily goal. It was insane." The sheer volume of three-hour volunteer shifts that organizers were required to recruit in the final weeks, as Malloy attests, was daunting.

Organizers had been making very different hard asks many months and even years in advance of the election. Dolginoff's recruitment call, for example, came in May 2011, fully a year and a half before the election. To arrive at the leadership ask in the early months of the campaign, organizers were required to put prospective neighborhood team leaders through a testing process. In most states, potential leaders had to successfully complete two organizing activities (host a house meeting, run a volunteer training, recruit five people to regularly perform voter contact) or two voter contact activities (lead a voter registration event, local canvass, or phone bank, as Dolginoff did). Below we show how these activities served as leadership "tests" that grew OFA's organizational capacity while enabling the volunteers to recognize their own power.

### House Meetings

House meetings, wrote Ari Berman, "combin[e] the social atmosphere of a Tupperware party with the intimate fervor of a church."[21] Organizers use house meetings as a mechanism for "building something from nothing," Ganz said, and in places that Colorado field director Gabe Lifton-Zoline described as "untouched turf." House meetings were opportunities to identify and develop entirely new leadership, turn diffuse social networks into an organized structure, persuade undecided voters, and activate existing supporters in the most personal of environments: a friend or neighbor's home.[22] In 2008 in Georgia, organizers facilitated over 4,000 house meetings to, as Cushman put it, "do what used to be truly American: sit around and talk about, 'What do we want for our family?' 'What do we want for our country?' 'What is our responsibility?' "[23]

The content of a house meeting was, however, always structured "in the service of movement building," Ganz said. Just as one-on-ones, hard asks, and volunteer testing included clearly delineated procedures, the gatherings were well-planned affairs. Lifton-Zoline, Colorado's field director, furnished 20 pages of documents describing how to run an OFA house meeting, including how to recruit attendees, sample agendas, and how to measure success.

Hosts were instructed to "invite their entire social network (as if you were planning a big event or wedding)" including any supporters or undecided voters in local precincts. In keeping with OFA's relentless focus on goals and data tracking, organizers asked hosts to make a "list of 50" potential invitees, which were to be entered into the MyCampaign repository of VoteBuilder, the campaign's database. Staff considered house meetings one of the most difficult asks to make, as hosts had to jettison their privacy and invite their friends, family, and mere acquaintances to their home to talk about the election. The invitation alone, according to the OFA documents Lifton-Zoline provided, "may be the most valuable contact the campaign can have with voters" because they were far more personal than a scripted television advertisement, direct mail piece, or mass email. Scholarship has repeatedly reinforced this claim: as the body of research outlined in chapter 2 suggests, neighborly conversations have been proven to be far more effective than any other form of political outreach.[24] As a tactic for OFA, building relationships among local groups of supporters and providing a forum for the public recognition of would-be volunteer leaders, the house meetings had the additional advantage of spurring the formation of neighborhood teams.

Despite the allusion to a wedding, OFA organizers were careful to stress that house meetings were just that—a meeting—and not a party. If the host wanted to serve refreshments, he or she was asked to do so at the end of the gathering. Three organizing goals underpinned each house meeting: to test would-be team leaders, to begin to build an interdependent group identity, and to obtain public commitments from two guests to host their own house meeting within two weeks. This means, as the OFA training materials read, "Your one house meeting could become 21 more house meetings and over 420 invitations in just 7 weeks." Such extrapolations were meant to show staff and volunteers that each organizing tactic was linked to OFA's longer-term capacity to mobilize more supporters, to build ever-larger neighborhood teams, and, therefore, as the strategy went, garner a winning margin of Obama votes.

House meetings were essential for developing a sense of community, particularly where there were no legacy teams from 2008 or OFA 2.0. The more time volunteers spent face to face and in groups, the more "people felt like they had been assigned to a team rather than, 'Okay, great, you want me to make phone calls once a week, but I don't know why it matters,'" Jasrasaria said. Bringing members of a community together to strategize toward OFA's explicit goals was one of the most effective ways to build a neighborhood team and test a potential leader. OFA's postmortem analyses of both the 2008 and 2012 campaigns, which yielded questionnaire responses from a million staff and volunteers, corroborated this view: Volunteers are more likely to show up to voter contact events if they are accountable to a group of people with whom they have relationships and with whom they have worked before. How did OFA create the conditions for such relationships to be built and sustained over time?

Ellen Gangnon, the neighborhood team leader from Wisconsin, provided an illustrative example. She recalls making two attempts at hosting a house meeting. The first one, she recalled, "I begged people who worked with me to come to the house party. Only four people came, and none of them were from my region." Undeterred, she tried again. With the help of her organizer and lists from VAN, she cast a much wider net, this time inviting more than 100 guests. "I ended up with 24 or 26 people at my second house party. And from there developed a really, really nice team. Some of the members are still with me today!" As host, Gangnon opened the second house meeting with her personal story. She told of voting "for George W. Bush twice" but feeling frustration with "the amount of lives that were being lost in wars" and "the economic status of our country." She talked about being "a wife, a retired teacher, a mother of four, grandmother of five, all [while]...taking care of my mom and my dad," but still feeling like she wanted to get more politically involved. She told this story as a way of trying to connect to other people at her party—others who may have voted for Bush, who were parents or educators, or who were retired. Since Gangnon's first house meeting, Kleppe, the Wisconsin field director said, "I mean it sounds like I'm exaggerating—but Ellen has volunteered at least 40 hours a week every single week since June of 2008."

Suzanne Trask, a volunteer leader in Colorado, said that the second item on the house meeting agenda was public introductions of guests. "One of the sort of standard OFA practices at the beginning of pretty much every house meeting [in which] you're bringing people together who maybe don't know each other, is you go around the circle and you ask a question and everybody tells their story." The airing of each guest's motivation was an attempt to build a sense of shared community, by identifying what people had in common.

Yet as with the one-on-one, if the sharing of stories was not followed by an explanation of the campaign's strategy and an associated hard ask, it did little to enhance the field program. To this point, Jasrasaria said, "The least successful house parties were the ones where people had a great time sharing their personal stories but didn't make solid commitments, and the best house parties were the ones where we were all about the hard ask [for volunteer commitments], all the time...I think that took some time to figure out," she said.

In both 2008 and 2012, the campaign provided a DVD with a video telling the OFA campaign story, which organizers cued up after all attendees shared an abbreviated version of their personal story. The clip was short—no more than 15 minutes—but allowed the attendees to peer into other OFA house meetings happening all over the country. The video showed them how their gathering fit into the larger campaign strategy of building teams to increase voter contact capacity. The OFA organizer debriefed the campaign video by sharing more explicit details about the neighborhood team program, and answering any questions from the audience about OFA's neighbor-to-neighbor strategy. The organizer or host then facilitated a discussion to plan a "day of action"—to register voters, canvass, or phone bank—together, as a budding neighborhood team. Finally, after reiterating the central role that house meetings play in building the organization that will turn out every supporter on

Election Day, the organizer makes a public hard ask: "We need to fight to protect our progress and ensure that every issue we surfaced in the introductions has a chance to become progressive legislations. [Insert the name of a guest], can I count on you to host the next house meeting at [this day and time] next week?" as the house meeting script went.

Once the OFA organizer had recorded the names of the next two hosts, he or she reviewed the plan for the action event and talked about the next steps required for forming a neighborhood team, highlighting the vacant leadership positions in the snowflake. Ideally, he or she would leave the house meeting not only having rigorously tested a neighborhood team leader, but also with two future house meetings on the books, a voter contact event, multiple one-on-one appointments with guests, and a less quantifiable but still palpable sense of whether the meeting could be the beginning of a high-functioning neighborhood team.

Steele described this process from the perspective of leadership testing: "If [the potential volunteer leader] agrees and hosts that house party in their neighborhood, that's your first test, and then ideally the second test [comes] out of that house party. This is just an example, but out of that house party, they hold a voter contact event... and if they do it successfully [then] they're confirmed as a neighborhood team leader." OFA's requirement for this type of testing grew out of the haphazard and rushed process Bird's team of organizers had used in the Pennsylvania primary, which identified leaders without first gauging their ability and commitment to the role.

Reflecting on dozens of OFA organizing trainings she led in advance of the 2008 election, Cushman cautioned that in the absence of aggressive follow-up, even the most beautifully executed organizing event was for naught. High-performing organizers left house meetings with a list of all attendees and called each person after the event, whether they had signed up for an upcoming volunteer shift or not. They would also take note of any policy questions that may have arisen but for which they did not have answers at the time of the meeting, and personally follow up with an answer for the house meeting participant.

One field director, Greg Jackson, described the challenge in hosting house parties: "The folks that may come to a house party but wouldn't come to a traditional [voter contact event], yes they would show up but once they leave they are just going to wait for the next house party right— unless you have a really hard pitch." Thus, while house meetings were intended to generate enthusiasm, to build public relationships, to create commitments to action, to test leaders, and to lay the groundwork for neighborhood team formation, they too are an example of an organizing practice that, as Ganz says, "can be done well" or "utterly screwed up."[25]

### Voter Contact

Thus far, we have dedicated limited attention to the mechanics of OFA's voter contact activities themselves, privileging instead the ways in which OFA built the capacity for its ground game through personal and public relationships. But, Bird notes, "You can't just be community organizing with depth and not also translating that depth into conversations with the number of voters you need to contact." Phone banks, voter registration, and door-to-door canvasses are the bread and butter of any field program, and these tactics were central to OFA's operation. Instead of adopting traditional strategies for voter contact wholesale, however, OFA revised them to fit the electoral-organizing model it was developing. Unlike previous campaigns, OFA sought to have volunteers perform the vast majority of voter contact. In addition, the campaign gained renown for enlisting what the *New York Times* called a "dream team" of behavioral scientists and organizations like the Analyst Institute, "a clearinghouse for evidence-based best practices in progressive voter contact," to refine the exact words that would appear on OFA's persuasion and turnout scripts.[26] For example, rather than call up a supporter on Election Day to remind them to vote, as had been done in campaigns past, volunteers asked the voter to visualize their day, describe when they would vote, how they would get to their polling place, and whom they might bring along with them. The wording of these GOTV scripts were the product of the efforts of the Analyst Institute and other scholars' controlled experiments, which sought to determine which questions and turns of phrases had the greatest positive effect on voter turnout.

OFA also used voter contact events extensively in the early organization-building period of the campaign (also called the "persuasion phase," which lasted until the beginning of October). Many of OFA's training personnel were well aware of the research that demonstrates the effect that personalized conversations at the door and on the phone have on undecided (or "persuadable," to use OFA 2012 terminology) voters.[27] One training manual translated these findings: "It means a lot to voters that someone would volunteer their time to talk with them about our country and our future together." Neighborhood canvasses, according to the document, are even more effective: "Face-to-face discussions at the door are one of the highest quality forms of contact a campaign can have with voters."[28] Through these conversations, OFA volunteers recorded which voters on their list were supporters, and which were not. Field organizers and data captain volunteers entered these "ids" (identifications) at the end of each canvass or phone bank. Those who affirmed their support for Obama were transferred from persuasion "call" and "walk lists" to OFA's turnout lists, only to be contacted again when the polls were open. Further, volunteers were trained to invite any supporters they found on persuasion lists to join their neighborhood team as volunteers, another way in which teams expanded their capacity in the organization-building phase of the campaign.

For OFA, then, voter contact was not only about producing persuasion calls, knocks, and voter registration, but also about helping to build and stress test the organization. Voter contact served as a useful barometer of the health of neighborhood teams. The ability to successfully launch a voter contact event, moreover, served as one of the most common tests for potential team leaders. From OFA field directors and to the highest levels of leadership in Chicago, the volume of voter contact in each field organizer turf was of paramount interest. Bird described the relationship between volunteer capacity and the volume of registration and persuasion coming from each turf: "Do they have team members? And were they on track? And then are they producing? A lot of people would have teams [in VAN] that just didn't do anything," he reflected. In the absence of meaningful and measureable outputs, such groups might have "nice group meetings" but little else, Bird said.

Voter contact thus enhanced both OFA's organization-building and persuasion work in the many months leading up to Election Day by fostering solidarity among volunteers and organizers. Motley groups of Obama supporters engaged in strategic action—in the form of voter contact—together. In the process, the teams acquired a group character and members formed new relationships with one another. Just as Gangnon's house meeting served as the venue that publically launched her team and her role as a leader within it, core team members grew into their roles in the weekly canvasses, voter registration drives, and phone banks. These roles were so entrenched in the campaign structure such that by GOTV, each volunteer leader was given a badge that specified his or her role on the team.

Shirley Bright, the neighborhood team leader from North Philly, recalls one weekend: "It was raining cats and dogs and we were supposed to go out and canvass, and an 82-year-old and this [other] team member whose father [had just] died, they decided that they weren't going to let a little bit of rain stop them, so they put on ponchos and went out to knock on doors and canvass.... When they came back, I wished I had a camera. They looked like drowned mice." The two volunteers thus set a standard of commitment on Bright's team: the election was too important to forgo voter contact, no matter the extenuating circumstances.

Farther north, in Pennsylvania Dutch country, team leader Kutscher described how his team cohered around voter contact events. Kutscher hosted the local volunteers on his team for Wednesday and Sunday phone banks. The core group—"all old friends of ours now," he said, "literally lived within a one-mile radius of each other." Kutscher's team regularly won the statewide voter contact competitions. Asked to what he attributed his team's success, he replied, "If you wanted to know the secret, it's because we're a bunch of friends. It's what we like to do together. Some people like to go out bowling. We like to do this. I know maybe it sounds strange, but people showed up because they didn't want to let the team down."

Kutscher's team exemplified the OFA model: It possessed a mix of meaningful relationships, a clear leadership structure, and disciplined actions for which team members held one another accountable. As we discuss in the next chapters, the transition from relationship building to voter contact was not without its difficulties, particularly when newly hired organizers were expected to begin producing apace before they had time to do the crucial relationship building work described throughout this chapter. Skilled organizers and volunteer leaders with ample time to organize often struck this delicate balance. In this way, they forged the relationships that, we argue, were the key to OFA's field capacity.

## "HE WAS REALLY DOING THIS FOR LOVE OF HIS COUNTRY"

As with most forms of organizing, relationships anchored the Obama ground game. OFA sent organizers into the field more than 18 months before the 2012 election with the express purpose of building relationships. Organizers used this time to get to know their turf and build up a pipeline of potential volunteers and leaders. OFA wanted volunteer leaders reaching out to people in their own community. To recruit, develop, and test these volunteer leaders, OFA used one-on-one meetings, public narrative, house meetings, and voter contact events. Relationships tethered each of those practices together; they made it possible for organizers to ask their volunteers to make hard commitments, and for the volunteers to accept responsibility for growing OFA's capacity.

In reflecting on the core lessons they learned from their work on the Obama campaign, several of our interviewees recalled the importance of relationships. Both Bird and Cushman noted that the best indicator of the strength of a neighborhood team was the extent to which members of the teams had real relationships with each other, and knew about each others' lives outside the campaign. When team members were personally invested in one another, Bird and Cushman argued that they generated the commitment to work together to help the campaign win.

Face-to-face connections became a crucial source of motivation throughout the campaign. Because of them, many volunteers report rising to new levels of commitment, and team members could tell stories about each other that compelled them to stay committed. Diviney, the volunteer from North Carolina, tells one such story about her fellow volunteer, Joe, who walked into the OFA field office on the Central Piedmont Community College campus in North Carolina.

He shows up one day and he starts scrubbing the ladies' room, and I thought, "Wow, there you are. Who are you?" And he's cleaning the ladies' room, he cleans the bathroom, scrubs the floors, he sorts out and reorganizes the supply room, he cleans the break room, he scrubs the microwave oven, the vacuums the floor. He's just doing housework. And then we discover that he's got computer capabilities, and he's getting our printer fixed for us, and he's getting all our phones charged up, and we just keep seeing Joe, and he's just doing all the drudge stuff.

So finally, one day his phone started ringing, and [the ring] was battle stations for a battleship. The only way I happen to know that is because of a connection I have through the Navy—long story, never mind—but I said, "Is that battle stations on a battleship?" And he said, "Yes."

Diviney struck up a conversation with Joe, "chatt[ing] like ordinary acquaintances who have something in common." She learned that he was a military veteran who served for nearly 30 years in the United States Coast Guard. Diviney continued,

He had gotten to a point in his military command where he was having to tell his subordinates things that he just could no longer, in good conscience, say to them. This was when George Bush was president, and he could no longer in good conscience give these orders to his men, to his sailors, and it was tearing him up.

So Joe made a decision. "He decided to give up his military career as an act of patriotism, because he felt he could no longer serve his country in the military with the things that George Bush was asking of his sailors," Diviney recounted.

After retiring from the United States Coast Guard, Joe "wandered in the wilderness for a long time," Diviney said, with respect to "how to engage in public service in a volunteer mode." Then, one day, "He just pulled his car in the parking lot and walked in and picked up a toilet brush and started scrubbing toilets because he just wanted to serve.... [Joe] became a team leader. He became a canvassing star." Diviney spoke of his bravery:

> He went out and did canvassing and voter registration in Matthews, North Carolina. "Oh my gosh, they're sending people to Matthews?".... I'll tell you, if you go out to those places, it's red, red, red. My own precinct is very red. But he was going out in places where people would come up to him, look around, make sure nobody else was around them, and then whisper in his ear, "Thank you so much for doing this. I am so glad somebody is doing this," and then run away.

In 2012, Joe was diagnosed with cancer. He transferred his OFA responsibilities to another volunteer while he underwent treatment. "As soon as he was physically able to do so," Diviney remembered,

> We saw him at an event with Vice President Biden, and there was Joe, and he was sitting on a chair, and he just looked—I was surprised he could even sit up. But he had gotten up from his cancer treatments and come to this event because he knew that he would see so many of us there, and he just wanted to say hello to everybody. And, of course, we were loving him up. But he was really doing this for love of his country, and he had been in service to his country all his working life, and that's what he was doing.

# 5.

# CREATING A STRUCTURE TO SHARE RESPONSIBILITY
## *Neighborhood Teams*

Volunteer recruitment and retention is the most important aspect of our field program. We cannot achieve the sheer volume of what we need in order to win without their help.

—*OFA-Ohio training document, 2008*

This is your subsection of it. This is your community.

—*Gabe Lifton-Zoline, Colorado Field Director 2012*

When looking through the rose-colored glasses of victory, observers across the political spectrum have argued that the Obama campaign was one of the most sophisticated field campaigns in memory. Bird describes it as "the strongest grassroots organization in the history of American presidential politics," and even GOP strategists concede that the Obama campaign, with its rigid yet transparent structure, was far superior to both the McCain and Romney operations. Yet many accounts of the campaign overlook the significance of the Obama neighborhood teams. The vice chairman of the Florida Republican Party, Blaise Ingoglia, said as much: "When people asked me what happened last November, why did we lose, I break it down like this: We got outworked, we got out-messaged, and we got out-organized. And to put it bluntly: we got our clocks cleaned.... Whether you like it or not, Barack Obama has changed the game when it comes to politics by using social media and microtargeting."[1]

130

As with many appraisals of Obama's campaign operation, Ingoglia's focus on OFA's technological prowess misses the human side of the campaign—the hundreds of thousands of people who devoted more than ten hours per week to the campaign for no pay. When Obama spoke to his campaign staff a few months before the 2008 election, he focused on the organizing. "When I started this campaign," Obama said, "I wasn't sure that I was going to be the best of candidates. But what I was absolutely positive of was the possibility of creating the best organization." He went on to repeat one of the hallmark refrains of his campaign:

> What I was always confident about, was that if people will to submerge their own egos, and bring their particular gifts, passion, energy, and vision to a common task, that great things can be accomplished. That's my old organizing mindset. It's not just a gimmick, it's not just a shtick—I actually believe in it.[2]

For OFA's field leaders, the success or failure of the field model hinged on enabling volunteer teams to take responsibility for organizing, persuading, and turning out voters. One of OFA's proudest feats was building 10,000 neighborhood teams composed of 30,000 dedicated core team members. But how did the campaign manage all of the volunteers with whom they were building relationships, and, moreover, ensure they stayed focused on the work of the campaign? Relying on volunteers to run the ground game was one of the biggest departures OFA made from previous campaigns. How could they make it work and avoid the pitfalls that are commonly associated with volunteers—"flakiness," lack of focus, disorganization, or low productivity?

This chapter describes the structure that OFA created to manage, motivate, coordinate, and empower volunteers: the neighborhood team. We show how the campaign used this structure to distribute responsibility for actual campaign outcomes to local Obama supporters. By opting for a framework that held teams—rather than a single heroic leader—accountable, OFA created the space for ordinary citizens to learn to work collectively to achieve their goals.

## MANAGING AND MOTIVATING VOLUNTEERS: THE NEIGHBORHOOD TEAM

The neighborhood team model uniquely solved many of the challenges OFA faced in organizing its volunteers. First, how do you cultivate volunteer motivation? Researchers argue that when people are organized to work in teams, they become committed not only to the cause, but also to each other.[3] Some scholars argue that Obama and his "words inspired millions to contribute to and work for his campaign."[4] Indeed, while one-third of our respondents cited their admiration for Obama himself as the reason they initially sought out OFA, none reported that the force of his personality motivated them through, in the case of organizers, 90-hour work weeks "for little pay and even less sleep."[5] Instead, what kept them going was the commitment they had to other people in their organizing region and on their team. Diviney, the volunteer from North Carolina, describes her team:

> [L]et me give you an idea of my team: When they found out my husband was in the hospital—we had been talking that after Christmas we would all get together and have a sort of a New Year's party. We'd had our Christmas party at my house. So after New Year's, my husband got sick. And so...my team members said to me, "We will not have our party until you can go. We'll wait until your husband is home from the hospital before we'll have our party so that you don't have to choose between going to the hospital and seeing your husband and going to the party."

Through the neighborhood teams, volunteers developed relationships with each other that became the basis of their commitment. It was not just their "affect toward the candidate," but also their relationships with each other that animated and sustained the field staff and volunteers' organizing and voter contact work.[6]

Second, if a field operation wants volunteers to assume real responsibilities—like running staging locations without staff support during GOTV—it has to enable that work. How do campaigns provide the clarity and coordination necessary for volunteers to take on leadership

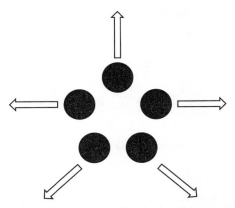

**FIGURE 5.1**: Leadership structure that lacks clarity and coordination
*A leadership structure without any authority often results in a lack of direction, efforts that work at cross-purposes, and, consequently, stymied capacity. Figure based on Marshall Ganz's teaching materials.*

roles in a national campaign? OFA recognized that motivation is not enough. Howard Dean, as we've described before, also had a feverish following of "Deaniacs," yet their enthusiasm did not translate into results. Figure 5.1, taken from OFA's 2008 General Election training manual, demonstrates the danger of working in a group of people that lacks coordination and clarity about its shared purpose. Originating from Ganz's course materials, the diagram illustrates how, in this system, nobody is responsible for coordinating everyone, for resolving impasses, or for taking "ultimate responsibility for the outcome," as the manual instructs. Without coordination, the team cannot produce strategic results for the campaign.

Third, how do you avoid overburdening your volunteers? Sometimes, the alternative to the uncoordinated model above is to have one person in charge, as depicted in Figure 5.2. As the OFA training manual writes (again, borrowing language from Ganz): "Sometimes, we think the leader is the person everyone goes to, which ends up looking like this:"

"But what does it feel like to be the 'leader' in the middle? What does it feel like to be the arrow that can't get through? What happens if the 'leader' in the middle drops out?"

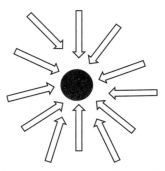

FIGURE 5.2: **Leadership structure with no shared responsibility**
*A single volunteer responsible for all leadership and execution also precludes capacity growth. In this situation, many voices are excluded and team performance can be reduced to a single person's efforts. Figure based on Marshall Ganz's teaching materials.*

To address these challenges, OFA relied on the neighborhood team model. It is no accident that when talking about the Obama field operation, people often refer to the entire program as the "team model." This was the core structural innovation of the OFA field campaign. The team model fosters relationships within groups of people while providing them with a structure for getting work done. By linking team members together in interdependent roles, the team structure provided the coordination and clarity necessary to help the team meet its goals without overburdening any one person. Interdependent roles meant that each person on the team had a unique role to play, but no one person could get her work done without coordinating with others.

Cheryl Ellis, who lives in a suburban, formerly farmland area outside of Raleigh, North Carolina, pointedly observed that, "[With OFA], people don't just have titles just to have titles. They have titles because they have shown that they're able to do the work and to make it happen and whatever the ask is, they're able to do it." Contrasting this model "side-by-side" with the Democratic Party in her county, Ellis said, "OFA is so much more effective because people know when they get involved with OFA, we are actually going to do the work that's going to make a difference."

In 2012, OFA charged field organizers with building, on average, three to four neighborhood teams. The leadership diorama of a FO

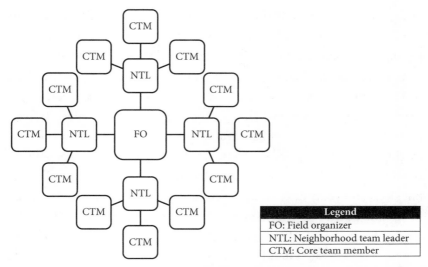

FIGURE 5.3: **A field organizer's interdependent neighborhood team structure, called a "snowflake"**

*Field organizers were responsible for building as few as two and as many as seven neighborhood teams. This range reflects the different phases at which the organizers joined the campaign, as well as the distinct turf types and demographics to which they could be assigned.*

would look something like Figure 5.3, with each neighborhood team leader representing the nucleus of a neighborhood team. The interlocking relationships among people on the teams gave this model its colloquial name, the "snowflake" model.

In the above, ideal scenario, a paid OFA field organizer would be the leader in the middle, guiding volunteer efforts and being held accountable for outcomes. However, his or her success was not about how much voter contact he could produce on his own. Instead, meeting goals was entirely contingent on his or her relationships with others—most importantly, with the volunteers who accepted the responsibility of becoming neighborhood team leaders. A further, crucial dimension of the organizer's success was his or her ability to support the neighborhood team leaders in getting their teams to work autonomously.

Thus, the only way staff and volunteers could meet their ground game goals was by developing the leadership skills of others. Neighborhood team leaders (NTLs) were directly responsible for the execution of OFA's most important field activities: registering, persuading, and mobilizing voters through millions of personal conversations. To execute such tactics successfully, NTLs had to recruit and train core team members (CTMs) who would oversee each of these voter contact activities, as well as ensure that the team had enough volunteer capacity to meet its ever-increasing goals as the election neared. Further, the NTLs (who became staging location directors, or SLDs, during GOTV) were responsible for reporting the number of voter registration forms collected, calls, and knocks on a weekly basis to their field organizer, and at hourly intervals in the final phase of the campaign. By design, the number of GOTV staging locations—5,117—matched the minimum number of volunteer leaders the campaign had to confirm, because NTLs were expected to transition into the role of running their neighborhood's staging location. This final number of staging locations was roughly half the number of neighborhood team leaders that OFA organizers had recruited nationwide. In the run-up to the election, many teams were fused because it often made more logistical sense to house two teams in one location and under one leader, a testament to how local the OFA field operation was in most battleground states.

Given this structure, our interviewees reported that weak or absent neighborhood teams corresponded with underperformance, and strong team leadership correlated with high levels of voter contact. Kutscher, the NTL quoted in chapter 4, described how his team consistently won the state's voter contact competitions: Each week, two times a week, he and his wife held a two-hour phone bank in their home. Kutscher's goal was to maximize the number of volunteer team members who attended. In this way, every Wednesday and Sunday evening leading up to the election, his house was abuzz with conversations with persuadable voters. "Our group was so powerful and the groups that spun-off of it were so strong that for a long time, Sean, who was our field organizer, beat every other field organizer in the state for months and months and months, and it was all because of us. He knew. I mean, he joked about it."

To build teams like Kutscher's, OFA began by teaching organizers the leadership model that depends, once again, on "enabling others to accept responsibility."[7] This approach to leadership was a dramatic shift for volunteers who had been exposed to the classic party-led field programs. Diviney recalled that "Kerry and Edwards put two paid staffers in the state of North Carolina. They operated on a wheel and spoke model [as depicted in Figure 5.1]....I worked through the county party framework, which I found to be a very dispiriting experience. So when my friend suggested we go to the Obama office, I knew that I was not going back to the county Democratic office."[8]

The core task for field organizers, then, was to identify, recruit, and develop people like Kutscher and Diviney to become leaders in the neighborhood team structure. "These leaders will be the backbone of your operation, and you must be able to trust them to delegate responsibility to other dedicated people, and to follow through on commitments," OFA's 2012 training materials read. Developing these leaders requires delegating responsibility (as opposed to tasks), and holding others accountable for carrying out that responsibility. OFA knew that its volunteers had the local knowledge and relationships that a newly arrived, fresh-out-of-college field organizer could never build in just a few months. One regional field director in Iowa, Kate Cummings, empowered her field organizers by telling them that "they were the field director for their turf." Field directors, the organizers knew, were not the ones going door-to-door. Cummings's framing meant that they were expected to build the infrastructure of the operation that would produce the results for which they would be held accountable—not to perform the voter contact work themselves.

Magnifying the snowflake model one degree further, according to 2012 training documents developed by OFA's national training director, Sara El-Amine, the ideal neighborhood team passes through five phases. The first is merely the potential for a team. When she first arrives in her turf, an organizer may have a list of 100 possible Obama supporters, none of whom she has a relationship with yet, and none of whom are organized among themselves in a leadership configuration, let alone in teams. In the second phase, "team formation," the volunteers pass through the early stages of growth and leadership development, the indicators of which are "active volunteers and perhaps one confirmed NTL or CTM," according to OFA's 2012 training materials. In the third phase, the team is formed and functioning, with a confirmed NTL but without a complete leadership core. In phase four, a "developed team" is well-established. This is the phase when it is most productive. The indicators for this phase are an experienced NTL with at least three CTMs. One top field staffer said that the final stage of development is when a team understands its roles and goals and can "help mentor new teams."

One state-level field staffer recalled one such team in Nashua: It was so complete that its volunteer leader traveled throughout the state to mentor new NTLs "because she understood her role so well that she was just there talking about it, as an organizer." In phase five, which "only large and developed teams might go through," new staff starts in a turf and teams are split in two, focusing on an even more locally demarcated team turf.

Figure 5.4 depicts what an OFA neighborhood team might look like in phase four.

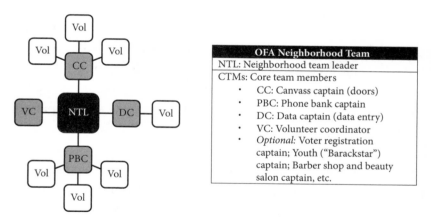

FIGURE 5.4: **A fully developed neighborhood team**

*In phase four of development, an OFA neighborhood team could count on a leader, 3–4 core team members, and half a dozen or more regular volunteers. While data, canvass, and phone bank captains were a constant presence across teams, other leadership roles, such as congregation or voter registration captains, were recruited as needed according to turf type.*

In phase four, the volunteer structure is in place such that each NTL is managing her own team and, in turn, each core team member manages her own subteam. Thus, in Figure 5.4 there is a core team member in charge of volunteer coordination, data, phone banking, and door knocking—and they each have their own sub-volunteer teams as well. The field organizer, not pictured in this diagram, is ideally managing between three and seven NTLs, all of whom have teams like this. Throughout the campaign, layers of leadership and team-building continually grow, so that the capacity of a given field organizer's turf depends on the number of active, functioning teams he or she has organized.

These figures, of course, represent the ideal type. One of the most consistent insights our respondents shared was the need to modify the responsibilities of the core team members depending on the turf type. Greg Jackson, the field director in North Carolina, described it this way:

> While originally there were some cookie-cutter models of "Oh you need a data director, you need a canvass captain, you need phone bank captain, you need a team leader"; we looked at it a little bit differently. So our actual neighborhood teams throughout most of the campaign—every team had a voter registration director, because there was so much voter registration that needed to happen [in North Carolina]....So the voter registration captain was a part of every team just like a canvass captain was. With our neighborhood team leaders, depending on what type of turf they were in, if they were in a turf that was heavy African American or heavy youth, then that was part of their responsibility as well. So while there might not have been a youth captain or an African American outreach captain, neighborhood team leaders were responsible for reaching out to barber shops and beauty shops and connecting with local administration and high schools if that was the type of turf that they were in.

In a 2013 interview, David Axelrod said something similar of the highest-level staff in Chicago: "Everybody understands what instrument they play and how to blend those instruments," an apt metaphor for the way in which a full-formed neighborhood team functioned at the ground level.[9]

## DISTRIBUTING RESPONSIBILITY FOR OUTCOMES

To make the neighborhood team structure work, OFA also had to "give people the keys to the car and let them drive," as Buffy Wicks said. For top field staff, that meant giving field organizers and volunteers a sense of ownership over the campaign and motivating them to take responsibility for their voter contact metrics. OFA created a culture in which all staff and volunteers had real goals they had to meet, and in which they held those around them to the same standards. As Alex Peña, an organizer in Durango, Colorado, said, "Everybody is trying not to let one another down."

How did the campaign allocate responsibility to volunteer teams? Throughout the campaign, OFA used metrics to distribute responsibility to staff and volunteer teams, providing a clear set of goals teams had to reach. A canvass captain was ultimately responsible for door-to-door activities, but whether or not his team met its goal also depended on the volunteer coordinator to recruit shifts, the phone bankers to confirm the shifts, the volunteers to show up and do the door knocking, the data captain to enter the voter contact numbers at the end of the day, and the neighborhood team leader to oversee the whole operation and report the numbers to the field organizer. Maintaining transparency about goals thus served to distribute leadership throughout the network of field staffers and neighborhood teams across nearly a dozen states. In describing this distribution of responsibility, Cushman said, "It really matters that we could give people *meaningful* goals" (emphasis added).

Many traditional campaigns dole out one-off activities to volunteers. In outsourcing tasks in this way, a volunteer might be asked to call voters for two hours, without being given any insight about who they are calling, what a successful contact rate is, and how many personalized phone calls needed to be made in their neighborhood in order to execute the campaign's national strategy. The volunteer served as an interchangeable phone banker, responsible for nothing more than sitting in a chair and making calls for a designated period of time. Giving someone responsibility for outcomes, by contrast, is like asking them to recruit 10 new volunteers. Such a responsibility requires the volunteer to use her own skills and resources to try to achieve the outcome by recruiting people to go door-to-door, ensuring that walk packets are prepared, and making contingency plans for inclement weather or difficult-to-access housing complexes. By giving neighborhood teams consequential goals, the Obama campaign increased their sense of responsibility and ownership over the outcomes. In doing so, OFA gave volunteer teams a "subsection" of the campaign, as Lifton-Zoline said.

To distribute responsibility to NTLs and their teams, the staff started first by identifying what consequential goals would be. Working with the analytics team, the field director and deputy field directors of each battleground state, divided the entire state into geographic units, called turf. Then, they calculated the number of votes each turf would need to generate for the campaign to win the entire state. Based on the number of votes needed, they then worked backward to create a plan for the amount of voter contact that would have to happen in each organizer's turf, and, correspondingly, the number of neighborhood teams needed to achieve that voter contact. Allison Zelman, the Pennsylvania field director, described some of the logic behind the goal-setting:

> The [number of] NTLs and CTMs [necessary for a given organizer turf] were by far the easiest just because...we were able to look at the number of MyCampaign people that existed within the turf and we knew we wanted an average of five [teams per FO turf].... We took into account diverse turf, but [figuring that out] was...just part of our turf cutting process. And we also knew how many NTLs we wanted in our state in order to win.

By breaking down goals geographically, the campaign gave each local organizer (and his or her volunteer leaders) an understanding of how their work could contribute to the larger victory. It broke it down to simple math. As LaCava said, "[I]f your wards go strong Democratic then maybe the city goes Democratic and then maybe the state goes Democratic and then you get those electoral votes for the President."

Field staff, neighborhood team leaders, and core team members were responsible for all the metrics achieved by the people they were managing. Field organizers were responsible for all of the capacity building and voter contact that took place in their turf, regional field directors for their entire region, deputy field directors for their pods (four to eight regions) and field directors for their entire state. For each individual leader to meet her goals, then, she had to support her direct reports in meeting theirs. Holding NTLs accountable for the metrics of their volunteers was another way in which the campaign encouraged leadership development.

Staff thus shared their goals with volunteers to distribute responsibility to them. Attempting over 2,000 households per week in rural turf, for example, could be equivalent to 10 percent of the county's electorate. If limited to staff or stalwart activist production alone, this was an impossible feat. "But," as Jenni Boyle-Smith offered, "when volunteers knew what my goals were, they wanted to help." Her volunteers "wanted to do better, so I did share my goals with [them]." Boyle-Smith understood that the state staff "figured out [our goals] statistically, and then broke that down to field organizer and then I would break it down to teams per night." Bird stressed this point: "You need to have volunteers who know their goals."

Giving teams responsibility for outcomes gave volunteers the sense that they owned a piece of the overall strategy. In Colorado, field director Lifton-Zoline "grounded goals in reality" for his staff. He said, "The people in Chicago are pretty good at this stuff. We think if we do all this work we will win. This is your subsection of it. This is your community. The most empowering other thing we can do is to be clear that no one else is going to do this work, so 'if you're going to do it, do it, and if not we'll get someone else do it'—and we're all doing the same thing."

Anna Cooper, a field organizer in Ohio, remembers that, "there were consequences for not meeting your goals, both as an organizer, and overall. If you weren't doing the work, then we're not going to win." Cooper, who described herself as "really self-motivated, really hard on myself," said, "If I didn't make goals I would be upset, or just like, 'What could I have done differently?'" Staff and volunteers knew that the goals really mattered. One New Hampshire organizer said, "I think the most important thing was you had to hit your goals, because they didn't make these numbers up just to make our lives hard; maybe these numbers came out of calculations of mass numbers in order for President Obama to win." Bird admitted that OFA "didn't even get all the way where we needed to be" on volunteer ownership of goals. However, the majority of NTLs whom we interviewed were acutely aware of their voter contact production numbers, and how that related to the state and national strategy.

Staci O'Brien first experienced how responsibility was allocated throughout the Obama campaign as a volunteer in Waukesha County, "the reddest county in Wisconsin," she said. A former college English teacher, O'Brien served as an NTL in 2008 and "saw first-hand how much the neighborhood team model empowers local citizens, brings them together, and gives them direction and some tools to make them feel like they're really making a difference." Yet after Obama was declared the winner in 2008, O'Brien said that instead of getting swept up in the inauguration festivities, she was pouring over turnout statistics. "I told myself, 'I am going to trust what [OFA] is telling me but if the day after the election it turns out that it wasn't any different in my little town [as compared to] the surrounding communities, then I'll never do it again, frankly,'" she recounted. O'Brien observed the raw vote total in her town increase by 20 percent, whereas her neighboring county— which had a less robust OFA presence—had turnout increases in the teens. "So, I became a believer," O'Brien said. She became so convinced of the efficacy of the electoral-organizing model that she changed her career path, working to organize 23 counties in Wisconsin during Organizing for America's health care fight in 2010 and 2011, and finally serving as a regional field director on the 2012 campaign.

Because O'Brien had experienced "first-hand" what it felt like to work on a team with "direction," she wanted the organizers and volunteers she oversaw in 2012 to have the same clarity of purpose. Goals, as we learned from many of our interviews, helped staff and volunteer teams alike understand why their work mattered. "In the run up to the election," O'Brien said, "it was all about building the thing, quite frankly, as big as we could, getting as many volunteers engaged as we could, having as many initial conversations, and collecting as much information as we could—the information would later inform the goals, and the volunteers we were able to recruit would help us achieve those goals." To further contextualize how OFA arrived at the "very high" goals, as she said, O'Brien would tell organizers and volunteers that,

> Number one, it's all going to end at 8:00 p.m. on Election Day, come hell or high water, but number two, you also know you have to get to 50 plus 1 percent, and you know how many votes you need, and you can mathematically calculate how many people you should talk to in order to achieve that goal. I always felt that our goals were very grounded in reality, so I think that's the biggest difference.

Austin Brookley, a field organizer in Florida, also found that providing his volunteers with evidence and context about what the goals meant increased his teams' productivity. OFA, he said, "actually has data to back up their beliefs in [the team structure and goals], which makes it a lot easier to buy into. It's a lot easier to buy into a process when there's evidence to support it. It was a very data-driven campaign," Brookley said, echoing the campaign's secondary mantra: people-focused, metrics-driven.

Even though they did not communicate directly with state and national headquarters, volunteers bore witness to the importance the campaign placed on their work. Blanca O'Leary, the team leader in Colorado, remembers being told "you have to knock on 'X' doors, make 'X' number of phone calls." Ann Cherry, the retired teacher who became a volunteer leader in North Carolina, used similar phrasing: "We had little goals all along. We had the goal for our phone bank—for example, we wanted to hit 'X' number of calls and 'X' number of contacts, which we could see because, especially those of us who were on the evening shift from seven to nine, and call times stopped at nine, we immediately had to tally so our field organizer could call in on the statewide conference call the number of calls we made, the number of contacts."

Because goals gave people a sense of ownership, some interviewees reported that they could also be a source of motivation. Neighborhood team leader Rick Baer noted parallels between OFA and his former union organizing days. "If you're on an organizing campaign, you have to lead the people, more or less, but they're the ones who have to do it. And if they don't get involved, you're not probably going to win, because they don't really take ownership of the campaign," just like OFA's neighborhood team model, he remarked. Field organizer Clinton Thomas noted how "giving [volunteers] that responsibility, giving them ownership of the campaign, empowering them...made them feel like they owned it more, so they were willing to put in 10, 15, 20 hours a week there at the end."

When volunteer teams had responsibility for meaningful outcomes, they reported being more motivated and committed to the campaign, since they felt ownership over their piece. But goals alone are not the source of motivation; what matters is how they are used. After helping incubate many of the transformative elements of OFA's ground game in 2008, Joy Cushman went on to become a national leader in progressive organizing at the New Organizing Institute and now PICO. She has seen "people try to replicate the [neighborhood] team structure in other instances, where they're just giving people call goals or door knock goals, and it just doesn't work." Metrics thus played a crucial role in coordinating the neighborhood teams because metrics reflected how field responsibilities were both shared and contingent on the work of others.

## MORE STAFF, LESS OWNERSHIP?

According to some volunteers, an increase in the number of field staff, particularly in 2012, undercut the campaign's efforts to give volunteers a sense of responsibility for consequential outcomes. This shift underscores the importance of distributing responsibility. To implement its field strategy, the campaign flooded battleground states with far more staff in 2012. As Bird pointed out, the aggregate number of field staff in 2008 was comparable to that of 2012, but they were concentrated in fewer states. Organizers who might have been deployed to Michigan, Indiana, or Georgia in 2008 were allocated to Ohio. As a result, the staff size in Ohio in 2012 increased by approximately 160 percent as compared to four years prior. In Colorado, field director Lifton-Zoline said that in 2008, the state "had about 100 FOs and...75 or 80 DFOs [deputy field organizers], whereas this time around [in 2012] I think we topped up about 500 people total in the field. So we were [almost] three times the size this time."

This large influx of staff meant that volunteers had fewer respon-sibilities. Alex Steele was among those 100 FOs from 2008 who wit-nessed how staff size could alter the field program.[10] Having organized for OFA for years before assuming his post in the state's Denver head-quarters in 2012, some of Steele's "old NTLs call me bugging me all the time now about what's going on with OFA." The way in which he had organized in 2008 through the team structure, he said, was the only "way of organizing that has been able to produce that kind [of] loyalty, that buy-in and instilling that sense of greater purpose amongst the volunteers, and they really do feel that passion for their turfs, for their communities." By contrast, in some areas, one of the consequences of the influx of paid organizers in 2012 was that "in some of the more dense, urbanized or very, very dense turfs where it really becomes a little more staff heavy—especially when you have 300 people—you have more of the staff just taking on the responsibilities themselves because they can," Steele said.

Even volunteers in rural areas agreed that the higher concentrations of staff meant volunteers had less responsibility. Jennifer Herrington, a neighborhood team leader from a town of 5,500 in Iowa, contrasted her relationships with her FOs in 2008 and 2012: "In [2008], we had a designated field organizer, and she was very good as far as partnering, and assisting organizing, and just provided a lot of support, and direc-tion." OFA's 2012 presence, according to Herrington, was "much more hands-on, I think, as far as our field organizer, much more intense, more staff in the last several months leading up to the election, and then a lot more phone banking" as compared to 2008. Sally Gasior, a long-time neighborhood team leader in Ohio, remembers that as more staff came on, she was not the one directly reporting and taking responsibility for her goals. Gasior said, "When I think about being accountable and hitting goals and targets and everything, that was prior to 2012. After that, once they brought in the paid staff, they were the ones doing all that reporting." Katie Keating, a veteran of both election cycles, recalled that the turf she organized by herself in 2008 in Colorado "was divided among five different organizers in 2012. But yet [organizers] still had astronomical goals."

Ellen Gangnon, the long-time neighborhood team leader in Wisconsin, identified a related trade-off: The more hyper-local the field organization, the fewer opportunities there were for coaching, relationship-building, and exchange beyond the handful of precincts to which staff and teams were assigned.[11] As more staff became responsible for increasingly smaller local areas, Gangnon felt her role contract. Before most 2012 field staff arrived in Wisconsin, she had been asked to assume a mentorship role because of her deep understanding of both the OFA model and the neighborhoods in her county. In her capacity as an experienced team leader, she mentored new organizers and new volunteers. "I was able to give some insight," Gangnon said. "It was more of a, 'Well did you know that this is going on or I want to share this, and what do you have to share?'" But, she continued, "when more and more staff came on the ground in our area my contact with the neighborhood team leaders diminished greatly.... It was definitely a shift, it was definitely a shift in my role compared to my issue organizing [OFA 2.0] role. As more and more staff came on board, they then became responsible for the teams."

Assigning only one or two neighborhood teams to each organizer also ran the risk of, as Steele indicated, staff displacing local volunteers in leadership roles. This was a pendulum swing in response to one of OFA's key lessons from 2008: "It was tough for an organizer to manage more than five to seven teams, and give them the kind of support and coaching that it takes, particularly on an accelerated time scale," according to

Grandone, who was part of OFA's 2008 postmortem taskforce. Yet, Grandone also noted, some of the most self-sufficient teams were those that were very rural, and therefore actually had less attention from FOs.

"Ironically," Grandone observed, "some of our strongest teams were where we had one organizer having to cover, in some cases, hundreds of miles of turf because, unlike an organizer in the heart of the city of Milwaukee, where they are right in the center or at the office and people are just coming [through the door], the rural organizers…had no choice because it wasn't humanly possible to be in all these places in the northern part of the state, with all their leaders and at all of their meetings." The premium on finding and empowering the right volunteer leader was thus higher in places where staff had to organize teams that could operate autonomously.

For example, in 2008, one organizer outside of Hayward, Wisconsin, had a "completely unreasonable" amount of turf to cover, Grandone said. The FO recruited a leader who also happened to own a hair salon, which they transformed into a campaign outpost. The organizer outlined what he could do, and how often he could come to Hayward. Realizing that his town was now his responsibility, the volunteer responded that his hair salon would be where they had regular meetings, "because I realize that you're on the road, Mr. Organizer," Grandone recalled the volunteer saying to the staffer. The NTL then conducted his own one-on-ones, leveraged his community contacts to get phones donated, and was forced to learn the VoterFile so his team could input their data in a timely manner. "It was that scenario that forced the organizer and those leaders to actually figure it out," Grandone said.

Thinner staff capacity in 2008 necessitated identifying and empowering a volunteer who could "think strategically and be able to coach others and run an arm of the campaign without an organizer being there as a crutch," Grandone said. Enabling volunteers instead of staff to lead the ground game was, as we have argued, one of the most important components of OFA's field model. Through stories like these, our respondents highlighted the importance of distributing real responsibility to volunteers to make the neighborhood team model work and sustain itself beyond Election Day.

## THE TRIBULATIONS OF TURF SPLITTING

More evidence of the importance of giving volunteers responsibility for strategic goals came up when discussing the campaign's commitment to creating hyper-local teams. Giving OFA a presence in every county of every swing state in 2012 meant that each organizer's turf was relatively smaller than it had been in 2008. Patrick Frank, who served as a field organizer in 2008 and regional field director in 2012, noted that "there was sort of an attitude, I think, from HQ, that more is better. And more *was* better, in general—like having more staff was always great—but some things, like, having another field organizer that I now have to give turf to, or getting somebody who doesn't have a car in a suburban turf causes more problems than it's worth."

The campaign would "on board" staff sequentially as they got closer to Election Day, progressively cutting down the size of each organizer's turf as more people were hired. This often strained the relationship between the original field organizer and their volunteers, at times increasing attrition rates. Frank articulates what nearly a dozen interviewees alluded to:

> We had two field organizers in the town of Fort Collins when I started, which is a big place. So by the end we had ten field organizers in Fort Collins. So you can imagine, as the hiring went on, how we kept splitting and we lost NTLs over it. There's no excuse for that. . . . I do think that there could have been more understanding of the situation and the unique relationship that field organizers have with their neighborhood team leaders.

Severing the relationship between early organizers and their volunteers could undermine the relationships that were responsible for the campaign's capacity. Frank noted that OFA "lost some time at the end of July into August taking a team out of a very good field organizer's hands and giving it over to somebody who didn't yet know what they were doing."

Shrinking turf sizes also meant that the pool of potential volunteer recruits per team diminished, making it harder for some organizers and leaders to build their teams. Jenni Boyle-Smith, the Ohio field organizer, said that the number of teams she was charged with building in her rural turf was "really ambitious up front. When I came in, they were like 'you are going to have 5 teams.' I was like, 'I don't have enough people to have 5 teams!'" As Election Day neared, Boyle-Smith was given permission to consolidate. "And once we [narrowed] it down to three, the neighborhood model worked perfectly," she said.

In addition, because of the pressure to build teams in ever-smaller numbers of precincts, some staff and volunteers were tasked with building teams in areas that were simply not "walkable," as the campaign described them. In very rural turf, it could take four hours to canvass only 15 houses, and speak to a handful of voters. When looking only at the numbers of teams and the geographic coordinates of staging locations, this meant that OFA was achieving its goal of hyper-locality. From the perspective of the volunteers, however, their time was being wasted. One regional field director said,

> [Headquarters] kept changing our goals and telling us that we were gonna build more teams, but at some point we knew this was what we had, so we started figuring out how to make it work like that, still looking for people, but I think you should always have a backup plan. So for us it was teams covering bigger areas, moving some people from suburban areas. We had one whole team that we told [headquarters] that their whole turf was unwalkable, but nobody believed us until the very end, and we just moved that whole team into another area, because their whole turf was unwalkable. They didn't need a staging location out there.

Where organizers could not find volunteers to fill roles on their neighborhood teams or in staging locations, they fell back on tactics that field campaigns had used in past campaigns. "We had some people from New York who came in and helped," the RFD said. "I had fellows that I moved [into staging location roles] from different areas. What ended up happening in a lot of areas is it looked like I told them it was gonna look before [headquarters] kept pushing me to make [the teams] smaller."

Bird agreed that turf splitting and staff handoffs were one of OFA's greatest challenges. "The whole turf breaking up, we probably struggled with that the most, because you never know how much money you were going to have for staff, so it's not like at the beginning I was able to say, 'Chris [Wyant, the Ohio general election director], you're going to have 700 staff, and here's when you're going to get them.'" Chicago never knew precisely how much money they would raise each quarter, so Bird could only tell field directors that "you're going to be able to get 250 [organizers] by X date, and if fundraising keeps going [you'll] get another." As mentioned in chapter 3, Bird and other top operatives in Chicago knew that *Citizens United* would change the game, and that the Republicans would spend a lot of money early on. "We were freaked out about it, so it was always a fight over how much money we got to put into the field program," Bird said. He was careful to add, however, that within OFA "it wasn't like the paid media people were trying to take all of our money. They were trying to do their job; we were trying to do ours."

Ultimately, the Obama campaign raised nearly $260 million in the final months of the campaign, a sum that allowed for a last-minute surge of field staff hires. As a result, states brought on full-time organizers through August and September, according to the field directors we interviewed. "We always would take more field staff," Jackson laughed. "I just think, and this is not just the case in North Carolina, but I think more staff earlier would have allowed us to be a lot stronger.... So I think most importantly if I were to do something differently for 2016 I think it would be to take a little bit more time to be there in the state and to make sure that the entire grassroots movement is growing a little bit faster than it was."

## THE NEIGHBORHOOD TEAM: A VEHICLE FOR COLLECTIVE ACTION

The challenges of turf splitting and balancing staff and volunteer responsibility arose only because OFA sought to empower its volunteers in the first place. In contrast to most campaigns that did not give volunteers real responsibility, or ask them to work collectively with each other, OFA wanted volunteers to work with each other to produce real work for the campaign. In OFA, the volunteer leaders took so much responsibility for campaign outcomes, that some veteran volunteers were the ones training new staff who joined the campaign. As Frank recalls, the volunteers would sometimes groan about having to manage up to the paid staffers. "[There was a time] right around August, where we'd introduce a new staffer and every [volunteer] NTL in the room would groan and go, 'Oh, God, who has to take the new guy?'" OFA had cultivated so much capacity among some volunteers that they were the ones who assumed responsibility for teaching the electoral-organizing model to the staffers.

The neighborhood team structure was central to OFA's program of developing capacity among volunteers. Through the team structure, volunteers and staff formed relationships with each other that became the basis of their commitment. The team became a vehicle for collective action. It served to coordinate the work of volunteers, while still holding them accountable to the outcomes the campaign cared about. OFA's highly disciplined and rigidly structured field hierarchy was, in other words, more than just that. Its strength still depended on meaningful human relationships, and an investment in the development of both the staff and volunteers.

It bears repeating that OFA's organizing practices were not in themselves revolutionary. Building relationships with constituents through one-on-one, direct conversations and entrusting those constituents with responsibility is exactly what Obama himself did on the South Side of Chicago in the 1980s, in the same way that countless other social movements, labor unions, and civic associations build power with communities. However, the tactics were unusual in their application (on two national presidential campaigns) and also for their scale: all told, the 2012 Obama campaign reports that it had over 4,000 people on its field staff payroll, over 10,000 neighborhood teams, and more than 30,000 core team members who produced over 400,000 manpower hours per week for the campaign.

# 6.

# USING METRICS TO GET
# TO SCALE

I remember my dad would call me up and be like, "Oh, did you hear about this thing on the news? How is that affecting the campaign?" And honestly it was like, I had no idea. I probably knew less about what was going on nationally once I started working there than I did before because I just didn't have time to follow the big-picture news. A lot of what you were doing was just really focusing on your area. The goal is basically to get as many votes out for the president as possible.

*—Nicholas LaCava, New Hampshire Field Organizer*

Toward the end of the summer of 2007, while Jeremy Bird was first developing the neighborhood team model in South Carolina, he almost caused a "mini revolt." For several months, he and his team had been pushing field organizers and the first cohort of neighborhood team leaders to build relationships and create teams in their communities. The OFA organizers and volunteers had grown so invested in this relational work that they were taken aback when headquarters staff convened them for a voter contact training. According to Bird, the campaign was, at the time, still learning how to prepare organizers and volunteers for making the switch from building volunteer teams to canvassing voters.

"This," Bird says, "is *the* tension of the model. You can't just be community organizing with depth and not also translating that depth into conversations with the number of voters you need to get to scale." The campaign had to figure out how to balance the twin goals of depth and breadth. How could they create capacity at the local level while still achieving national scale?

OFA's answer to this predicament was an intense focus on metrics. The Obama campaign was "as data driven as any presidential [campaign] in modern times."[1] "I didn't care where you organized, what time you organized, how you organized, as long as I could track it, I can measure it, and I can encourage you to do more of it," campaign manager Jim Messina said.[2] Headquarters staff and strategists in Chicago used the daily (and during GOTV, hourly) quantitative reports from the field to monitor progress toward the campaign's ultimate goal of "50 percent plus 1" of the vote in each of the states Obama needed to win. "Every day we got to see a snapshot of every state in the country," Dan Grandone said of the 2008 campaign. Even Bird, the highest-ranking field staffer in the 2012 campaign, remembers feeling beholden to micro-level metrics. Whenever he advocated for more resources to be funneled to the field, "we'd have to go make our case for why we needed X and Y," using analytics and evidence, "as you should," Bird affirmed.

Discrete roles—from Bird's as national field director in Chicago to the sign-in captain at a staging location in Appalachian Ohio—had attendant responsibilities, all of which were rigorously translated and evaluated against OFA's benchmarks. Throughout the campaign, Chicago headquarters established voter contact goals for each state, region, FO turf, neighborhood team, and even volunteer shift. Those numbers were passed down the chain of command to the FOs on the ground, and staff and volunteers at each level were held strictly accountable to those numbers. As Nicholas LaCava notes, he and many of his peers focused single-mindedly on their local goals. "I just didn't have time to follow the big picture news.... The goal is basically to get as many votes out for the president as possible."

LaCava's commitment to his particular turf was not unusual. Through an almost obsessive focus on metrics, OFA was able to take its locally rooted neighborhood team model to scale and ensure that a sprawling field program spread throughout battleground communities across the nation worked in concert with each other. In chapter 5, we described how the campaign broke its metrics down geographically. Here, we show how it broke them down over time, to change the focus of the field program as the campaign moved closer to Election Day. In addition, we describe the way the campaign used metrics to provide clarity to each team about what its role was, but also to ensure that all the activity at the local level added up to something bigger.

## THE TEMPORAL DIMENSION OF METRICS

OFA used metrics not only to distribute responsibility but also to track how close it was to achieving its goal of building a massive volunteer infrastructure. Each state's in-house analytics team generated thick daily reports on field metrics, which compiled the number of voter registration forms collected, door knocks, phone calls, conversations, support identifications, one-on-ones, leadership tests, and house meetings in every field organizer's turf. The reports also calculated each organizer's percentage progress toward their weekly goal in each of these categories. The campaign used metrics to distribute responsibility at the organizer level, hold them accountable, and gauge the health of the field organization from the moment its staff deployed to their assigned turf.

Over time, the campaign held staff and volunteers accountable to a shifting set of goals, indicating what the campaign valued at any given time. Through the lens of these metrics, OFA's field campaign unfolded in four, interrelated phases: capacity building, persuasion, expansion of the electorate, and, finally, mobilization (described in Table 6.1).

For the majority of the campaign, OFA held staff and volunteers accountable to metrics associated with building capacity, persuading voters, and expanding the electorate. They wanted organizers to be identifying and developing leaders who could serve on neighborhood teams, reaching out to "persuadables," and registering new voters. In 2008, for instance, field staff in select states, including Ohio, Georgia, and Wisconsin, chose "not to measure voter contact before Labor Day," Cushman said. They would, of course, track data on door knocks and calls if people were doing it, "but what the campaign was sending out across the

TABLE 6.1: **Field Metrics and Phases of the 2012 Campaign**

| OFA Campaign Phase, 2012 | Associated Metrics* |
|---|---|
| *Capacity building* <br> January through October | One-on-ones (15 per week, per FO, which reduced to 10 in October), house meetings, team meetings, neighborhood team leader (2 tests per volunteer), core team member tests (1 per volunteer), volunteer leadership confirmations (until snowflake is full), volunteer recruitment calls (500 per week, per FO) |
| *Persuasion* <br> January through October | *Persuasion calls* (for all teams in a given FO turf): <br> Rural: 300 → 2200 <br> Suburban: 450 → 2400 <br> *Persuasion knocks:* <br> Rural: 300 → 1100 <br> Suburban: 800 → 1600 <br> Urban: 0 → 1400 |
| *Expanding the electorate* <br> January through registration deadline | Voter registration forms collected**: (60–150 per FO, per week. This number varied based on proximity of college campuses and turf demographics.) |
| *Mobilization and GOTV* <br> October through November 6 | GOTV shifts, early vote pledge cards, absentee ballot request forms |

*Numbers are informed estimates, and varied based on state and turf type.*
**Some RFDs opted to "pool" voter registration goals, which were as high as 1,000 forms per week per region in the latter half of the summer.*

states was 'how many volunteers do you have and how much voter registration have you done?'" In Ohio in 2008, Bird and then-field director Jackie Bray held organizers accountable to just two metrics through the end of summer. Both were measures of capacity building: house meetings and neighborhood team leader confirmations.

"You know," Cushman said, "that was pretty risky. But from the top down, people were getting the message that capacity matters more than voter contact, right now." Grandone concurred: "There was a huge learning around how important it is to take the time on the front end of an organizing effort particularly if you want to bring it to scale—[you have] to focus almost exclusively on building your organization." If all of the early staff and volunteers focused immediately and exclusively on voter contact, OFA would have contacted hundreds of thousands more voters in the summer months before the election. Instead, they engaged in the relational organizing described in chapter 4. "That," Grandone said, "translates into identifying and training new leaders and doing all the groundwork of putting your structure in place so you have something to really turn on when you want to run your full program" in the mobilization phase.

To lay this groundwork, each organizer was charged with building between two and seven neighborhood teams, or "snowflakes." As such, a total of 12 to 28 committed volunteers were needed to fill all of the leadership positions in each snowflake for which an FO was responsible. To facilitate this leadership development, in 2012, field organizers were responsible for holding between 10 and 15 introductory or maintenance one-on-ones per week, a distinction introduced by training director Sara El-Amine. A one-on-one held by one of the FO's volunteers (most often, between a neighborhood team leader and a potential recruit) counted toward this weekly goal. In a fully developed turf, the field organizer might conduct weekly maintenance one-on-ones with his or her neighborhood team leaders and office "walk-ins," while their volunteer leaders filled the rest of the quota and, most importantly, expanded their team's voter contact capacity. To prioritize leadership development, in other words, the campaign held organizers and their volunteers responsible for relationship-building work. This made staff accountable for turning volunteers into leaders who were, in turn, enabling other leaders. If done well, this process would build the volunteer infrastructure needed for Election Day and beyond.

By what they tracked, the campaign signaled what they cared about. Cushman says that in the absence of a bright line between organizing goals and mobilizing goals, "people don't have a really keen sense of what is strategic and consequential and what is not." Organizers like

Ohio's Tony Speare, who was considered one of the best recruiters in his state, seemed to grasp this concept: "The main goal—speaking generally—was just to build up more volunteer capacity," Speare explained. The metrics reflected priorities. Grandone noted that "you can't give a field team 20 different metrics to focus on at the same time. There is something very significant about prioritizing what are the most important two, three metrics…to focus on. Because if we are able to accomplish these top couple of metrics, then everything else is going to fall into place," he said.

The metrics thus became a way for the campaign to guide the work it wanted its staff and volunteers to do and to avoid. For instance, a number of states in 2012 suspended the use of house meetings as a tactic for which organizers were held accountable. Some field staff who worked in 2012 had no idea what they were, and even some field directors, like Greg Jackson, questioned their efficacy: "But just basic house parties, we only used them when we needed to get a surge of interest around the campaign to help us decentralize, but it was not a very regular tactic because we found that volunteers were just as likely to come out to a phone bank or to a canvass or to a voter registration drive as they were a house party." Why would an organizer, who is not being held accountable for a house meeting quota—but is indeed being held accountable for immense voter contact goals—make a hard ask for the former instead of the latter, particularly if they were equally likely to elicit a commitment?

The goals grew geometrically as the election neared. Table 6.1 shows a sample table of the number of organizing and mobilizing metrics staff were responsible for distributing to their volunteers, broken down by time period and turf type. In August, the campaign asked organizers to focus on developing and testing potential NTLs and CTMs, doing one-on-one meetings to identify new leaders, making recruitment calls to build the prospect pool, and registering voters. They also wanted organizers to make persuasion calls and knocks, but framed them as a way to test potential leaders. By October, the campaign wanted organizers to continue to identify and cultivate volunteer leaders—at that point, for GOTV staging location teams—but held them accountable for fewer one-on-one meetings. The volunteer teams were expected to make far more persuasion calls and knocks that incorporated asks about Early Vote.

The associated metrics in Table 6.1 complement more familiar graphs of field metrics, which most often show the exponential growth of persuasion call and knock attempts over time. The fact that OFA's goals changed qualitatively even as they increased quantitatively speaks to its differential strategic priorities, and shows how it sought to build capacity, instead of exclusively holding high-volume phone banks and canvasses. The two were, as we have described, intimately related.

The field organizers we interviewed could lucidly recall, months after the election, the precise metrics for which they were held accountable. Jenni Boyle-Smith, the Ohio organizer, described how she balanced her call output with the relationship building work we discussed in chapter 4:

> I was held accountable for my recruitment calls and my voter contact numbers. My voter contact numbers were what my volunteers were doing on the phones and on the doors. We had to do X number of phone calls per week and knock on X number of doors, which grew rapidly as we started approaching Election Day. I was held accountable for the number of recruitment calls I made and that was consistent. It was 500 calls a week, which was basically 100 calls a night from 5:00 to 9:00 and... for people who have never done recruitment calls before, you have to sit and focus to get through 100 calls in that amount of time, especially because when you do talk to someone you want to have that real engaging conversation to get them to come in and volunteer. When you are on the phone it can turn into a lengthy conversation, so it takes a lot of focus to get through that.

As the persuasion and organization-building phase came to a close, the topline metric the field program tracked was the number of shifts recruited for GOTV: that is, the number of boots OFA would have on the ground in the final mobilization of the campaign. Colorado RFD Nina Anziska said that "voter registration forms became like the Holy Grail of metrics" as the registration deadlines neared. "And then," she said, "it switched to doors, obviously, when we got closer to GOTV. Because we had Early Vote in Colorado, door-to-door contact was huge earlier on," she said, referring to the six to eight weeks before November 6, in which field staff deployed volunteers to collect absentee ballot request forms and Early Vote pledge cards—"votes in the bank," as the campaign refrain went.

By the final stage of the campaign, each neighborhood team had its own staging location, which took the form of a field office, an empty storefront the campaign had rented on leaseback, a church basement, a community center, or, in many cases, a volunteer's garage or living room. This was the stage at which OFA's hyper-local presence was most visible. Each staging location went into GOTV with the highly refined lists of voters in a five- to ten-precinct radius, its "neighborhood." These final turnout lists represented the collective effort of the analytics team in Chicago as well as the sweat labor of the volunteers who had contacted hundreds of thousands of voters in the months prior. Those on the turnout lists had confirmed their support of Obama, and OFA canvassers had likely already attempted to talk to them about the ways in which they could cast their ballot early (and therefore not be bothered again by the campaign). Those who OFA's analytics team deemed as necessary to attempt to contact up to three times on Election Day were called sporadic voters, often generalized as "the Obama supporter who had registered to vote for the first time in 2008 but did not turn out in the 2010 midterm election." Or, they were simply the voters who could not be persuaded to cast their ballot early, like "the [one] who wants to take his kids to the polling place and pull the lever," as field organizer Patrick Cronin put it.

Because of the sustained emphasis on metrics throughout the campaign, each team knew "which precincts they were responsible for, how many volunteers had been trained, how many leaders were trained and tested," Cushman explained. Moreover, they knew that the precious turnout lists had been harvested thanks to their arduous work, and that each voter whose name they could not reach at the doors was an Obama vote they left on the table. Vigilant about conducting stress tests of its massive operation, OFA conducted two dry runs of GOTV in the weekends preceding the election, "to see how many had phone lines, where was the staging location, was it going to be open at the right hours of the day?" Cushman said. The dry runs were "not just *telling* [the organizers] they should be on the ball, but *testing* whether they were or not by getting data back from them," she observed. Armed with this knowledge and the field-tested scripts, OFA's 2.2 million Election Day volunteers sought to get out the vote.

## BALANCING NATIONAL PURPOSE WITH LOCAL ACTION

How did local organizers and neighborhood teams adapt to this strict system of metrics created by OFA's national headquarters? In some ways, top-down control over output seems to be at odds with the "respect, empower, include" mantra of the campaign. To provide counterbalance, OFA used several different strategies to synchronize its strict control over metrics with its philosophy of empowering volunteers at the local level.

First, it allowed FOs and neighborhood teams to use a nested strategy. Figure 6.1 provides an example. Imagine that a region within a state is divided into four FO turfs, as depicted by each of the four subtriangles outlined in bold—each FO has responsibility for all of the turf within that subtriangle. All FOs are handed a set of metrics they must reach, but they are given autonomy in strategizing within their turf about *how* they will reach those metrics. Similarly, within each FO turf, there are four neighborhood teams, denoted by the varied shades of gray. Each team has a certain geographic area for which they are responsible, but are allowed to use their local knowledge, networks, and relationships to strategize about *how* to reach their goals for that neighborhood. Each local team, thus, has some autonomy for strategy within its own neighborhood, but their work is nested in the work of the larger area. As team leader Shirley Bright put it, "We were basically told how things should run and what needs to be accomplished, but how we accomplished that was up to us."

Second, to ensure that field organizers did not short-circuit the team approach and did, indeed, invest in building neighborhood teams, Chicago

FIGURE 6.1: **Nested strategy in the OFA field structure**
*Although OFA imposed uniformity on its field strategy through metrics cre-ated at the national level, local regions, turfs, and teams had autonomy in strategizing about how to achieve those goals.*

held FOs accountable for metrics that had more to do with team-building than with voter contact during certain phases of the campaign. The only metric most field campaigns measure is voter contact: how many doors were knocked, how many phone calls made, how many conversations had with undecided or base voters. To be sure, OFA measured these as well, but also asked FOs to report things like the number of one-on-one meet-ings they had with new volunteers when recruiting them to the campaign, the number of volunteers they had in a leadership testing and confirmation process, and how many trainings and house meetings they had led in order to launch and empower teams. They paid attention to these organizing metrics particularly in the first half of the campaign, when their goal was building capacity. By prioritizing these metrics, the national headquarters ensured that FOs were building local capacity even as they adhered to elec-toral imperatives.

The metrics that OFA used to evaluate its local capacity reveal its philosophy. Because one of the fundamental assumptions of the field program was that leadership—or individual and collective capacity—was built first on relationships, they wanted to assess how strong the relationships were in the neighborhood teams. High-level field staff realized early on that one of the most effective ways to evaluate the health of a neighborhood team was to sit down with an organizer and "ask simple questions" as Bird put it: "'How is your team leader? Tell me something about her.' And if they could tell you, 'She has kids; and she's a writer,' and these sorts of things, usually that team was really good." If, on the other hand, the organizer replied with an easily observable fact, as in, "she comes in on Tuesdays," it was clear that the organizer had not built a real relationship, or simply did not understand how to build volunteer capacity.

Third, OFA used its training program to make it very clear to organizers that their job was to empower volunteer leaders through relational organizing. It was not, in other words, about recruiting other people to do your bidding, but instead about enabling people to act with common purpose. When field organizers touched down in their turf, some as much as a year in advance of the election and others just a month before, they were told some variation of the following phrase, as explained in OFA's 2008 General Election training manual: "We do not have enough volunteers and supporters to win right now. To contact enough voters, we need to spend time this summer identifying, recruiting, and developing volunteer leadership. That is your main job."

In this way, OFA's volunteer teams, not its paid staff, accounted for its output. We asked each of the 19 field organizers we interviewed to describe a "day in the life" on the campaign, and none said that they spent more than 10 of their 90 working hours per week engaged in voter contact. Instead, they spent their time organizing: calling potential volunteers, holding one-on-one meetings, conducting house meetings, or training volunteers to recruit more team members to lead their own canvasses, phone banks, or voter registration drives.

The FOs were thus the lynchpin of the field program in many ways, because they were directly responsible for developing volunteer capacity. Evidence of this fact was what Bird described as his only non-negotiable point with respect to the budget, as in "we need this, or we're going to lose": the number of field organizers OFA would hire. "We had one morning where it was early summer [2012], and they really wanted to hold the start dates of a lot of our [field organizers]...one of our last waves of people." Delayed field staff start dates reflects the old-style of turnout campaigning, where staff pour into battleground states in the final weeks to boost voter contact numbers with their own labor. Bird asked the deputy battleground states director, Mark Beatty, to quantify the opportunity cost of the proposed delay. "We [Stewart and Bird] really had to go to battle," Bird said. He told Messina and others, " 'If we hold off those staff by a month, we're going to register probably 300,000 fewer people,' based on the [organizing] work they do per day." Furthermore, he pointed out, "It takes a month for the organizer to know what the hell is going on, to understand their turf. We were able to show that the longer somebody had been there, the more fruitful their [numbers] were overall. So we had to make our case—as you should—with lots of analytics." Stewart, Bird, and Beatty's case for allocating funds to bring organizers on earlier rather than later demonstrated how committed OFA field was to capacity building as opposed to merely mobilizing, and how the two were closely related.

All of this focus on capacity building came to fruition in the weeks before the election and, ultimately, on November 6, 2012. On Election Day, the campaign's local capacity was put to the test as the teams worked to ensure that Obama voters cast their ballots. Across the country, each state's headquarters received reports four separate times as to precisely how many volunteers were out knocking on doors, and in which precincts. They could cross-reference these numbers with voter turnout statistics and adjust future GOTV shift locations accordingly. Instead of relying on an automated smartphone system, they used a people-based reporting system that could either troubleshoot the issue at each link in the chain-of-command, or surface urgent issues—such as voter protection concerns at a particular polling place—to the appropriate person within minutes.

This human-centric reporting system during GOTV operated in exactly the same way that all canvass shift and phone bank numbers had functioned in the year prior to the election. As a result, the volunteers and staff were well-accustomed to the procedure. The field organizers would designate specific times in a 15-minute interval in which they would "call down" to each of the neighborhood team leaders at their staging locations. The team leader would report the metrics—number of canvassers on the doors, number of walk packets out—and the field organizer would hang up and dial the team leader at a different staging location. In the subsequent 15-minute interval, the field organizer would expect a call from his or her regional field director at the exact, agreed-upon minute, until the RFD had collected all organizers'—and therefore all teams'—numbers.

The regional field directors in each state pod found themselves stationed around a large conference table in a bunker together, beginning at 4 a.m. on Election Day. This handful of sleep-deprived campaign staffers would call down to each of their organizers to collect numbers. In this 15-minute stretch, the RFDs of a given pod aggregated the numbers of over 70 field organizers, and therefore the canvassing capacity of nearly 300 neighborhood teams. Moments later, their phones would ring in two-minute intervals—it was the deputy field director calling down to collect the near real-time data about how many volunteers were on the doors in Las Vegas, the Florida Glades, or Philadelphia. The deputy field directors then reported their numbers live to the state field director who, in turn, would report them to Marshall and Bird in Chicago. The whole process took less than 45 minutes.

Colleen Cunningham, a neighborhood team leader from Grove City, Ohio, remembers, "We had smart local volunteers and didn't rely on technology or shy away from the grunt work. [On Election Day], one of Romney's volunteers tried to get one of my volunteers to show her how to use the smartphone app they were given. He just looked at her and smiled. No prep, no training, no Romney."[3] Creating a GOTV system that relied on people allowed the campaign to respond to events like four-hour lines at polling places on college campuses, voter intimidation, or the need to redirect volunteers to low-turnout precincts with greater speed.

This Election Day GOTV operation put the relationship between the field organizer and volunteer leaders to the test. After all, in the Election Day scenario described above, the volunteers were the only actors who were actually doing GOTV work, and were unquestionably performing the most difficult task: running a staging location and reporting numbers up the chain at non-negotiable intervals. All OFA staff, true to the campaign's motto of "organizing staffers out of a job," were secluded in law offices, supporter housing bedrooms, or the statewide boiler room merely collecting and reporting numbers to their superiors and troubleshooting problems at the polls from afar.

## HOLDING PEOPLE ACCOUNTABLE

To capitalize on the sense of shared responsibility, OFA made its voter contact data accessible throughout its behemoth organization. All OFA staff, as well as all volunteers who had data entry responsibilities, had a VAN account. This meant that they also had access to the reports of the number of calls, knocks, contacts, and voter registration forms produced down to each volunteer shift. Every field organizer's percent-to-goal progress was circulated at the national, state, and regional level, in addition to appearing on NationalField (in 2008) and Dashboard (in 2012), OFA's digital platforms. Thus, in addition to the interpersonal accountability at the team and regional level, voter contact data were widely available within OFA, yet strictly withheld from press and outside observers. This degree of access and trust created "transparency and accountability with organizers," Grandone said, in addition to serving OFA's electoral goals.

Communal access to voter contact numbers was a prominent feature of OFA's internal accountability model. Alex Peña remembered how he was attuned to how his voter contact numbers compared to others:

> You could also measure yourself up against how the state was doing as well as how the rest of your region was doing. As a result, there were a lot of Saturdays where the expectation was to record a high number of door knocks, because everybody was home. A conservative goal would be to motivate canvassers to knock around 150 to 200 doors. Let's say one Saturday, you were only able to record 120 doors. You automatically wouldn't feel too good because you knew the rest of the state, at the end of the day, would meet on a conference call to report how every

region did. These conference calls allowed you to see the average amount of door knocks across other districts across the state. And if the state only had an average of 130 knocks per district, then you knew you weren't too far from the average. If the average was much higher than your recorded numbers, than you knew you underperformed. Your attitude and mindset all depended on how you compared your results to the rest of the state and obviously if you met the expectations set up by your regional field director based on the composition of your district.

One 2012 field organizer said that the numbers culture engendered a productively competitive spirit on the campaign. The campaign leadership, he said, "did a very good job of making it a huge competition. You wanted to be on those weekly emails—shout-out emails—to people who were at 100 percent-to-goal from the week before. You didn't want to be seen as the person making the lowest amount of dials. You wanted to be the person recruiting the most shifts."

There was, the organizer continued, "a big competition among all the field organizers to be the best. And so, we did it, number one, because we knew we had to hit these numbers in order to get the president reelected, and number two, because each of us wanted to be the best field organizer in the state."

Steele, the deputy field director in Colorado profiled in chapter 4, said that the sky-high goals and the constant surveillance of each organizer's progress-to-goal made the reelection campaign comparatively more difficult. "I think [the field organizer's] jobs were harder than our jobs were [in 2008] in a way. I think they were saddled with a lot more responsibility in terms of the organization-building aspect. I mean it was very, very strict, like you need to be confirming this many CTMs every week. You need to be confirming this many NTLs every week in order to hit your org building goals." Other organizers and regional field directors we interviewed said that they too grappled with the quality and quantity of pressures they faced.

Most states followed a probationary rubric if goals were not met. One expectations document from Ohio warned, "Goals are to be hit every week. If an organizer does not hit 3 of their 5 goals in a given week," the process is as follows:

Week 1—Meeting with RFD to discuss plan for meeting goal

Week 2—Meeting with DFD to discuss plan for meeting goals

Week 3—Formal write-up

Week 4—Progress review & possible termination

If at any point in this process 3 goals are hit, the process will end and start over again, the protocol indicated.

Peña observed that "one of the consequences" of public goal tracking was that people knew when you weren't performing well, and this led to follow ups—sometimes in front of your colleagues. Once in a while, he said, "you would get called out in a morning conference call." It would sound something like this:

"Hey, what can we do? We are here to help you out. You obviously are not hitting your numbers." And so those were the consequences, and obviously if you kept missing then you would get personal phone calls from the regional field director or deputy field director and sometimes as much as getting a phone call from the state director. Nobody wanted that call.

Supplementing this enforcement system was a system of coaching and support within the campaign hierarchy. Field organizer Anna Cooper remembers,

I had a really good working relationship with my regional field director...she always wanted us to succeed, so we'd talk about what went wrong, or not necessarily what went wrong, but what can we do next time, next week to make this not happen again, or to improve upon that. So, a lot of direct accountability there.

The relationships that existed between organizers and their managers, and staff and their volunteers, helped create a parallel, interpersonal system of accountability that focused more on learning than the external accountability system created by the campaign hierarchy.

Staff and volunteers also used the metrics as a way of communicating about the work that needed to get done. One field director we interviewed described how she used goals to break into manageable parcels the work that needed to get done:

> I think the best way to describe [goals]: not only understanding that they need to do voter contacts but actually getting it, like we need 20 canvass shifts and we're going to get these 20 shifts because you're gonna call people, and I'm gonna call Ted, and you're gonna call Rob, and it's kind of understanding and owning goals.

Similarly, Shirley Bright remembered that she and her field organizer, "had a weekly meeting, you know, we had a set day of the week and time where he would call, and we would talk over our goals, our concerns. He would want to know what was going on with the team, what was going on with me. It was an ongoing support structure. I never felt that I was there by myself."

Seeing these interactions made volunteers understand how their work was valued. Team leader Ann Cherry and her teammates were not only aware of the number of calls they needed to make to fulfill their share of attempts, they were also cognizant of what a desirable contact rate was. "We worked hard to make sure every call turned into a contact. Not to let somebody blow you off and not answer a question, at least try to get a 'yes or no, do you support Senator Obama' out of them, so we could count it as a contact. We definitely, you know, had goals that we worked on."

## "Metrics were to live and die by"

OFA arrived at "the organizing approach that was ultimately used for the general campaign [in 2008]," Grandone said, "through a lot of trial and error." By 2012, as Wicks said, OFA had "a much crisper model of organizing." The longer lead time allowed for "a more well-defined strategy that [was] easier to really develop in the grassroots because you have paid staff... [who] know how to do this stuff and are trained on it and are able to work in the community and know the local grassroots politics, know how to engage people, and have been trained." What appear to be unqualified assets—more staff, more resources, more time, more technology, and more accountability—did indeed translate into more volunteers and more contact with voters in 2012 than 2008.

Some felt that by 2012, however, OFA was relying too heavily on its voter contact metrics at the expense of long-term capacity building. The centrality of call and knock goals went hand-in-hand with an influx of organizers because the campaign could exert more control over staff than volunteers. As a result, some of our interviewees reported that these first-blush advantages—more staff, resources, time, and technology—were not necessarily covalent with a more empowered, energized, and enduring campaign. From the perspective of some of the local volunteers and organizers we interviewed, this pursuit for scale was simultaneously one of the campaign's most impressive features and one of its vulnerabilities.

"Metrics," RFD Kate Malloy said, "were to live and die by. They were used to shout people out; they were used to shame people if they were behind. They were used on a daily basis both in conference calls and emails for the entire staff to say, 'This person's been great, you people are doing horrible.'" One 2012 regional field director, who also worked on the 2008 campaign, agreed. The reelection, she remembered "was very metrics-driven right out of the gate. That was a big difference I noticed between 2008 and 2012."

Creating a positive culture around metrics required the campaign to strike tricky balances between discipline and autonomy, healthy competition and shame, and what we previously described as national purpose and local action. More than a third of our respondents who worked or volunteered in 2012 noted that the campaign shifted too far toward a centralized system that emphasized national purpose at the expense of local action. Campaigns have clear goals they must meet; they have time constraints and a bottom-line goal of a winning vote share. From the start, OFA argued it would achieve this end by investing in local relationships—"we build relationships because they are the only way to win," they declared in their 2008 and 2012 training documents. By 2012, some of our respondents reported that the focus on the number of door knocks, voter registration forms, and phone calls overshadowed the relational dimension of organizing that had set OFA apart.

Veterans of the 2008 campaign who returned to work in 2012 noted a subtle change in the campaign's oft-cited maxim, "respect, empower, include." In 2012, OFA tacked one more word on the end of that mantra: "Win." Zack Davis spoke about this ideological shift: In 2012, "OFA itself was, I think there were more, I don't want to call them professional politicos or anything like that, but there were more people who, like, this is what they did. They do politics and they do it really well and they're here to win. There was, I think, more of a presence of those type of folks as opposed to '08." This shift created a different organizational culture in 2012 as compared to 2008.

What some of our interviewees perceived as top-down, staff-driven control of local action through metrics created what they described as a demotivating culture in 2012. Malloy said that even when her organizers did well, they said, "'I don't even care. I don't want to hear it. I don't want to be shouted out.' They hated it so much—the shaming outdid the congratulatory tone of everything." Dylan Roberts, a DFD in Colorado, also noted that "a lot of people, a lot of new staff got really turned off by [the focus on metrics]." The competitive focus on metrics created an atmosphere of stress that Peña, the field organizer in Colorado, describes:

> Because of the nature of the campaign, [there was] a lot of stress between everybody trying to hit goals. Essentially, everybody is trying not to let one another down. And the competition obviously was very intense between regions and field staffers etcetera so you had to balance it out between being fair to your colleagues in your own region and being fair to the volunteers. Without [the volunteers], none of it was possible. It was just something that became part of your skill set: dealing with the pressures of a high level of competition while leading a team of volunteers based on moving our country forward.

Several of our interviewees noted that the campaign sometimes ignored staff and volunteer insights about local conditions. Stephanie Monahon, the RFD in Pennsylvania, noted that although the campaign had clear voter contact and voter share targets in 2008, they gave the local organizers more autonomy in strategizing about how to reach them. "[T]here was something that they wanted from us, but if we were getting our numbers and hitting our goals, I remember it being like, okay…there was more of an acceptance of the organic nature of organizing." By 2012, however, she said the campaign had a more prescriptive approach to organizing. "I feel like there was more of a push to make everything look exactly the same so that we can measure it," she said. Such tactics did not make sense, however, because they ignored local strategic variability. Monahon provided one example.

One of her field organizers was stationed in Allentown, Pennsylvania's third most populous city. Situated in the Lehigh Valley, it has a Hispanic population that nearly doubled from 24 to 43 percent between 2000 and 2010. "We should have had zero call goals in Allentown. It made no sense. Nobody ever picked up the phone. We were making all these phone calls for nothing." Instead of futile dial attempts, Monahon said, "What we should have been doing is every night we should have been canvassing." High-volume phone banks and inflexible team roles tended to work best in upper-income suburban neighborhoods, she said. But "what works in suburbia may not be the best model everywhere else. And I feel like we kind of took a suburbia model and tried to apply it everywhere." By creating what Monahon (and earlier, Jackson in North Carolina) called a "cookie-cutter" model in 2012, the campaign, in some places, lost the balance it had struck in 2008 between national purpose and local action.

At times, our interviewees reported, metrics became more important than learning. Malloy noted that the organizers who were given the time to shadow veteran organizers and learned to build capacity before producing knocks and calls were far better positioned to build successful neighborhood teams. One organizer who worked under Malloy in New Hampshire remembered how these early coaching relationships could form organically as OFA was "continually hiring people" in the summer months. The result was that you had "the advice of people who were older, and had been around, more seasoned...and then you had these new folks bringing in a new different type of energy—that was really phenomenal, and it really kept things shaking," the organizer said. Grandone noted that it was important to give organizers "enough room to actually fail and fall off the bike so they can learn from it." However, as the focus on metrics increased, the time for organizers to learn decreased. Malloy says, "[Earlier on] we had the luxury of [a new] FO having two weeks goalless. But that went away toward the end of the summer where they started immediately having goals." In June and July, new organizers had a grace period with respect to their voter contact goals. After all, as soon as FOs land in their turf, before they build relationships, the only capacity on which they can count is their own. By September, that two-week grace period disappeared—which, according to people like Malloy, was problematic.

The intense focus on metrics and production from the top created a sense among organizers that they could do nothing but work. Boyle-Smith recalls of her time as an OFA staffer:

It was just absolutely exhausting. It felt like you were never going to catch up and you never could get enough sleep. There was never enough Red Bull in the world....It was really all-consuming and that was something I didn't really...I knew it was going to be long hours, but I didn't have any idea how all-consuming it would be and how isolated I would become. It was 100% campaign all day everyday. If you took time out to call your mom you might fall behind. So that was my biggest frustration. I felt like I had to let go of my entire world, of everything I knew, and had to be 100 percent focused on the campaign.

Boyle-Smith was not alone. Several interviewees noted that basic functions, like eating and sleeping, fell by the wayside. Matt Caffrey was a campus neighborhood team leader in 2008 before being hired as staff for 2012. On both cycles, he said, he "didn't really sleep a lot." In 2008, he remembers "the day after the election going home to my dorm and I didn't know any of the people I lived with and it was sort of like, 'Hi, I know we have been roommates for two months, but nice to meet you.' It was pretty weird." In 2012, Caffrey continued, "I always forget when did I eat during those days because there is not really a break anytime in the day when you can just go get food. So often we would just eat whatever volunteers were kind enough to bring to the office." Brookley agreed—meals were often afterthoughts. "By the time you get home around midnight you realize that you've only eaten one meal for the day so you try to eat something but you really don't feel like eating anything because you're extremely exhausted so you just end up going to sleep." Brookley said he "probably lost a good 25 pounds on the campaign, which I couldn't afford to lose because I was already skinny."

The intense pressure to hit metrics led some organizers to meet their goals by taking shortcuts, sometimes by straying from the careful relational and capacity-building practices described in previous chapters, or importing buses of volunteers from safe states, or relying on incentives programs to fill volunteer shifts. In some cases, top staff suggested that organizers motivate volunteers with rewards instead of building a culture of commitment through relationships. In Ohio, which received no fewer than a dozen principal visits in the final months of the campaign, field staff offered VIP tickets to rallies for supporters who signed up for a determinate number of shifts. Shifts acquired in this way, however, were filled at a lower rate than those that had been recruited through one-on-ones and interpersonal connections.

Despite all this pressure, many FOs held fast to the organizing principles they were taught, even if it meant not meeting their voter contact goals early on. "In the summer," Ohio organizer Speare recalled,

Sometimes campaign leadership was pushing to try and recruit more people to come out to canvass or try and recruit more people to come make phone calls. But sometimes that doesn't work just because it's so hot outside. It's like 100 degrees. It's humid. People are in their 60s and 70s. And so sometimes rather than try and force people to come out and canvass in the middle of the summer, I would instead spend a lot of my time just asking people to come meet with me and just using my time rather than trying to get them to initially just go out and knock on doors, especially when the weather is really unpleasant, I would spend my time instead talking about what we're doing, what we're planning, how they can get involved, and emphasizing it doesn't have to be right this second.

Volunteers would often not return if you asked them right off the bat, as Speare said, "to just go out and knock on doors," without first investing in a relationship. Colorado FO Clinton Thomas echoed this sentiment. "The most rewarding thing about building the teams was the relationships that you made with people, and I think that was also the most rewarding for the volunteers, knowing that you're making friends in this process that you're probably going to talk to for the rest of your life, or you're going to go to their kids' wedding, or those kinds of things." For many interviewees, these relationships were a greater source of sustained motivation than material rewards like a credential or VIP ticket to campaign events.

### "I hope that has a lasting effect. I think that's what's important"

This system of carrots and sticks was not universal. One field organizer noted that while metrics were OFA's abiding focus, each region developed its own culture and norms around numbers. She recalled the three regions in her county, which she described as "a really interesting microcosm of the whole state. The northern region in the county was very focused on numbers, using goals and competition to drive results." At the other end of the spectrum, she said, "The southern region didn't worry about who was ahead of who." It was, she continued, "one of the highest performing [regions in the state], maybe because they deemphasized competition." The field organizer understood her region as somewhere in between: "We definitely cared about meeting our goals, but we tried to downplay ranking among organizers within our region, focusing on collaboration and training instead."

Monahon, the RFD in Pennsylvania, describes another variation. The organizers and volunteers in her turf found that the phone numbers associated with voters in VAN were often inaccurate or had been disconnected. "Phone numbers just simply—they just aren't correct. They don't work." As a result, Monahon decided to shift her regions' strategy, and justify it to her superiors:

> In Allentown we just changed the way we canvassed. We would print walk lists, but we would knock every door. So we did [what was called] a blind canvass, and then we would just record every bit of information, because it's like, you know, 90 percent Democratic. So we just knocked on every single door, and there's a lot of houses that they label not fit for habitation, so like condemned homes. That allowed us to go ahead and get all of those out of the [database].

Monahon's experience emphasizes how OFA's field program made significant contributions to the quality and precision of the campaign's data about voters, and therefore, its microtargeting. First, her volunteers were "scrubbing" lists of disconnected phone numbers and abandoned houses—which would be removed from the database and would therefore maximize GOTV volunteers' time when every second counted. Second, the organizers, having understood the dynamics of their turf through relational organizing, knew how best to reach and track voters. Unfortunately, the data volunteers in Monahon's region had to enter each of those contacts one voter at a time, rather than in an expedited format available on preprinted lists from VAN. The result, she said, was that, "sometimes our numbers didn't reflect everything we did," and it often appeared that the Latino canvassing teams in Allentown were coming up short of their door knock goal.

What appeared to be low numbers in VAN were cause for concern for the data-driven elements at the top. Monahon explained the strategy to her deputy field director, who, in turn, advocated on behalf of the region to headquarters staff. Although they were no doubt alarmed at the seemingly lower knock numbers in one of Pennsylvania's most important turfs, they acceded. "It's really important to be metrics-based and to report what you do, but it's more important that we win, you know?" Monahon said. "But we were actually accomplishing so much more, and they [campaign higher-ups] could see. And I hope that has a lasting effect. I think that's what's important."

Metrics became the tool by which the campaign delegated responsibility to volunteers and staff, gave them ownership over their subset of the campaign, and held them accountable for meeting consequential goals. The campaign used metrics to make visible to everyone what responsibility they had in helping Obama win. In doing so, they helped people understand how and why their work mattered. They also used rewards and penalties to maintain strict adherence to the metrics.

Limitations existed. Some of our interviewees argued that it created a hierarchical culture that ran counter to the campaign's stated values of respect, empowerment, and inclusion. Others noted critical elements of the field program that could not be captured by the numbers. OFA's database made no distinction, for example, between canvass attempts made by out-of-state volunteers—who were often activists who resided in solidly blue states like California, New York, and Massachusetts—and local volunteers. Were a group of nearly 40 college students from George Washington University, bused in to Columbus, as effective in their conversations with persuadable voters as were local volunteers? The campaign was aware that they were not, but justified these deployments because they filled what the campaign considered to be capacity vacuums. Most often, out-of-state volunteers were shipped to heavily Democratic urban wards, which were also far more likely to be low-income and therefore, as we also discuss later, had fewer supporters with disposable time to volunteer within the constraints of the team model.

Similarly, an untrained organizer might engage in a brisk, 15-minute chat with a volunteer and report it as a one-on-one, while others spent 45 minutes investing in the craft of building a public relationship. Another might feel incentivized to bend the rules on what constitutes a volunteer test in order to meet his or her strictly enforced quota of leadership confirmations. In fact, Bird acknowledged that quality control of the testing process, often compromised by time pressure, strained management, and conflicting notions of what constitutes a test, was one of the data points OFA field struggled to universalize. One high-ranking field staffer spoke plainly to this fact:

> [To] push those [organizers] that had to fill in gaps...we had to be, like, you know, "At the end of the day who do you want running your [staging] location?" And they'd say "This person" and you're like, "Great they're your NTL, tag them, get them in, go."

In a database, there is no distinction between volunteers who appeared as the result of a functional-for-the-moment decision as in the quote above, and volunteers who had gone through the rigorous leadership testing process the campaign created.

Theorists have long wrestled with the ways in which institutions and organizations convert qualities into quantities, a practice the Obama campaign engaged in to strictly monitor its organizers' activities as part of its electoral project. This is a process that some scholars term commensuration, the goal of which, as Wendy Nelson Espeland and Mitchell Stevens write, is to "reduce and simplify disparate information into numbers that can be easily compared."[4] In OFA, an organizer who recruited a local minister to hold a meeting at his predominantly black church would report this event as a house meeting in the campaign database, equivalent to a gathering of mostly white suburban moms in a wealthy suburb. Training its organizers to classify and report the fruits of their relational and organic labor as mechanically objective information was crucial to the functioning of the campaign organization. As we've chronicled throughout this chapter, however, volunteers and staffers found OFA's commensuration practices frustrating or even demotivating at times because they placed undue "emphasis on results at the expense of the process."[5]

Despite the campaign's focus on the hard numbers, the staff and volunteers on the ground with whom we spoke said that delegating responsibility to volunteers was, for them, ultimately about investing in their capacity. Colorado neighborhood team leader Suzanne Trask, for instance, said, "What made OFA different from other campaign organizations" was its "social dimension." She elaborated: "Even though it's about getting someone elected, it's also about building something that can go on into the future as an organization." The result, Trask concluded, is "people who are stronger and who know how to do organizing and know that they can do it. So, they're there for whatever comes next, which is, to me, incredibly exciting." Steele echoed Trask:

> This older woman named Jeannie—our office was her dining room. We called it the war room, and it had pink wallpaper in it and we installed computers. We had a printer in there. We had everything we needed and we converted it into our little office, but we had this: "respect, empower, include" on the wall, and that was in every [OFA] office I've ever worked in whether I was running the office or it was someone else's office. Those three words were penned and handed to anyone who came into the organization from the field director on down to the neighborhood team leader.

This feeling is not easily distilled into a metric, yet it resonated in many of our interviews. Wicks, providing her own assessment, said, "It's fairly difficult to track, but my gut tells me that people are much more engaged in the political process than they were before, and that's going to be a legacy of the 2008 and the 2012 campaigns."

# PART THREE

# OBAMA FOR AMERICA'S LEGACY

# 7.

# REFLECTION

The volunteers. We were the core of the strategy.

   —*Jennifer Herrington, Neighborhood Team Leader, Iowa*

I don't think I have ever seen a campaign that people actually felt more that they had a part in than this one. People felt like they had a stake in it. People felt that their voice was heard; they had an opinion and wanted to express it. It was heard and valued.

   —*Deidre Reynolds, Neighborhood Team Leader, New Hampshire*

For people like Jennifer Herrington, Deidre Reynolds, and legions of other volunteer leaders across America, the Obama campaign was not a typical campaign. For these volunteers, the campaign was a journey through which they discovered their own power. By enabling people to "[feel] like they had a stake," that "their voice was heard," and by providing a structure that harnessed the energy and talent of millions of ordinary people, the Obama campaign engaged more people with more depth than previous campaigns—and they did it at scale. In so doing, according to our interviewees, the 2008 and 2012 Obama groundbreakers not only elected a president, they also transformed themselves, their communities, and future field campaigns around the world.

  This book described how they did it. How did they inspire people to "interrupt" their lives and put long hours into the campaign? How did they train volunteers to produce real work for the campaign that helped it meet its electoral goals? How did they manage the work of volunteers, and hold them accountable? And, above all, how did OFA leaders learn to do all this? This book described the historical roots and evolution of the OFA ground game, and the mechanics of the field program. It addresses questions that are at the heart of studies of political campaigns, civic engagement, movement building, organizational behavior, and volunteerism. In all of these fields, scholars and practitioners alike ask how organizations can recruit, develop, and deploy people with breadth and depth to effectively meet consequential goals.

There is no silver bullet. Instead, early field staff in the Obama campaign learned to build a ground game whose success depended on investing in the capacity of volunteers, leaders, and staff, then harnessing their collective capacity to win. By building motivating relationships, organizing volunteers into interdependent teams, giving those teams responsibility for real outcomes, training them to achieve their goals, and holding them accountable with metrics, the campaign was able to build both breadth and depth. Doing so, however, required balancing multiple tensions: between deep, relational organizing and mobilizing at scale; between standardization and local variation; between discipline and creativity. Even when they stumbled in striking the right balance, however, OFA staff built a ground game that, in the words of our interviewees, not only helped win elections, it also empowered ordinary people to take action in their own communities.

OFA's blend of community organizing and modern electioneering was at once derivative and distinctive. While it drew heavily from the community organizing canon, it also emerged as a modern method for enlisting real people—not pundits, pollsters, or private power—in the long-term project of democracy. Thus, we argue that the legacy of the Obama campaigns includes the effect on the groundbreakers—the millions of volunteers who, in 2008 and 2012, got involved in the trenches. Focusing only on OFA's pioneering use of technology, analytics, or data would provide an incomplete picture of the innovations that the Obama campaign bestowed on future organizing and electoral efforts. One neighborhood team leader said, "I was hoping somebody would ask what happened at the ground level because I'll be honest with you:

I don't really think the national media got it. I don't think they really understood the level of organizing and the kind of volunteers who were working on the campaign nationally. I really don't think they got that." Below, we synthesize our findings into key lessons of the model for grassroots practitioners, for other campaigns, for scholars, and for democracy.

## LESSONS FOR PRACTITIONERS

We have begun to see that other campaigns—electoral and issue advocacy campaigns on both the left and right—are adopting the practices of the Obama campaigns. Congressional candidates enlisted Obama field alumni to run their 2014 midterm campaigns. Gubernatorial hopeful Steve Grossman hired former OFA regional field director Matt García to run his ground game in Massachusetts. After the 2012 election, Jeremy Bird and Mitch Stewart founded the consulting firm 270 Strategies, staffed by many of OFA's former top brass. 270 Strategies works with clients domestically and internationally, online and offline, organizations both public and private, and, inevitably, high-profile electoral races. In a January 2014 email, 270 Strategies reported helping win "some historic campaigns," including that of Cory Booker for U.S. Senate and Terry McAuliffe for governor of Virginia, while "help[ing] dozens of organizations" like the SEIU win the minimum wage vote at SeaTac airport and promote equality in the Boy Scouts.

There are more than hints that the lessons of the 2008 and 2012 Obama field campaigns will permeate the 2016 presidential election. Sasha Issenberg predicts that "every Democrat who runs for president in 2016 is likely to tell advisers, donors and the media that they want an 'Obama-style ground game.'"[1] Ready for Hillary, the Super PAC whose aim is to "lay the groundwork for [Clinton's] candidacy," hired Bird and Stewart to design and implement the organization's field and volunteer training strategy. Bird, quoted by CNN, said, "We know from years of leading the Obama organization that empowering people and engaging grassroots volunteers are the most critical components of building a winning, 21st-century campaign...That's why we're pleased to be working with the Ready for Hillary team to help tap into the organic grassroots energy we're seeing around the country from voters of all ages who are already inspired by the notion of a potential Clinton candidacy."[2] In January 2014, Buffy Wicks was named the executive director of Priorities USA Action, the former Obama Super PAC that pundits suggest will soon become a paid media effort for Clinton.[3] Meanwhile, the GOP commissioned a post-2012 election review and determined that one of its top priorities would be to "[build] a permanent, year-round ground game."[4] Bearing striking similarity to OFA's terminology, Republican National Committee Chairman Reince Priebus said in early 2014 that the GOP had

> recruited more than 12,000 [precinct] captains nationwide. Those captains have teams of volunteers whose job it is to maintain lasting relationships with sets of people in their communities. They're listening to their concerns and making sure they hear about the issues they care about.[5]

Through OFA spinoff organizations like 270 Strategies and OFA alumni-led grassroots efforts, multiple campaigns have begun to adopt the principles and practices of the Obama ground game. OFA's reach, however, goes beyond that. Even campaigns not explicitly contracting with former Obama field staff have tried to adopt pieces of the Obama field model—undergraduate students have told us stories of internships they have done with local, state, and federal campaigns trying to implement the "neighborhood team model."

In addition, the tens of thousands of trained organizers and volunteers from the Obama campaign continue to take action on issue-based campaigns and in their communities, and not only under the aegis of OFA 4.0, dubbed Organizing for Action. "Our local party is not organized the way OFA is," Colorado NTL Pat Bruner said, "but we're using what we learned from the campaign to start laying the infrastructure for our own local campaign. We have a little community of people who are working on local issues together."

Beyond Bird and Stewart's firm, hundreds of former OFA staffers work for non–candidate centered, grassroots campaigns. Joy Cushman is now the campaign director of PICO, the national network of faith-based community organizations. Ohio field director Jenn Brown now serves as the executive director of Battleground Texas, the PAC working to organize communities in Texas to make it a swing state. And Marshall Ganz, in many respects the forefather of the OFA model, launched the Leading Change Network after the 2008 campaign, an international community of practice composed of organizers, educators, and research-ers. After 2012, dozens of other organizations and campaigns circulated hiring announcements on listservs and job post boards, indicating that experience with the OFA organizing model is "highly preferred." One former OFA staffer, now working for a grassroots organization called Students for Education Reform, said that she and her superiors were specifically interested in "Obama campaign all-stars." Colorado field di-rector Lifton-Zoline agreed: There is a premium on people who "speak the OFA language."

As the Obama model and approaches like it begin to spread, it is worth thinking carefully about the core lessons that emerged from 2008 and 2012. First, the case of OFA shows that campaigns can invest in building capacity while still getting to scale. By integrating its field pro-gram symbiotically with data and technology, the Obama campaign fig-ured out ways to combine the old with the new. The OFA campaigns revived shoe-leather politics, but unlike campaigns that preceded them, they were able to do voter contact on a national scale with volunteer manpower, rather than paid staff. As a result, they were able to achieve the depth that face-to-face campaigns of previous generations used to achieve. Through this depth, the Obama campaigns had the kind of transformative effect on volunteers and leaders that many of our inter-viewees described. In this way, OFA cultivated a ground game organi-zation that was distinct from many other modern campaigns, which seldom develop these kinds of transformative relationships with the in-dividuals or communities in which they work.

To achieve this balance of depth and scale, the Obama campaign in-vested in its *human* capital by building relationships, engaging people in collective action through neighborhood teams, giving them consequen-tial responsibilities, and holding them accountable to real outcomes.

Throughout the book, we described the nuts and bolts of each of these features of the model.

It can be tempting to export discrete pieces of the model to other organizations. Leaders and managers who opt for this approach, however, risk losing the benefits to be gained from applying the practices interdependently, as OFA did. One challenge in replicating the Obama ground game, therefore, is understanding how these pieces are all interrelated. As some of our interviewees found, setting up neighborhood teams without making the upfront investment in building relationships will not be nearly as effective. For instance, one regional field director in Colorado remembered a team snowflake composed of

> [a] Latino, a Latina, an African-American woman, and a white middle-aged woman. They came from such different backgrounds and had such different ideas. But they all something in common: [their field organizer] being a leader. They had all developed a relationship with her, and then they all were all so passionate about their team's work.

Relationships alone are not enough, however. The relationships may have been the glue to hold the people together, but the structure, training, delegation of real responsibility, and metrics made those volunteers productive. Using metrics to hold people accountable without providing them with the technical, emotional, and skills-based support to achieve their goals can be more destructive than constructive.

Likewise, the power of big data is diminished when it is not coupled with a robust ground game. As Jonathan Alter writes in *The Center Holds*, "the Koch brothers couldn't just buy a first-class field organization from afar; it had to be painstakingly built at the local level. That explained why OFA was so obsessed with building a million-plus corps of volunteers."[6] The persuadability scores that Chicago indexed—versions of which Republicans, Democrats, and the private sector have used for years—were most meaningful in the hands of local organizers and neighborhood team leaders who knew where young people congregated, knew how to facilitate house meetings, could build relationships that enabled political discourse, and were willing to commit to the grueling but gratifying work of leading a team. Learning how to put all the pieces together in a way previous campaigns had not was one of the key innovations of the Obama ground game.

Several important tensions that the campaign itself experienced must be managed to make the Obama field program work. One key challenge for practitioners is having the patience to invest in building capacity upfront. Community organizing and, by extension, the Obama field model, depends on an initial investment in building capacity. This can be a risky approach for practitioners who are eager—or under pressure from donors—to demonstrate results right away. The early work of equipping organizers with the skills and practices of one-on-ones; telling public narratives; facilitating house meetings; making hard asks; identifying and developing volunteer leaders; and learning to execute voter registration drives, phone banks, and canvasses is what permits exponential growth during the campaign's peaks of action. This implies a major, organization-wide commitment to leadership development and training. "The biggest innovation of 2012 was the training program, and nobody's talked about it," said Bird. "If you're running a business, one of the first things they tell you is that a significant amount of your resources should be spent on the people." If you invest in them, he continued, "you're going to be successful."

Another key challenge is balancing national purpose with local action. Our interviews implied that the Obama field model worked most successfully in places where teams bought into the goals the national campaign developed, but had local autonomy in figuring out how to implement them. In this way, the campaign sought to do community organizing at scale. They imposed uniformity on staff and volunteers by giving them responsibility for clear goals that made the electoral math work. Beyond that, Chicago embraced (or willfully overlooked) heterogeneity in the model's implementation up until GOTV. NTL Ann Cherry said: "It was interesting to see, you know, that the campaign had sort of a strategy that allowed us to develop the tactics on a local level, and that made them successful, because it depended on our knowledge of our area, and exactly how you could carry out a strategy." Each state, organizer, and team developed an internal logic that corresponded with the electoral metrics for which they were held accountable.

Third, although the health of a neighborhood team was signaled by its autonomy—its ability to fill out the leadership positions, to re-cruit and train new volunteers, to perform voter contact, and to enter and report data on its own—the goals were collective. When used as a mechanism to motivate and strategize in groups, metrics enabled OFA organizers to delegate their monumental call and knock goals, turning individual resources into collective power. This made the volunteers with whom we spoke feel as though they were doing their work not as an individual cog in a machine, but as part of something bigger.

Finally, there is the challenge that both campaigns and civic organiza-tions face: maintaining an ongoing spirit of learning that makes possible the kind of innovation we saw on the Obama campaign. In reflecting on the Obama field program, Joy Cushman said, "There's a point at which this structure... and this whole way of organizing becomes ideology or model. And at that point it loses a lot of value, I think.... We have some work to do to understand, like, once you get this structure going and it proves itself, how do you continue to remotivate it and give people space to innovate?" Some of the differences between the 2008 and 2012 campaigns reveal the danger of losing this willingness to experiment. As many of our interviewees tell the story, the 2008 ground game was about innovation and 2012 was about implementation. Staff and volunteers conveyed their experiences in 2008 as exploratory and pioneering, part of a "movement moment," as Dan Grandone described it. The "energy and motivation people had throughout the country to actually get engaged..., particularly after eight years of George W.," was palpable, Grandone said. By contrast, 2012 was "much more a well-oiled machine," according to Buffy Wicks. One staffer who worked on both cycles, said, "[I]n 2012, I didn't feel like we were changing anything." As Cushman points out, once the approach becomes "ideology," it can "[lose] a lot of value."

The differences between OFA's field program in 2008 and 2012 were not only about routinizing a model, but also about a changing electoral context. In 2008, Obama was the underdog. Lulu Gould, a neighborhood team leader from Steamboat Springs, Colorado, said, "[In 2008,] there was just so much...hope and all those lovely things that were being thrown around and [2012]—it was the real deal. I mean it was *really hard, hard work* and really got...more and different volunteers," she said. By 2012, Obama was the establishment candidate. For Bird, the biggest question at the outset of the reelection campaign was whether or not OFA could inspire people to volunteer at the same levels as 2008. During Obama's first term, voter registration among OFA's base demographics had declined precipitously. "It was bad," Bird said. "From 2008 to 2010 we were just hemorrhaging Democratic voters...[in 2012] we registered 361,000 people in Florida and we [still] didn't get back to the margin we had in 2008 in terms of the D to R. That's nuts." According to Bird, the Republicans "could have caught up after 2010 if they had run a voter-rich program. That was extremely nerve-wracking to me." Figuring out how to implement the Obama ground game with a sensitivity to the specific conditions of any campaign and a critical awareness of the interrelated tensions of the electoral-organizing approach is thus a key strategic challenge for practitioners.

## LESSONS FOR SCHOLARSHIP

Aside from its practical implications for campaigns and organizations, the Obama campaign case study also has important implications for scholarship. To contextualize these implications, we should first discuss the limitations of our case study.

First, the fact that we relied on a single case means that we do not know how features of Obama's candidacy or the unique political circumstances of 2008 and 2012 affected the ground game. For instance, how much did Obama's background as an organizer and the values on which he centered his campaign affect the ability of the campaign to recruit new organizers or unlikely volunteers? Likewise, how much was the success of the electoral-organizing model predicated on the fact that Obama was building a coalition that depended on demographic groups like youth and African-Americans? In addition, the Obama campaign operated with unprecedented financial resources. By 2012, the campaign had nearly 5,000 paid organizers and the biggest war chest in campaign history. Can campaigns that do not have as much money, staff, and media attention achieve the same successes? Our analysis of the way in which OFA harnessed volunteers implies that it is not payroll that limits the ability of small campaigns to build a formidable voter contact operation. One-on-ones, house meetings, trainings, and team meetings can be virtually free of cost after fixed outlays for organizing staff and training. Still, without more comparative case studies of other campaigns, we cannot precisely answer these questions. The consistency of our findings across diverse communities across America and two election cycles, however, gives us some confidence. To further study these effects, however, we hope that this book opens up an avenue of research on field programs across a variety of campaigns in America and around the world.

Second, to track the involvement and experiences of volunteers in the Obama campaign, we relied extensively on the campaign's own data. Given OFA's rigorous focus on data and metrics to track progress toward its goals, we have confidence that their internal data was as accurate as possible. Nonetheless, internal data are always subject to some bias, and it would be helpful to have additional data sources to corroborate the information we get from the campaign's own records. Many data sources exist to help us track the financial and technological resources campaigns raise and deploy. Insofar as we care about campaigns' human resources, analysts ought to develop resources that would help us better ratify and contextualize the campaign's reports. In building this resource, we urge researchers and campaign leaders to consider measuring outcomes beyond the final vote tally. The type and degree of volunteer involvement, the profile of the people performing the work (paid or unpaid, demographics, policy views), and the practices campaigns use to engage ordinary citizens can offer important insights into the quality of the country's civic infrastructure. New resources to help track these data could range from clearinghouses of campaign data on volunteer activity to better, more complete surveys of campaign staff and volunteers.

Third, much of the data that we used was retrospective. Any post hoc analysis of electoral campaigns is subject to bias generated by the outcome of the election itself. If Obama had lost in 2008, would field directors have discarded the neighborhood team model as ineffectual? Conversely, because he won twice, have campaign operatives put too much stock in OFA's field strategies? To ameliorate the effects of retrospective overestimation, we tried throughout the book to examine the critiques that staff and volunteers on the ground surfaced about the OFA ground game. Their words and stories are just that—their own views about what worked and did not work. Although they do not provide fixed answers about the Obama campaign's shortcomings, they nonetheless contain important perspectives. Future studies of field programs could gather data in real time, to minimize this bias.

Thus, while this case study of the Obama ground game has some key limitations, it also opens up pathways for additional research. For scholars interested in political participation and civic engagement, it reinforces findings from a burgeoning body of literature that demonstrates that participation is best understood as "dynamic social expression," a way for people to convey who they are in the context of social relationships and interpersonal interactions.[7] Much recent scholarship has begun to understand the social, interactive nature of political behavior and political participation in particular. The Obama campaign bolsters these findings, showing how a campaign can intentionally structure the social interactions and collective experiences people have, thus shaping the type and extent of their participation.

To be sure, some researchers have already begun investigating these trends. A group of scholars at the Fielding Institute published observational findings that argue that a long-term investment in civic power and capacity building can affect electoral outcomes:

> In the fall of 2010, Citizen Action of Wisconsin Education Fund (Citizen Action) conducted voter education efforts in 25 precincts where they had conducted year-round civic engagement over the previous two years. Those precincts experienced a 29% increase in voter turnout over 2006—21% higher than precincts where a more traditional get-out-the-vote only approach was conducted.[8]

Similarly, a team of researchers at the University of Southern California has begun studying the type of campaigning that OFA developed and scaled, calling it integrated voter engagement (IVE). They describe IVE as a method by which organizations—not only electoral campaigns—build up their contact lists by knocking on doors and a year or more later, work to turn those contacts out for policy campaigns. IVE bears great resemblance to the ideal-typical version of the Obama model we have described:

> [IVE] takes neighborhood concerns and addresses them by equipping community members to get the people and policies into place that will positively affect their neighborhood. [It also] requires social movement organizations to reach beyond their own comfort zone—to mobilize thousands, not hundreds—it creates a practice of "moving the middle" through values-based approaches that can widen the base of supporters for social justice.[9]

This case study raises a number of questions about how the organizational mechanics of a campaign's field operation influence people's levels of engagement and participation. What is the effect of having people work in teams, as opposed to working alone? What is the effect of using stories to motivate people, instead of policy discussions? What is the effect of asking volunteers to take responsibility for consequential outcomes, as opposed to discrete tasks? What can campaigns do to best develop leaders? The list could go on. All of these questions point to a stream of research on the effect that organizations so familiar to the American polity—from political campaigns like Obama's to civic associations—can have in shaping citizen participation in their own governance.[10]

For scholars interested in campaigns, the case of OFA points to a field of study that has largely been dormant in recent decades: ground games. Much scholarship has focused on the financial, technological, and other resource investments that campaigns make, while far less research examines their investment in human resources. Those who do study field operations tend to limit their analysis to the GOTV period, asking whether last-minute phone calls and door knocks contribute to a winning margin of votes. Further study is needed to understand how different kinds of field campaigns work in the many months leading up to Election Day, how they interact with political contexts to succeed, and what the unique elements of different field programs are. In addition, this case broadens the scope of campaign effects to look not only at whether a campaign wins or loses, but also at what impacts it has on the people and communities in which it works. Often, we evaluate for-profit companies at the end of the year based not only on the profits they made in a given year, but also in terms of the assets they have going forward. For democratic associations, evaluating assets means looking at the civic and human resources they have in addition to their electoral or organizing balance sheets. This book shows how campaigns can develop those resources even as they seek victory. As Nielsen observed, "Elections come and go, but local politics carry on year after year."[11] There is much more to be written about the relationship between campaigns and the strength of a democracy.

Finally, for scholars interested in community organizing and organizational learning, this case study profiles one of the many local, state, national, and international campaigns that have taken root in recent years. As a case study, it provides rich learning for those interested in how community organizing works, but also raises a number of questions for people seeking to enrich the way we organize. One key question is how modern campaigns can organize in ways that involve diverse constituencies. In our interviews, we heard some organizers and volunteers talk about the class and race differences as they affected voluntarism.

One regional field director shared the story of a volunteer leader that speaks to the inequalities in volunteering. The volunteer "works in a chocolate factory, she goes in at 5:00 a.m., she stands on her feet processing chocolate bars all day long, and she would literally tell [her field organizer], 'Okay, I will call you at 1:07 because that's when I'm allowed to clock out and take my break.' She would call [the field organizer], check in, then she would finish the rest of her break registering people at the chocolate factory, and then get off work and do stuff for OFA." When the on-the-ground field staff were pressured to squeeze their volunteers for more time and more commitment, the response from volunteers like the one in this story was, "I can't do this." There was, the interviewee said, "no other hard ask that we can make of her."

In Pennsylvania, by contrast, NTL Harlan Kutscher, a retired surgeon, hosted his phone banks and team meetings in his home. "We did [events] in our house, which I think really makes a difference. We have a big house, which is why we could have so many people over, a big open contemporary house and it was easy to have all those people." As an added bonus, volunteers donated food, and, Kutscher said, "We wound up having two professional pastry chefs who brought in desserts that were to die for....You can never have too much food and variety," he said. His team celebrated their successes: "At the end of our competition nights, we had beer and wine for people who wanted it to celebrate our victories because we were always winning."

Our interviews provided some qualitative insights into the ways in which class and race served as important mediating factors in volunteer participation and production.[12] A typical NTL dedicated more than 30 hours a week to leading his or her team, a time investment that, according to field staff and volunteers, was often not feasible in lower-income turf where many supporters worked unforgiving hours or had multiple jobs. This contradicted what field director Greg Jackson called the "assumption that an urban African American community may be fruitful for [an OFA] neighborhood team." It can be "fruitful in support," Jackson said, "but not necessarily fruitful for folks to pour a lot of volunteer hours into the campaign.... that was one trend that we saw and we were challenged with sometimes." The organizing model that the Obama campaign used had its roots in the civil rights movement, the migrant farmworkers movement, and other collective undertakings that have successfully engaged disadvantaged and economically marginalized constituencies. The problem is not that electoral organizing is antithetical to working with marginalized constituencies. Instead, the challenge is for organizers to develop campaigns that maintain the same commitment to developing leaders among a diverse set of voices who are entrusted to shape the campaign itself to fit their particular circumstances.

## LESSONS FOR DEMOCRACY

Elections govern the rhythm of our democratic life. Every two years, federal elections dominate headlines and news reports, and candidates seek the votes of millions of Americans across the country. In between these national elections, we have countless local and state elections that present opportunities for mobilization. Elections mediate many of the interactions people have with the democratic system but too often, we see elections that focus only on winning and not on the impact they are having on the community.

Whether it was for normative or practical reasons, the 2008 and 2012 Obama campaigns focused not only on what they did, but also how they did it. In that sense, they resembled a social movement—seeking not only to achieve an electoral victory, but to do so in a way that built the strength of its constituency. Perhaps the most important legacy of the Obama campaign, then, is evidence that campaigns can be run in ways that reinforce some of the building blocks of our democracy.

Unlike other campaigns, the OFA gave people an experience of shared power, and a sense of ownership over what they accomplished. Rival political campaigns' field operations were different, a fact thrown into sharp relief by the underwhelming investment both McCain and Romney made in volunteers and their respective ground games in 2008 and 2012. Yet while the Obama campaign was distinct from its contemporary Republican counterparts, it was derivative of local, organizing-intensive efforts that dated back to the 1960s. "The very first electoral campaign I ever did was the East Los Angeles GOTV for RFK in 1968," Marshall Ganz remembered, "where I was trained by Fred [Ross] and Cesar [Chavez]. It went like this":

> You go door-to-door and as you're identifying supporters, what you're really looking for is the person you can *get to take respon-sibility* for contacting the rest of the voters in that precinct, reporting back to you, coming to a training on X day, turning their house into a precinct headquarters, and taking the day off work to get a couple of friends to help them get the people they've identified out to vote: one poll watcher keeping track of who voted and the other two calling and visiting until they've all showed up.

The GOTV operation Ganz described taking place exactly 40 years before the Obama campaign's 2008 efforts reflects the underlying principles of what we now know as the OFA electoral-organizing model. As we have shown throughout this book, although the Obama ground game was unparalleled in its scale and sophistication, the core principles sprang from old sources rooted in the community organizing tradition.

Because no organizer had ever knocked on her door to ask her to "take responsibility for contacting the rest of the voters in her precinct," Nevada NTL Kara Freeman said that she "had never really had the idea that I could get involved and do things. When President Obama took the oath, to sit there and say, 'I was involved in helping this happen'—that was a really neat feeling." As select, smaller campaigns had done many decades ago, the Obama campaign sought to give ordinary people responsibility for a real electoral outcome, and then supported them in helping them meet those goals. In doing so, the campaign tried to teach people they could make a difference in their communities. NTL Laura Diviney put it this way:

> [I wanted] to be a part of something that I could respect, that I could admire, that I could have a clear conscience in engaging in. [I wanted to] have my efforts put to the best test, to learn and grow, and to serve my country. The Obama campaign gave me all of those things.

"Giving people the keys and letting them drive," as Buffy Wicks put it, thus not only helped Obama win, it also helped change the way the groundbreakers we interviewed for this book conceived of their democracy. Balancing the tension between winning an electoral victory and building a movement—between what you do and how you do it—is no easy feat. Campaigns are frenetic and unwieldy by nature, and trying to build a movement at the same time only exacerbates the problem. As Nielsen writes, "Ground wars are full of sound and fury; adversarial, unequal, and plagued by internal conflicts, they are far from poster children for a picture-perfect democratic process."[13]

Questions still remain about what kind of infrastructure the Obama campaign left in the communities in which it worked. Nowhere is this more evident than in the postcampaign organizations that emerged from both election cycles. After 2008, OFA became Organizing for America (shorthanded to "OFA 2.0"), a community organizing project housed in the DNC, whose objectives followed in lockstep with those of the Obama administration. After 2012, OFA became Organizing for Action ("OFA 4.0"). In both of these postelection incarnations, Obama supporters were eager to see the powerful campaign machine morph into an organization that would not only further President Obama's legislative agenda, but also strengthen the progressive movement. In its first year of operation, 2013, OFA 4.0 reported that its volunteers held 10,697 "grassroots action events," drawing largely on the volunteers who participated in the 2008 and 2012 election cycles. According to the 501c4, led by Jon Carson, OFA 4.0 volunteers delivered 1.4 million petition signatures demanding action against gun violence, aggressively phone-banked climate change deniers in Congress, and "[told] the story of how millions of Americans have better, more affordable health care thanks to health reform."[14] Many others, sometimes called "Obama orphans," were disappointed. Farhad Ebrahmi, a long-time supporter, said that he was "hoping to see those tools and that amazing development of skillsets applied to something that was going to be responsive to bottom-up energy." Instead, he said, "it seems like they're still just running it like electoral campaigners and saying, this is the menu you can order off of. But it's not a potluck."[15]

Whether in an electoral- or issue-based organizing context, doing the work of building a field program that "respects, empowers, and includes," is difficult. Wicks notes, "If you're doing a team model versus paid canvassers or more traditional models of organizing it takes—it's a labor intensive process. You're testing team leaders. You're making sure that they're going to be up for the task. You're really trying to make sure you have the right people in the right roles and that they constantly feel engaged and they're a part of something bigger than themselves. All of that takes an enormous commitment and human resources to make sure that that happens."

OFA is thus an example of what journalist and author Gail Collins calls the work of "heroic people doing really boring and frustrating things" behind "almost every great moment in history."[16] Despite the inevitable fatigue that accompanies the round-the-clock campaign rhythm, Wicks said, "[the team model] is a far more effective way of organizing communities than any other model that I've worked with." And, as the late Senator Paul Wellstone once remarked, "If we consign ourselves merely to the poetic, utopian discussion of what should be and neglect the prosaic, practical work of the electoral politics that is, we doom ourselves to the margins of political life."[17] It takes deep, skilled, and tireless effort to build an infrastructure that productively engages millions of people in the democratic process, a key challenge for our democracy and for grassroots practitioners and campaigners who plan to draw from the OFA model.

## OBAMA'S MULTIPLE LEGACIES

Because OFA does not fit neatly into any taxonomy of voluntary, political, or campaign organizations, conflicting accounts of its legacy persist. While we have focused on the campaign's impressive engagement of ordinary citizens, others marvel at its pioneering use of technology. While some applaud its victories, others point to the defeats Obama has suffered as president. Disentangling the many legacies of Obama for America is nearly impossible, not least because organizations are not static entities. Instead, as the OFA story attests, people-powered assemblages consist of fallible human beings with competing interests, evolving goals, and dynamic activities that can either reinforce or reconfigure existing power relations.

What we hoped to do in this book is tell what has been, until now, a largely untold story—the story of how ordinary Americans got involved in a campaign and experienced the collective power of democracy. As we have argued, many of the Obama field program's strategies and tactics originated from a long and storied tradition of community organizing. At different times and places, OFA's field operation could be characterized as a social movement, a transactional vote-getting operation, or a new kind of ground campaign. These variations aside, a basic truth about OFA's field operation is that, unlike many campaigns that came before it, the field program depended on the leadership and commitment of regular citizens.

The story of Obama for America is one of spontaneity, experimentation, failure, reflection, and, ultimately, victory. It contains key lessons about the choices that campaign managers make, but it is also about the choices that ordinary citizens can make. The Obama campaign capitalized on a political moment to build a structure that enabled thousands of individuals to understand and act on their capacity to shape politics in their communities, in Washington, and beyond. The sprawling, if temporary, civic infrastructure that OFA staff and volunteers built serves as a forceful reminder that democracy can work when people are given power. For that reason alone, it is an important story to tell.

# NOTES

## CHAPTER 1

1. These numbers come from a survey conducted by the campaign and reported by Obama for America's successor organization, Organizing for Action 2013, pp. 20–21. The campaign reports that this number increased dramatically in the final weeks of the campaign, when volunteer leaders committed upward of 30 hours per week. These numbers also do not account for the hundreds of thousands of hours invested by rank-and-file volunteers who did not have an official role (team leader or team captain) listed in the campaign's database, VoteBuilder.

2. One of the reasons that the acronym OFA is so widely used is that it does not distinguish between Obama for America and Organizing for America, a legal distinction without a difference. As in 2008, state parties served as the official employers of field staff in 2012. Wherever there was a heavy Obama campaign field presence, Obama for America funded their hires by paying the state Democratic Party through a transfer-down account. Generally only a handful of "Obama for America" employees were stationed in each state: a state director, communications staff, and a digital team, all of whom reported to Chicago. The remaining 200 to 500 employees, depending on the state, had their paychecks signed by "Organizing for America," a project of the state's Democratic Party.

3. Organizing for Action 2013, 32.
4. Some scholars have attributed America's enervated political life to the decay of civil society (Gerber and Green 2000; Putnam 2001; Sander and Putnam 2010), a shift from "membership to management" in civic associations (Skocpol and Fiorina 1999; Schier 2000; Skocpol 2003), and the fact that "ordinary people—their ideas, time, energy, and commitment—have come to count for very little in determining who is nominated for public office" (Weir and Ganz 1997, 165). Even in 2012, turnout remained stubbornly low: Fewer than 60 percent of eligible voters cast their ballots in the presidential election, still among the lowest rates of established democracies worldwide. This percentage varies wildly by state, with Minnesota (71.9), Wisconsin (69.8), and New Hampshire (68.7) earning the top three spots in voting age population (VAP) turnout, and Texas (41.9), Hawaii (40.1), and Mississippi (39.7) recording the three lowest rates (2012 *Election Administration and Voting Survey*, 9). Yet the nationwide average is still below that of other industrialized democracies that do not have (or do not enforce) compulsory voting, as evident in statistics from the most recent general elections in other countries: France (80.35, 2012), Germany (71.5, 2013), UK (65.8, 2010), Mexico (63.1, 2012), and Canada (61.4, 2011) (data from IDEA 2013).
5. Cooper and Meckler 2008.
6. Quoted in Berman 2010, 228.
7. Barone 2013, 1.
8. Precise figures on the number of volunteers previous campaigns had engaged are hard to estimate. Nonetheless, the estimates that do exist differ by an order of magnitude. The *Almanac of American Politics* estimates that the Democratic National Committee involved 233,000 people in the 2004 campaign (Barone and Cohen 2006, 22), and Rasmus Kleis Nielsen notes that 115,000 volunteers from ACT were Kerry's main canvassers in 2004 (Nielsen 2012). Other scholarship citing the unique breadth of the Obama campaigns include Masket 2009, Barone 2013, Sides and Vavreck 2013, and Darr and Levendusky 2013. Even this research, however,

makes little mention of OFA's sprawling network of neighborhood teams, which were the heart of the field program. Most of this research focuses instead on the field offices. While OFA had over 700 field offices in 2008 and 813 field offices in 2012, it had more than ten times as many hyper-local, volunteer-led neighborhood teams, the majority of which operated largely independently of the offices that housed field staff. The field offices thus provide an important but "blunt" picture of the ground game (Sides and Vavreck 2013, 222), one that focuses more on staff resources than the central contribution volunteers made.

9. This quote is taken from a real-time transcription of Johns's speech at the OFA Legacy Conference in Washington, D.C.

10. See Nielsen 2012 for a history of field campaigns.

11. Quoted in Nielsen 2012, 26.

12. Speer et al. 2010; Ganz 2010; Smock 2004; Warren 2001.

13. Personal communication, December 10, 2013.

14. Balz 2013; Kreiss 2012; Issenberg 2012; Carey 2012; Rutenberg 2013.

15. Hebdon 2013.

16. Balz 2013.

17. See, e.g., Snow, et al. 2004; Snow and Soule 2010; Wood 2002; Speer and Christens 2011; Klandermans, et al. 1988; Goodwin, et al. 2001; Warren 2001; Han 2014; Musick and Wilson 2008.

18. See, e.g., Gerber and Rogers 2009; García Bedolla and Michelson 2012; Sinclair 2012; Nickerson and Feller 2008.

19. Klein, et al. 2009; Baggetta, et al. 2013; Hackman 2012.

20. See, e.g., Sides and Vavreck 2013; Darr and Levendusky 2013; Thurber and Nelson 2010; Hillygus 2005. As Sides and Vavreck write, "It was difficult for one candidate to move enough votes to shift the polls or, ultimately, to win the election outright," given the two fundamentals that undergird all American elections: the power of partisanship and the state of the national economy (8–9). A rich body of literature examines the effect of campaigns, even if they move vote shares only at the margins (Bartels 1988; Popkin 1991; Holbrook 1996; Iyengar 2000; Holbrook and McClurg 2005;

Popkin 1991). Some scholars suggest that "across the battleground states, Obama's network of field offices netted him approximately 200,000 votes (or about 7% of his margin in these states)" in 2008 (Darr and Levendusky 2013, 12). Masket's examination of data from 11 battleground states in 2008 found that "those counties in which the Obama campaign had established field offices during the general election saw a disproportionate increase in the Democratic vote share…[an] increase was large enough to flip three battleground states from Republican to Democratic" (Masket 2009, 1023).

21. Sociologist Jeffrey Alexander (2010, 46) quotes one of the Obama campaign's senior Latino staffers who cited a similar bump: "The ground game is worth 2 percent on voting day—all over in Nevada, New Mexico, Colorado, and Florida."

22. Gerring 2007.

23. Ragin and Becker 1992; Yin 2002; Small 2009.

24. Hart 1973; Brazile 2004; Hughes 2004; Plouffe 2009; Muir and Axelrod 2013.

## CHAPTER 2

1. Nielsen 2012, 50.

2. Cushman, et al. 2010, 12.

3. Palmer 1986, 638.

4. Lariscy, et al. 2004; Shea 1996; Thurber and Nelson 2010.

5. Nielsen 2012, 15.

6. Nielsen 2012, 15.

7. Quoted in Nielsen 2012, 18. The sample of panelists at Harvard's "Campaign for President" conference, held after every general election since 1972, mirrors this trend. The gathering convenes top political operatives from both major parties to reflect upon the decisive moments of the campaign. Before 2004, field directors were not even invited, and campaign spokespersons said very little about the person-to-person operations, even while "money, media, and individual events were discussed in great deal" (Nielsen 2012, 41). Now, the ground game is a topic of each election postmortem.

8. Forthal 1946, 32.

9. Key 1956, 367.

10. See, for example, Cutright and Rossi 1958. Mid-century, "precinct captains who were well integrated into the social milieus of their precincts were the most effective workers for their parties" (179). Moreover, the authors found, "how committed the precinct captain is to his party is also related to the vote obtained for both Democrats and Republicans. When a committeeman does not care a 'great deal' whether the other party wins, his own candidate suffers a loss of a little more than 0.5 per cent, while the candidate gains slightly in a precinct in which the committeeman says that he cares a great deal if the opposition wins" (175).

11. Unions provided much of the manpower necessary for Democrats' registration drives and Election Day mobilization in the post–New Deal era, particularly in the rust belt states. In 1960, beneath the Democratic Party leadership of Adlai Stevenson, Lyndon Johnson, and the Kennedys were "layers of imposing strength," namely, the trade union movement (Wade 1973, 2839). The labor movement's efforts were rewarded with kickbacks from winning politicians. At the same time, unions played the critical role of aggregating voters on the basis of class (Weir 2004; Verba, et al. 1978). Beginning in the 1970s, however, patronage power began to drift toward Washington, local organizations were left with a "dwindling share of public jobs" (Wade 1973, 2830), and union membership dropped precipitously. As a result, the unions' political influence plateaued, even though Democrats continued to lean heavily on labor for their field operations for many years. Scholars and pundits on both sides attributed heavy union campaigning to Vice President Al Gore's victories in Michigan, Pennsylvania, Wisconsin, and Iowa, all battleground states that were crucial to his popular vote win (Freeman 2003). John Kerry's ground operation, which we examine later in this chapter, relied heavily on a 527 political organization called Americans Coming Together (ACT).

12. Cohen, et al. 2008, 131.

13. Cohen, et al. 2008, 118.

14. Cohen, et al. 2008, 157.
15. Cohen, et al. 2008, 141.
16. Cohen, et al. 2008, 158.
17. Polsby, et al. 2012, 191.
18. See Hart 2012. Some argue that the new, visible primary system thus ushered in an era of amateur activists who crusaded for causes—antiwar, prolife, civil rights, tax reduction—rather than for winning or losing on behalf of their political team, Democrat or Republican. Other scholars disagree that issue activism was unique to the latter half of the 20th century, pointing out that such developments reflect America's perennial reform mentality. Cohen and colleagues write, "The Democratic clubs of the 1790s, the Jefferson-Jackson ideologues of the 1820s, and the abolitionists of the 1840s and 50s may also be seen as precedents for the amateur activism of the post–World War II period" (124).
19. Like Obama, McGovern and Carter were lesser-known candidates who were eager to take advantage of the new rules, and they announced their candidacy nearly two years in advance of the 1972 and 1976 elections. An examination of formal candidate filing and announcement data from the FEC, however, shows that the lengths of the McGovern and Carter campaigns are historical anomalies. Campaigns are ever increasing in length. Brendan Doherty writes of the pernicious effects of the "permanent campaign," arguing that we should "carefully consider whether we need to reform the system that incentivizes a perpetual focus on electoral concerns" (Doherty 2012, 72).
20. Nielsen 2012, 44.
21. Nielsen 2012, 44.
22. In his 1989 book *Democracy Without Citizens*, Robert Entman argued that politicians face a "no-win choice" with respect to mass media. If they "manage the news, they will almost inevitably oversimplify and mislead," unable to tell the public complex or painful truths. "But," he continues, "if they do not self-consciously play to the media's biases and limitations, their opponents will; and journalists seeking to hold officials accountable in the way they can—by

quoting those opponents—will inadvertently penalize public servants who fail to manage news skillfully" (Entman 1989, 126).

23. Nielsen 2012, 39.

24. Quoted in Green and Gerber 2008, 26. Scholars have also examined the normative impact of the rise of mass media. According to Arthur Schlesinger, technological advances "now presented the politician directly to the voters; computerized public opinion polls now presented the voters directly to the politicians, and the mediating agencies, the traditional brokers of politics were left to wither on the vine" (Schlesinger 1973, 209). Others argue that television and the Internet have given ordinary citizens a new sense of entitlement in the political process, stimulating activism (Hands 2011; Downing 2011; Karpf 2012). No longer the product of back-room deals among party leaders, elections see voters select their candidates based on information they acquire from the comfort of their homes. Tempering this optimistic view of the democratizing forces of technology, numerous studies have also pointed out that citizens selectively absorb news from news media or their peer groups' digital posts in a way that reinforces their existing political biases (Jones and Sugden 2001; Smith 2010; Smith 2011). Contrasting the "vital" democratic rituals of the 19th and 20th centuries, scholars have linked the decline of popular and deliberative politics to the rise of new media "advertising campaigns" (McGerr 1986).

25. Green and Gerber 2008, 44.

26. Green and Gerber 2008, 44, 10.

27. Goodwin 2005, 89.

28. See Silver 2012, 9. As campaigns have improved their microtargeting, they have integrated big data with field operations. Findings from the computer algorithms are transformed into geocoded lists, which are then printed, collated, and given to organizers and volunteers to use in their phone banks and door-to-door canvasses. The "targets"—or voters—are continuously updated by the response data generated by the online and offline canvassing efforts of the campaigns themselves.

29. Shea 1996, 126.

30. The next largest line item—in excess of $10 million for both campaigns—was for "consultation," a class of electioneering professionals or "consultocracy" (Berman 2010, 37), a now-predictable part of presidential campaigns. In 1996, the Clinton campaign spent $4.2 million on his cadre of just 10 political consultants (Tenpas 1998, 764). Professional pollsters, advertisers, tech wizards, and in 2012 a "dream team" of behavioral scientists delivered research-based advice on how to "counter false rumors, like one that President Obama is a Muslim," how to "characterize the Republican opponent, Mitt Romney in advertisements" (Carey 2012).

31. Ganz 1994, 5.

32. Baldino and Kreider historicize the case. The U.S. tax code has "long exempted nonprofit and not-for-profit organizations from paying taxes even as they participated on the margins of electoral campaigns" (Baldino and Kreider 2011, 326). Yet in no other time in history have Political Action Committees (PACs) given such large sums—from $223 million in 2006 to the nearly $2 billion spent in 2012 (Baldino and Kreider 2011, 326). Moreover, as a result of *Citizens*, donors "desiring anonymity can give generously to 501(c)4s without fear of disclosure, even while voters are deprived of information necessary to evaluate the credibility of political commercials sponsored by the groups" (Baldino and Kreider 2011, 331). *Citizens* thus reversed decisions from the 20th century, such as the Tillman Act of 1907 and the Taft-Hartley Labor Act of 1947, which restricted corporations; and labor unions' independent expenditures on federal campaigns.

33. Nielsen 2012, 6.

34. Berman 2010, 34.

35. Herrnson's studies suggest that parties still play a critical role in congressional field operations. Fifty-two percent of campaigns reported that local party committees were "moderately to extremely important" in recruiting volunteers for their ground efforts. His findings showed that Republican House candidates were slightly more likely to rely on the party infrastructure than were Democrats, who could still turn to organized labor (Herrnson 2009, 203).

36. Green and Farmer 2003, 2 and 14.

37. Some analysts place the blame for the debilitated Democratic party squarely on Bill Clinton's "dogged pursuit of a second term," which "drained the party of finite, precious resources" and left it "poorly positioned to improve its national strength and status" (Tenpas 1998, 765). The state-level Democratic Coordinated Committees, part of what scholars have described as the DNC's "modernization" efforts (Blumberg 1999, 166), were designed to be voter mobilization machines. But the coordinated campaigns suffered from activist infighting, outsourced voter contact, staff cutbacks, and perhaps most perplexing, the exclusion—or inability to absorb—ordinary people into party-run field efforts (Weir and Ganz 1997, 150).

38. Ganz 1994, 14.

39. Dulio and Thurber 2003, 220.

40. Hillygus and Shields 2008.

41. E.g., Gerber and Green 2000; 2001; Nickerson, et al. 2006.

42. Green and Gerber 2008.

43. Green and Gerber 2008, 37.

44. Green and Gerber 2008, 42.

45. Green and Gerber 2008, 10.

46. In addition to removing the hourly wage from the return-on-investment equation Green and Gerber used to calculate the efficacy of door-to-door canvassing, other scholars have investigated what is considered received wisdom among campaign staff—that is, that local volunteers are more persuasive than outsiders. Sinclair's *The Social Citizen* (2012) is one of the most recent pieces of evidence: findings from a field experiment demonstrate that volunteers canvassing in their own zip code were more effective at mobilizing votes than their nonlocal counterparts. Sinclair's findings are corroborated in Lisa García Bedolla and Melissa Michelson's research (2012), which found that "neighbors increased turnout by 8.5 percentage points (SE = 3.00), while nonlocals increased turnout by 5.2 percentage points (SE = 2.9)" (García Bedolla and Michelson 2012, 102).

47. Rosenstone and Hansen 1993.

48. Panagopoulos and Wielhouwer 2008.

49. Berman 2010, 6.

50. Beckett 2008, 3.

51. Berman 2010, 33.

52. Berman 2010, 144.

53. Berman 2010, 27.

54. Berman 2010, 97.

55. Meyers 1993; Bimber 1998; Davis 1998; 2009; Klinenberg and Perrin 2000.

56. Nielsen 2012, 28.

57. Personal communication, November 20, 2013.

58. Berman 2010, 35.

59. Berman 2010, 35.

60. Berman 2010, 35.

61. Historical notes from personal communication with Marshall Ganz, January 18, 2014. In chapter 4, we discuss how the Obama campaign deployed the house meeting tactic to capture what Ganz called its "real magic": the relational, leadership developing, geometric scale achieved through disciplined and number-based work.

62. Berman 2010, 39–40.

63. Purdum 2004.

64. Keeter, et al. 2007, 154.

65. Berman 2010, 47–49.

66. Cohen, et al. 2008, 294.

67. Nielsen 2012, 42.

68. Polman 2004.

69. Nielsen 2012, 50.

70. Barone and Cohen 2006, 22.

71. Barone and Cohen 2006, 23.

72. Quoted in Nielsen 2012, 41.

73. Quoted in Nielsen 2012, 55.

74. Balz and Allen 2003.

75. Balz and Allen 2003.

76. Peter Ubertaccio provides a clear description of the how the Bush field operation imported Amway's multilevel marketing techniques

in 2004, noting that the crux of the "multibillion dollar enterprise" rests on the fact that "people are much more likely to fall for a sales pitch from a friend or relative, or a stranger in a home setting, than they are from a stranger in the shop or market, or an advert in a paper, magazine, or on the Internet" (Ubertaccio 2007, 175).

77. Embedded in the 72-Hour project, as Sasha Issenberg writes, was the Republicans' then cutting-edge interest in developing "an intellectual infrastructure for their field operations" (Issenberg 2012, 158). Mysteriously, the set of PowerPoint slides that detailed Rove's new endeavor in turnout targeting fell into Democratic hands in the winter of 2002, Issenberg reveals (ibid.). Although it was not called microtargeting at the time, Republicans were eager to, as Bush White House staffer Adrian Gray said, "take geography out of the equation" (97), and instead rely on tailored, narrow messages to individual voters of a certain profile. This was analogous to the objective of OFA's impressive Narhwal project, which triangulated data about voters from all information repositories such that it was available—and useful—to OFA's digital, paid media, fundraising, analytics, and field teams.

78. Berman 2010.
79. Nielsen 2012, 49.
80. Berman 2010.
81. Nickerson and Feller 2008 .
82. Barone and Cohen 2006, 23.
83. Nielsen 2012, 51.
84. Barone and Cohen 2006, 23.
85. Barone and Cohen 2006, 23.

## CHAPTER 3

1. Quoted in Berman 2010, 109.
2. Ganz 2010; Speer and Christens 2011.
3. In order for a candidate to remain viable in an Iowa caucus, he or she must have the support of at least 15 percent of the caucus participants. Supporters of "nonviable candidates" must then decide whether

to shift their vote to another candidate or abandon the caucus. Each "viable" candidate then elects delegates to the county convention, after which the Iowa Democratic Party compiles the results in Des Moines.

4. Berman 2010, 110.

5. Obama took 37.6 percent of the vote to Edwards 29.7 and Clinton's 29.4. Fifty-seven percent of 17- to 29-year-olds caucused for Obama, compared to Clinton's 11 percent.

6. After working together on the Dean campaign, former political director Paul Blank enlisted Bird and Wicks for the Wake Up Wal-Mart campaign. Part of the United Food and Commercial Workers' (UFCW) union effort, the group sought to hold Wal-Mart accountable for paying poverty wages to its employees. According to the UFCW, the average full-time Wal-Mart associate makes roughly $15,500 a year, and an increasing number of employees are relegated to permanent part-time positions. Meanwhile, the UFCW points out, "the six members of the Walton family—heirs to the Wal-Mart fortune and near majority owners of the company—have a combined wealth of $93 billion. That's more than the bottom 30% of Americans combined" (UFCW 2011). Bird, whose mother worked at the company for four years, had a personal stake in the cause. He devised the campaign's field strategy while Wicks assumed the role of political director.

7. Green and Gerber 2004; 2008.

8. Ganz 2010.

9. The race had narrowed to Clinton and Obama, and Super Tuesday contained the promise of 1,681 delegates, more than enough for either candidate to assume a decisive lead in their quest for 2,118, the threshold for claiming the nomination. Because states were eager to have a greater influence, 23 had moved their primary or caucus date to February 5, the earliest date permitted by the DNC. For this reason, in 2008, the media dubbed it "Super Duper Tuesday" or "Tsunami Tuesday." The results were expected to determine the party's presidential nominee.

10. "Production" in the context of OFA, as we discuss further in chapter 5, translates to voter contact (phone calls, door knocks, voter registration) and volunteer leaders identified and trained.

11. Berman 2010, 133.
12. Ganz 2010.
13. For a first-person account of a Latino Camp Obama in Colorado, please see Alexander 2010, 45–59. Volunteers from 30 field organizer turfs across the state convened in Su Teatro, "a well-kept, working-class Hispanic neighborhood of Denver." As with Burbank, participants were trained in leadership skills and charged with returning home to organize 300 neighborhood teams of five to ten people each. Alexander describes how, over the course of the weekend, "the Obama campaign's script of civil repair [was] made to walk and talk…the lines between audience and actors, organizers and organized, paid staff and volunteers—all these have broken down" at Camp Obama (55).
14. The VAN (short for Voter Activation Network)—interchangeably called the VoterFile or VoteBuilder by campaign staff and volunteers—refers to the database that the Democrats use. (Its counterpart for the Republicans is called GOP Data Center.) From the user-interface perspective, VAN has two separate "tabs," MyVoters and MyCampaign. The former is the campaign's repository of voters, and the latter lists known or likely supporters and therefore prospective volunteers.
15. Quoted in Berman 2010, 121.
16. Berman 2010, 118.
17. Memo from Ganz to Steve Hildebrand entitled "Organization, Organizing, and Movement Building," dated July 17, 2007.
18. Papa, et al. 2006.
19. Scola 2011.
20. In 2013, NationalField was acquired by VAN.
21. Barone 2013, 1.
22. Ganz 2009.

CHAPTER 4

1. Speer, et al. 2010; Warren 2001; Smock 2004; Ganz 2010.
2. Warren 2001.
3. Camp Obama Participant Guide, Orlando, FL, August 8–9, 2008.
4. Warren 2001, 220.

5. Warren 2001, 222.
6. Warren 2001, 224.
7. See Han 2014 for further discussion of the distinction between mobilizing and organizing.
8. In the final two months of the campaign, Chicago headquarters staff deployed to the battleground states in "closer" roles, such as GOTV directors or as support for staging locations that lacked volunteer capacity.
9. Fall Fellows also learned how to engage potential volunteers through calls and canvassing, how to hold a one-on-one to develop relationships, share goals and develop strategy with supporters, empower new voters, perform data entry in the database, and hold house meetings, among others. We describe each of these skills and tactics in detail in chapter 4.
10. OFA-Ohio 2008.
11. OFA-Ohio 2008.
12. OFA-Ohio 2008.
13. Alexander 2010, 54.
14. Ganz 2009.
15. See Ganz 2009, 2010 for a further explanation of how and why stories can be so powerful.
16. Marcus 2002.
17. Chen 2012, 312.
18. OFA-Ohio 2008.
19. O'Brien went on to become a regional field director where her turf encompassed Madison, one of the most liberal communities in the country.
20. Adapted from a February 2013 interview with a field director who wished to remain anonymous, general election training videos, and participant-observer fieldwork.
21. Berman 2010, 38.
22. Some scholars argue that evidence of the decline of participation in America is not to be found in empirical evidence about the diminishing membership rosters of unions and civic associations, but rather in how politics themselves are practiced. As sociologist

Nina Eliasoph writes, "When the public spirit evaporates from [the] public discourse, the only 'moral' voice left in public is the voice that calls for citizens to abandon the public good" (Eliasoph 1998, 262). OFA house meetings sought to counteract this trend.

23. Cushman 2008.
24. Nickerson, et al. 2006; Nickerson and Feller 2008; Green and Gerber 2008; García Bedolla and Michelson 2012; Sinclair 2012.
25. Ganz 2006.
26. Carey 2012.
27. The intricacies and efficacy of mobilization activities on turnout has been extensively and ably studied elsewhere, as mentioned in chapters 2 and 3. See, for example, Green and Gerber 2008; Arceneaux and Nickerson 2009; Issenberg 2012; Enos, et al. 2013. Additionally, it is common for scholarly treatments of political campaigns, not only the 2008 and 2012 general elections, to disproportionately scrutinize field programs' GOTV tactics rather than the people who perform the work and their campaign activities in the months prior to the election. GOTV, however, lasted just four days in states without an early voting period. Measured chronologically, that is less than 1 percent of the length of the campaign, launched 578 days before. For this reason, we instead examine OFA's organization-building practices in most of this book.
28. OFA-Ohio 2008.

## CHAPTER 5

1. Man 2013.
2. Obama 2008a.
3. Hackman 2002.
4. Toal 2009.
5. The first of many times Obama uttered these words publicly was during his victory speech in 2008, as quoted at the outset of this book: "[The campaign] drew strength from the young people who rejected the myth of their generation's apathy, who left their homes and their families for jobs that offered little pay and less sleep" (Obama 2008b).
6. Rapoport 1997, 186.

7. Ganz 2010.

8. Diviney's observation highlights the expanded roster of states that OFA would contest, as compared to the Clinton, Gore, and Kerry campaigns. A critical piece of the strategy was to change the electorate in previously "safe" Republican states like North Carolina, Missouri, Georgia, and Indiana. In 2012, the Obama campaign's battleground states were Colorado, Florida, Iowa, Nevada, New Hampshire, North Carolina, Ohio, Pennsylvania, Virginia, and Wisconsin.

9. Muir and Axelrod 2013, 247. In chapter 7, we give particular attention to how socioeconomic and geographic constraints affected how well the team model functioned in different turf types, in spite of—or perhaps because of—staff and volunteer leaders' disposable time and income, skill level, and/or commitment to the experimental facet of organizing. We surface this and other implications for how future campaigns and organizations might improve upon OFA's practices.

10. As mentioned in chapter 4, Steele started on the campaign in Iowa in 2007, was a field organizer on the 2008 general, remained on staff of OFA 2.0, and was one of the deputy field directors in Colorado in 2012. He was later hired as the field director of Battleground Texas, the grassroots organization headed by OFA veterans that aims to turn the state blue in future elections.

11. These "turf splitting" measures, as they were known, could artificially divide neighborhoods and towns that did not recognize the boundaries drawn by each state's analytic teams. We probe turf splitting and the resultant staff transitions in further detail in the next section.


CHAPTER 6

1. Balz 2013.

2. Balz 2013.

3. Cunningham's choice of the phrase "my volunteers" demonstrates the ownership and responsibility that she—a volunteer herself—felt over the training and performance of the people on her team.

4. Espeland and Stevens 1998, 316.
5. Espeland and Stevens 1998, 330.

## CHAPTER 7

1. Issenberg 2014, 3.
2. Steinhauser and Liptak 2013.
3. Haberman 2013.
4. Priebus 2014.
5. Priebus 2014.
6. Alter 2013, 109.
7. Rogers, et al. 2013.
8. McClintock, et al. 2013, 1.
9. Pastor, et al. 2013, 2.
10. See Han 2014 for more discussion and research on this point.
11. Personal correspondence, November 2014.
12. The composition of OFA's staff, too, was not very diverse. According to Nielsen's study, campaign volunteers and staff "tend to be white, college-educated, older, and often affluent. They are typically motivated by political partisanship, a sense of citizenship, and sometimes a love of the game" (Nielsen 23). Indeed, this demographic was disproportionality represented in our qualitative data, and corroborated in statements from top campaign staff about the class and racial make-up of the field staff and volunteer base. Still, as Issenberg reports, there is some evidence that the Obama campaign was more inclusive than those that came before it. One study found that five times as many blacks reported that they were working for a candidate or party in 2008 as compared to 2004 (Issenberg 2014). In *Paint the White House Black*, sociologist Michael Jeffries treats these tensions in greater depth, providing an insightful account of the racial ramifications of the Obama presidency, as well as the ways in which "the policies and practices of banks, schools, health care providers, courts, and corporations"—and, we would add, campaigns, civic organizations, and social movements—"must be changed if we are to do away with unjust racial hierarchy" (Jeffries 2013, 162).

13. Nielsen 2012, 34.
14. Organizing for Action email, January 17, 2014.
15. Graves 2013.
16. Collins 2010.
17. Quoted in Franken 2012.

# WORKS CITED

Alexander, Jeffrey. 2010. *The Performance of Politics: Obama's Victory and the Democratic Struggle for Power*. New York: Oxford University Press.

Alter, Jonathan. 2013. *The Center Holds: Obama and His Enemies*. New York: Simon & Schuster.

Arceneaux, Kevin, and David Nickerson. 2009. "Who Is Mobilized to Vote? A Re-analysis of 11 Field Experiments." *American Journal of Political Science* 53: 1–16.

Baggetta, Matthew, Hahrie Han, and Kenneth Andrews. 2013. "Leading Associations: How Individual Characteristics and Team Dynamics Generate Committed Leaders." *American Sociological Review* 78: 544–73.

Baldino, Thomas, and Kyle Kreider. 2011. "U.S. Election Campaigns: A Documentary and Reference Guide." Santa Barbara, CA: ABC-CLIO.

Balz, Dan. 2013. "How the Obama Campaign Won the Race for Voter Data." *Washington Post*, July 28.

Balz, Dan, and Mike Allen. 2003. "Bush Campaign Is Now: Early Efforts to Amass Voters." *Washington Post*, November 30.

Barone, Michael. 2013. *Almanac of American Politics: 2014*. Chicago: University of Chicago Press.

Barone, Michael, and Richard Cohen. 2006. *The Almanac of American Politics, 2006*. Washington, DC: National Journal Group.

Bartels, Larry 1988. *Presidential Primaries and the Dynamics of Public Choice*. Princeton, NJ: Princeton University Press.

Beckett, Charlie. 2008. *Supermedia: Saving Journalism So It Can Save the World*. New York: Blackwell.

Berman, Ari. 2010. *Herding Donkeys: The Fight to Rebuild the Democratic Party and Reshape American Politics*. New York: Farrar, Straus, and Giroux.

Bimber, Bruce. 1998. "The Internet and Political Transformation: Populism, Community, and Accelerated Pluralism." *Polity* 31: 133–60.

Blumberg, Melanie. 1999. "Do the Grassroots Matter? The Coordinated Campaign in a Battleground State." In *The State of the Parties: The Changing Role of Contemporary American Parties*, eds. John Clifford Green and Daniel Shea, 3rd ed. Lanham, MD: Rowman & Littlefield. 154–67.

Brazile, Donna. 2004. *Cooking with Grease, Stirring the Pots in American Politics*. New York: Simon & Schuster.

Carey, Benedict. 2012. "Dream Team of Behavioral Scientists Advised Obama Campaign." *New York Times*, November 12.

Chen, Katherine. 2012. "Charismatizing the Routine: Storytelling for Meaning and Agency in the Burning Man Organization." *Qualitative Sociology* 35: 311–34.

Cohen, Marty, David Karol, Hans Noel, and John Zaller. 2008. *The Party Decides: Presidential Nominations before and after Reform*. Chicago: The University of Chicago Press.

Collins, Gail. 2010. "My Favorite August." *New York Times*. http://www.nytimes.com/2010/08/14/opinion/14collins.html?_r=0.

Cooper, Christopher, and Laura Meckler. 2008. "Obama Takes in a Record $150 Million, but McCain Narrows Gap in Some Polls." *Wall Street Journal*, October 20.

Cushman, Joy. 2008. "Organizing for Change." Paper presented at the Netroots Nation, Austin, TX. July 17–20.

Cushman, Joy, Susan Markham, Doug Hattaway, R. J. Bee, Karen Hicks, and Judith Freeman. 2010. "Campaigning to Engage and Win: A Guide to Leading Electoral Campaigns." Washington, DC: The New Organizing Institute. http://neworganizing.com/content/page/campaign-managers-manual.

Cutright, Phillips, and Peter Rossi. 1958. "Grass Roots Politicians and the Vote." *American Sociological Review* 23: 171–79.

Darr, Joshua, and Matthew Levendusky. 2013. "Relying on the Ground Game: The Placement and Effect of Campaign Field Offices." *American Politics Research* 41: 529–48.

Davis, Richard. 2009. "The Internet in U.S. Election Campaigns." In *Routledge Handbook of Internet Politics*, ed. Andrew Chadwick and Philip Howard. New York: Routledge. 13–24.

Davis, Richard. 1998. *The Web of Politics: The Internet's Impact on the American Political System*. New York: Oxford University Press.

Doherty, Brendan. 2012. *The Rise of the President's Permanent Campaign*. Lawrence: University Press of Kansas.

Downing, John. 2011. *Encyclopedia of Social Movement Media*. Thousand Oaks, CA: SAGE.

Dulio, David, and James Thurber. 2003. "The Symbiotic Relationship between Political Parties and Political Consultants: Partners Past, Present, and Future." In *The State of the Parties: The Changing Role of Contemporary American Parties*, ed. John Green and Rick Farmer. Lanham, MD: Rowman & Littlefield. 214–23.

Eliasoph, Nina. 1998. *Avoiding Politics: How Americans Have Produced Apathy in Everyday Life*. Cambridge: Cambridge University Press.

Enos, Ryan, Anthony Fowler, and Lynn Vavreck. 2013. "Increasing Inequality: The Effect of GOTV Mobilization on the Composition of the Electorate." *The Journal of Politics* 76: 1, 273–88.

Entman, Robert. 1989. *Democracy without Citizens*. Oxford: Oxford University Press.

Espeland, Wendy Nelson, and Mitchell Stevens. 1998. "Commensuration as a Social Process." *Annual Review of Sociology* 24: 312–43.

Forthal, Sonya. 1946. *Cogwheels of Democracy: A Study of the Precinct Captain*. New York: The William-Fredrick Press.

Franken, Al. 2012. "Paul Wellstone's Legacy, 10 Years Later." *The Atlantic*. http://www.theatlantic.com/politics/archive/2012/10/paul-wellstones-legacy-10-years-later/264086/.

Freeman, Richard. 2003. "What Do Unions Do to Voting?" Working Paper. Cambridge, MA: National Bureau for Economic Research.

Ganz, Marshall. 2006. "Learning Organizing in Web Module on Online Organizing." Working Paper. Cambridge, MA: Hauser Center for Nonprofits at the Harvard Kennedy School of Government.

Ganz, Marshall. 2010. "Social Movement Leadership." In *Handbook of Leadership Theory and Practice*, ed. Nitin Nohria and Rakesh Khurana. Cambridge, MA: Harvard Business School Press. 527–68.

Ganz, Marshall. 1994. "Voters in the Crosshairs: How Technology and the Market Are Destroying Politics." *The American Prospect* 16: 1–17.

Ganz, Marshall. 2009. "Why Stories Matter." *Sojouners Magazine* 3. http://sojo.net/magazine/2009/03/why-stories-matter.

García Bedolla, Lisa, and Melissa Michelson. 2012. *Mobilizing Inclusion: Transforming the Electorate through Get-out-the-Vote Campaigns*. New Haven, CT: Yale University Press.

Gerber, Alan, and Todd Rogers. 2009. "Descriptive Social Norms and Motivation to Vote: Everybody's Voting and So Should You." *The Journal of Politics* 71: 178–91.

Gerber, Alan S., and Donald P. Green. 2001. "Do Phone Calls Increase Voter Turnout?" *Public Opinion Quarterly* 65: 75–85.

Gerber, Alan S., and Donald P. Green. 2000. "The Effects of Canvassing, Telephone Calls, and Direct Mail on Voter Turnout: A Field Experiment." *American Political Science Review* 94: 653–63.

Gerring, John. 2007. *Case Study Research: Principles and Practices.* New York: Cambridge University Press.

Goodwin, Doris Kearns. 2005. *Team of Rivals: The Political Genius of Abraham Lincoln.* New York: Simon & Schuster.

Goodwin, Jeff, James Jasper, and Francesca Polletta. 2001. *Passionate Politics: Emotions and Social Movements.* Chicago: University of Chicago Press.

Graves, Lucia. 2013. "OFA Refuses to Push on Keystone." *The Huffington Post*, May 16. http://www.huffingtonpost.com/2013/05/16/ofas-keystone-grassroots_n_3276622.html.

Green, Donald, and Alan Gerber. 2008. *Get out the Vote: How to Increase Voter Turnout.* Washington, DC: The Brookings Institution.

Green, Donald, and Alan Gerber. 2004. *Get out the Vote!: A Guide for Candidates and Campaigns.* New Haven, CT: Yale University Press.

Green, John Clifford, and Rick Farmer. 2003. *The State of the Parties: The Changing Role of Contemporary American Parties.* Lanham, MD: Rowman & Littlefield.

Haberman, Maggie. 2013. "Buffy Wicks in Talks to Be Priorities USA Director." Politico: http://www.politico.com/story/2013/11/buffy-wicks-priorities-usa-director-100218.html.

Hackman, Richard. 2012. "From Causes to Conditions in Group Research." *Journal of Organizational Behavior* 33: 428–44.

Hackman, Richard. 2002. *Leading Teams: Setting the Stage for Great Performances.* Cambridge, MA: Harvard Business Review Press.

Han, Hahrie. 2014. *How Organizations Develop Activists: Civic Associations and Leadership in the 21st Century.* New York: Oxford University Press.

Hands, Joss. 2011. *@ Is for Activism: Dissent, Resistance, and Rebellion in a Digital Culture.* London: Pluto.

Hart, Gary. 2012. "Remembering George McGovern." *The Huffington Post*, October 21.

Hart, Gary. 1973. *Right from the Start: A Chronicle of the McGovern Campaign.* New York: Quadrangle Press.

Hebdon, Chris. 2013. "Obama's Re-Election Strategist Lauds Tech-Driven Campaign as Game Changer." *GW Hatchet* (February 21).

Herrnson, Paul. 2009. "Field Work in Contemporary Election Campaigns." In *Campaigns and Elections American Style*, ed. James A. Thurber and Candice J. Nelson. Boulder, CO: Westview Press. 193–206.

Hillygus, Sunshine. 2005. "Campaign Effects and the Dynamics of Turnout Intention in Election 2000." *Journal of Politics* 67: 50–68.

Hillygus, Sunshine, and Todd Shields. 2008. *The Persuadable Voter: Wedge Issues in Presidential Campaigns*. Princeton, NJ: Princeton University Press.

Holbrook, Thomas. 1996. *Do Campaigns Matter?* Thousand Oaks, CA: Sage.

Holbrook, Thomas M., and Scott D. McClurg. 2005. "The Mobilization of Core Supporters: Campaigns, Turnout, and Electoral Composition in United States Presidential Elections." *American Journal of Political Science* 49: 689–703.

Hughes, Karen. 2004. *Ten Minutes from Normal*. New York: Viking.

IDEA 2013. "International Institute for Democracy and Electoral Assistance." http://www.idea.int/vt/.

Issenberg, Sasha. 2014. "Dept. of Experiments." *Politico*. February 27. http://www.politico.com/magazine/story/2014/02/campaign-science-dept-of-experiments-103671_Page4.html#.U5Zsz5RdUSA.

Issenberg, Sasha. 2012. *The Victory Lab: The Secret Science of Winning Campaigns*. New York: Crown Publishers.

Iyengar, Shanto, and Adam F. Simon. 2000. "New Perspectives and Evidence on Political Communication and Campaign Effects." *Annual Review of Psychology* 51: 149–69.

Jeffries, Michael. 2013. *Paint the White House Black: Barack Obama and the Meaning of Race in America*. Stanford, CA: Stanford University Press.

Jones, Martin, and Robert Sugden. 2001. "Positive Confirmation Bias in the Acquisition of Information." *Theory and Decision* 50: 59–99.

Karpf, David. 2012. *The MoveOn Effect: The Unexpected Transformation of American Political Advocacy*. New York: Oxford University Press.

Keeter, Scott, Cary Funk, and Courtney Kennedy. 2007. "Deaniacs and Democrats: Howard Dean's Campaign Activists." In *The State of the Parties: The Changing Role of Contemporary American Parties*, ed. John Green and Daniel Coffey, 5th ed. Lanham, MD: Rowman & Littlefield. 153–69.

Key, Valdimer O. 1956. *Politics, Parties, and Pressure Groups*, 3rd. ed. New York: Thomas Crowell Co.

Klandermans, Bert, Hanspeter Kriesi, and Sidney Tarrow. 1988. *From Structure to Action: Comparing Social Movement Research across Cultures*. Greenwich, CT: JAI Press.

Klein, Howard, Thomas Becker, and John Meyer. 2009. *Commitment in Orga-nizations: Accumulated Wisdom and New Directions*. New York: Routledge.

Klinenberg, Eric, and Andrew Perrin. 2000. "Symbolic Politics in the Informa-tion Age: The 1996 Republican Presidential Campaigns in Cyberspace." *Information, Communication, and Society* 3: 17–38.

Kreiss, Daniel. 2012. *Taking Our Country Back: The Crafting of Network Politics from Howard Dean to Barack Obama*. New York: Oxford University Press.

Lariscy, Ruthann Weaver, Spencer Tinkham, Heidi Hatfield Edwards, and Karen Ogata Jones. 2004. "The 'Ground War' of Political Campaigns: Non-paid Activities in U.S. State Legislative Races." *Journalism and Mass Com-munication Quarterly* 81: 477–97.

Man, Anthony. 2013. "Republicans Get Tough Talk from One of Their Own." *Sun Sentinel*, May 7. http://articles.sun-sentinel.com/2013-05-07/news/sfl-republicans-get-tough-talk-from-one-of-their-own-20130507_1_hispanic-voters-african-american-voters-message.

Marcus, George E. 2002. *The Sentimental Citizen: Emotion in Democratic Poli-tics*. University Park: Pennsylvania State University Press.

Masket, Seth. 2009. "Did Obama's Ground Game Matter? The Influence of Local Field Offices during the 2008 Presidential Election." *Public Opinion Quarterly* 73: 1023–39.

McClintock, Charles, Linda Honold, and Ileana Marin. 2013. "Grassroots in New Soil: A Case Study of Year-Round Civic Engagement in Milwaukee, Wisconsin." In *Secondary Grassroots in New Soil: A Case Study of Year-Round Civic Engagement in Milwaukee, Wisconsin*. Working Paper. Santa Barbara, CA: Fielding Graduate Institute for Social Innovation.

McGerr, Michael. 1986. *The Decline of Popular Politics: The American North, 1865–1928*. New York: Oxford University Press.

Meyers, Dee Dee. 1993. "New Technology and the 1992 Clinton Presidential Campaign." *American Behavioral Scientist* 37: 181–84.

Muir, David, and David Axelrod. 2013. "Obama Campaign: An Insider's View." *Public Policy Research* 19: 245–52.

Musick, Mark, and John Wilson. 2008. *Volunteers: A Social Profile*. Blooming-ton: Indiana University Press.

Nickerson, David, and Avi Feller. 2008. "Can Voter Turnout Contaminate a Neighborhood?" Paper presented at the Harvard Networks in Political Sci-ence Conference, Cambridge, MA, June 13.

Nickerson, David, Ryan Friedrichs, and David King. 2006. "Partisan Mobiliza-tion Campaigns in the Field: Results from a Statewide Turnout Experiment in Michigan." *Political Research Quarterly* 59: 85–97.

Nielsen, Rasmus Kleis. 2012. *Ground Wars: Personalized Communication in Political Campaigns*. Princeton, NJ: Princeton University Press.

Obama, Barack. 2008a. "Barack Speaks to HQ Staff and Volunteers." Available on *BarackObama.com* YouTube channel. https://www.youtube.com/watch?v=bnhmByYxEIo

Obama, Barack. 2008b. "Obama's Victory Speech: Transcript." *New York Times*. November 5. http://www.nytimes.com/2008/11/04/us/politics/04text-obama.html?pagewanted=all.

OFA-Ohio. 2008. "Campaign for Change Field Staff Training Manual." Columbus, OH: Obama for America.

Organizing for Action. 2013. "Obama Campaign 2012 Legacy Report." Internal Memo. Chicago: Obama for America.

Palmer, Robert. 1986. "Campania: Book Review." *The American Historical Review* 91: 638.

Panagopoulos, Costas, and Peter Wielhouwer. 2008. "The Ground War 2000–2004: Strategic Targeting in Grassroots Campaigns." *Presidential Studies Quarterly* 38: 347–62.

Papa, Michael, Arvind Singhal, and Wendy Papa. 2006. *Organizing for Social Change: A Dialectic Journey of Theory and Praxis*. Thousand Oaks, CA: Sage.

Pastor, Manuel, Gihan Perera, and Madeline Wander. 2013. "Moments, Movements, and Momentum: Engaging Voters, Scaling Power, Making Change." University of Southern California: PERE Publications. http://dornsife.usc.edu/assets/sites/242/docs/M3_web.pdf.

Plouffe, David. 2009. *The Audacity to Win: The Inside Story and Lessons*. New York: Viking.

Polman, Dick. 2004. "In Ohio, a Political Fight Like None Before." *The Philadelphia Inquirer*, November 1.

Polsby, Nelson, Aaron Wildavsky, Steven Schier, and David Hopkins. 2012. *Presidential Elections: Strategies and Structures of American Politics*, 13th ed. Lanham, MD: Rowman & Littlefield.

Popkin, Samuel. 1991. *The Reasoning Voter: Communication and Persuasion in Presidential Campaigns*. Chicago: University of Chicago Press.

Priebus, Reince. 2014. "Why the RNC Built a Year-Round Ground Game." *CNN Opinion*. March 18. http://www.cnn.com/2014/03/18/opinion/priebus-rnc-ground-game/.

Purdum, Todd. 2004. "Outside Campaigners Flood Iowa, Sharing Their Candidates' Styles." *The New York Times*, January 13.

Putnam, Robert. 2001. *Bowling Alone: The Collapse and Revival of American Democracy*. New York: Simon & Schuster.

Ragin, Charles and Howard Becker, eds. 1992. *What Is a Case?* Cambridge: Cambridge University Press.

Rapoport, Ronald. 1997. "Partisanship Change in a Candidate-Centered Era." *Journal of Politics* 58: 185–99.

Rogers, Todd, Craig Fox, and Alan Gerber. 2013. "Rethinking Why People Vote: Voting as Dynamic Social Expression." In *The Behavioral Foundations of Public Policy*, ed. Eldar Shafir. Princeton, NJ: Princeton University Press. 91–107.

Rosenstone, Steven J., and John Mark Hansen. 1993. *Mobilization, Participation, and Democracy in America*. New York: Macmillan.

Rutenberg, Jim. 2013. "Data You Can Believe In: The Obama Campaign's Digital Masterminds Cash In." *New York Times*, June 20.

Sander, Thomas, and Robert Putnam. 2010. "Still Bowling Alone? The Post-9/11 Split." *Journal of Democracy* 21: 9–16.

Schier, Steven. 2000. *By Invitation Only: The Rise of Exclusive Politics in the United States*. Pittsburgh, PA: University of Pittsburgh Press.

Schlesinger, Arthur M. 1973. *The Imperial Presidency*. Boston: Houghton Mifflin.

Scola, Nancy. 2011. "National Field: The Private Social Network That the Reinvented the Ground Game." *Tech President*, May 13. http://techpresident .com/blog-entry/nationalfield-private-social-network-thats-reinventing-ground-game.

Shea, Daniel. 1996. *Campaign Craft: The Strategies, Tactics, and Art of Campaign Management*. Westport, CT: Praeger.

Sides, John, and Lynn Vavreck. 2013. *The Gamble: Choice and Chance in the 2012 Presidential Election*. Princeton, NJ: Princeton University Press.

Silver, Nate. 2012. *The Signal and the Noise*. New York: Penguin.

Sinclair, Betsy. 2012. *The Social Citizen: Peer Networks and Political Behavior*. Chicago: University of Chicago Press.

Skocpol, Theda. 2003. *Diminished Democracy: From Membership to Management in American Civil Life*. Norman: University of Oklahoma Press.

Skocpol, Theda, and Morris Paul Fiorina. 1999. *Civic Engagement in American Democracy*. Washington, DC: Brookings Institution Press.

Small, Mario Luis. 2009. "'How Many Cases Do I Need?' On Science and the Logic of Case Selection in Field-Based Research." *Ethnography* 10: 6–38.

Smith, Andrew. 2011. *The Deliberative Impulse: Motivating Discourse in Divided Societies*. Plymouth, UK: Lexington Books.

Smith, Andrew. 2010. "On the Epistemic Incentives to Deliberate Publicly." *Journal of Social Philosophy* 41: 454–69.

Smock, Kristina. 2004. *Democracy in Action: Community Organizing and Urban Change*. New York: Columbia University Press.

Snow, David, and Sarah Anne Soule. 2010. *A Primer on Social Movements*. New York: Norton.

Snow, David, Sarah Anne Soule, and Hanspeter Kriesi. 2004. *The Blackwell Companion to Social Movements*. Malden, MA: Blackwell.

Speer, Paul W., Peterson, N. Andrew, Zippay, Allison, and Christens, Brian D. 2010. "Participation in Congregation-Based Community Organizing: Mixed-Method Study of Civic Engagement." In *Using Evidence to Inform Practice for Community and Organizational Change*, ed. M. Roberts-Degennaro and S. J. Fogel. Chicago: Lyceum.

Speer, Paul, and Brian Christens. 2011. "Contextual Influences on Participation in Community Organizing." *American Journal of Community Psychology* 47: 253–63.

Steinhauser, Paul, and Kevin Liptak. 2013. "Former Top Obama Campaign Aides to Advise Clinton Effort." *CNN Political Unit*. July 10. http://politicalticker.blogs.cnn.com/2013/07/10/former-top-obama-campaign-aides-to-advise-clinton-effort/.

Tenpas, Kathryn Dunn. 1998. "The Clinton Reelection Machine: Placing the Party Organization in Peril." *Presidential Studies Quarterly* 28: 761–67.

Thurber, James, and Candice Nelson, eds. 2010. *Campaigns and Elections: American Style*. Boulder, CO: Westview Press.

Toal, Gerard. 2009. "In No Other Country or Earth: The Presidential Campaign of Barack Obama." *Geopolitics* 14: 376–401.

Ubertaccio, Peter. 2007. "Machine Politics for the Twenty-First Century? Multilevel Marketing and Party Organizations." In *The State of the Parties: The Changing Role of Contemporary American Parties*, ed. John Green and Daniel Coffey, 5th ed. Lanham, MD: Rowman & Littlefield. 175–86.

UFCW. 2011. "United Food and Commercial Workers: A Voice for Working America." http://www.ufcw.org/category/industries/retail/walmart-retail/.

Verba, Sidney, Norman Nie, and Jae-On Kim. 1978. *Participation and Political Equality: A Seven-Nation Comparison*. Cambridge: Cambridge University Press.

Wade, Richard. 1973. "The Democratic Party, 1960–1972." In *The History of U.S. Political Parties*, ed. Arthur Schlesinger. New York: Chelsea House Publishers. 2827–68.

Warren, Mark. 2001. *Dry Bones Rattling: Community Building to Revitalize American Democracy*. Princeton Studies in American Politics. Princeton, NJ: Princeton University Press.

Weir, Margaret. 2004. "Challenging Political Inequality." *APSA Task Force Report and Commentary* 2: 677–81.

Weir, Margaret, and Marshall Ganz. 1997. "Reconnecting People and Politics." In *The New Majority: Toward a Popular Progressive Politics*, ed. Stanley B. Greenberg and Theda Skocpol. New Haven, CT: Yale University Press. 149–71.

Wood, Richard. 2002. *Faith in Action: Religion, Race, and Democratic Organizing in America*. Chicago: University of Chicago Press.

Yin, Robert. 2002. *Case Study Research*. Thousand Oaks, CA: Sage.

# INDEX

*Figures, notes, and tables are indicated by f, n, and t following the page number.*

Electoral-organizing model (*continued*)
lessons for scholarship of, 191
neighborhood teams in, 69, 152
to scale, 48
shared responsibility in, 143
tensions within, 191
top staff for, 80, 85
voter contact in, 124
Eliasoph, Nina, 216–217n22
Ellis, Cheryl, 134
Empowerment
in 2008 vs. 2012, 171
accountability and, 15
in balancing national purpose with
local action, 161
in campaign motto, 44, 78
community organizing and,
93–94
in historical roots of OFA, 50–55
lessons for democracy and, 199
metrics and, 177, 179
relationship building and, 92
at scale, 15
"Engagement' campaign," 24
Entman, Robert, 208–209n22
Espeland, Wendy Nelson, 178
Evolution of OFA, 44–85
balancing national purpose with
local action, 79, 81–83
continuing to build capacity
pipeline in, 79–81
convening and reflecting in, 76–79
getting to scale quickly in, 71–75
investment in training in, 63–70
learning through 2008 primaries.
*See* Democratic primary
campaign (2008)
lessons from 2008 in, 84–85
motivation of people through
relationships and neighborhood
teams in, 56–61
"old school" command-and-control
model discarded in, 55–56
people-focused but metrics-driven
approach, 61–63

respect, empowerment, and
inclusion of volunteers in, 50–55
transparency with volunteers
about data in, 70–71
Executive coaches for field directors, 99
"Extreme case," Obama campaign as, 16

Fabio, Shenelle, 101
Face-to-face contact
in Bush campaign, 40
effectiveness of, 33, 42, 125
in Kerry campaign, 33
motivation and, 127
with "persuadable" voters, 7
relationship building via,
107–109, 187
in South Carolina primary, 57
Fall Fellows program, 100–101,
216n9
FDs. *See* Field directors
Fellows programs, 80–81, 100–101,
216n9
"Field activist," 23
Field campaigns
Bush's 72-Hour Program as, 39–42
central challenge of, 8
for general election, 76–81
importance of, 24–26, 206n7
Kerry's outsourced, 38–39
leeway for innovation in, 78
media on, 4–5
metrics for, 77, 162
neighborhood teams in, 9, 134
new era of, 34–38
Obama on, 3
OFA as model for, 11–12
in Pennsylvania, 72–73
relationship building in, 91
resurgence of interest in, 32–34
structure for staff in,
99–100, 100f
training in, 102
turf splitting in, 150
volunteer recruitment and
retention in, 8–11